Walking Between Raindrops

Memes of Heaven and Hell

Dr. David Summers

Copyright © 2023 by Dr. David Summers

All rights reserved.

No part of this book may be reproduced in any form or by any electronic or mechanical means, including information storage and retrieval systems, without permission in writing from the publisher, except by reviewers, who may quote brief passages in a review.

This publication contains the opinions and ideas of its author. It is intended to provide helpful and informative material on the subjects addressed in the publication.
The author and publisher specifically disclaim all responsibility for any liability, loss or risk, personal or otherwise, which is incurred as a consequence, directly or indirectly, of the use and application of any of the contents of this book.

WORKBOOK PRESS LLC
187 E Warm Springs Rd,
Suite B285, Las Vegas, NV 89119, USA

Website: https://workbookpress.com/
Hotline: 1-888-818-4856
Email: admin@workbookpress.com

Ordering Information:

Quantity sales. Special discounts are available on quantity purchases by corporations, associations, and others. For details, contact the publisher at the address above.

Library of Congress Control Number:

ISBN-13:   978-1-961845-31-2   (Paperback Version)
            978-1-961845-32-9   (Digital Version)

REV. DATE: 11/29/2023

Walking Between Raindrops

MEMES OF HEAVEN AND HELL

DR. DAVID P. SUMMERS

MBA, PhD, FACA (Angiology)

David Summers, in his new book, "Walking between the Raindrops – Memes of Heaven and Hell" takes us on a cultural journey, showing us a very raw and brutally-honest part of Pentecostal Christianity in America (primarily in the 1950's and 60's). There are parts of our history as members of the human species that are … uncomfortable, and even a bit odd if we are honest. We are humans, and humans will be humans – in much the same way as ducks will be ducks and dolphins will be dolphins.

So much of American Christianity in those days was about how being human was somehow … wrong, or perhaps "sinful in the eyes of God Almighty." Several authors have written about these things, but this writer is doing what is long overdue – saying that it is time to talk about what this passing culture has cost so many. Ironically, a life-long pursuit of God that usually ends when the searcher finally finds themselves. This is a book about overcoming terrible theological thinking from generations past, and finally accepting the beauty that is you.

A bold work. –

Ken Dahl, author of
Honesty: The Final Frontier,
and other books

Table of Contents

	Page
Acknowledgements	1
Praise for *Walking Between Raindrops*	3
Preface	5
Foreword	7
About the Author	11
Chapter 1	13
The Leader of the Parade	13
Chapter 2	31
The "Big Time!"	31
Chapter 3	39
Build 'em and They Will Come!	39
Chapter 4	59
But Hope Springs eternal	59
Chapter 5	73
Busted Again!	73
Chapter 6	81
The Meeting on the Beach	81
Chapter 7	89
He Maketh Me to Lie Down in Green Pastures	89
Chapter 8	103
Walking Between the (first) Raindrops	103
Chapter 9	107
Here Comes the Bride (and Groom)	107

Chapter 10 119
Something Old, Something Borrowed 119

Chapter 11 121
Making the Cut 121

Chapter 12 127
Stranger in a Strange Land 127

Chapter 13 131
Will Someone Pinch Me? 131

Chapter 14 141
First, One Journey's the Dark Night of the Soul 141

Chapter 15 143
Looking for Truth in All the Wrong Places 143

Chapter 16 163
A Silver Lining in a Dark Cloud 163

Chapter 17 181
Haven't We Met Before? 181

Chapter 18 189
Bye-the-way, How does the Cotton Grow? 189

Chapter 19 195
Keeping the Faith 195

Chapter 20 213
God Realization 213

Chapter 21 217
Flathead Lake (Again) 217

Chapter 22 221
Games Religions Play 221

Chapter 23 229
Dead and Alive -- Can They exist Cooperatively? 229
Chapter 24 235
Why Do We Die? 235
Chapter 25 241
The Gift Must be Opened! 241
Afterward 247
The end. (Really) 249

Acknowledgements

To Dorothy Louise, my ever-present soul mate and life-companion…forever!

Thank you to Nathan Hassan, my poetry editor

Dr. David P. Summers

Praise for
Walking *Between Raindrops*

Dear Dave,

I have just finished, and so much enjoyed your book! Wow, what huge and life molding experiences you have come through and described so very well. Indeed, all life IS experience no 'right or wrong', but an ever-deepening awareness of was is…. and finding that we are part of It, whatever we call it, bringing us eventually full circle… home. I was right there with you and had no idea of your globe-trotting career - so different from the piece of your life with which I was familiar. Terrific!

Thank you, Dave, as ever….

Rev. Jane Sorbi, President and Lodge Mother
White Eagle Lodges of the Americas

David Summers, in his new book, "Walking between the Raindrops – Memes of Heaven and Hell" takes us on a cultural journey, showing us a very raw and brutally-honest part of Pentecostal Christianity in America (primarily in the 1950's and 60's). There are parts of our history as members of the human species that are … uncomfortable, and even a bit odd if we are honest. We are humans, and humans will be humans – in much the same way as ducks will be ducks and dolphins will be dolphins.

So much of American Christianity in those days was about how being human was somehow … wrong, or perhaps "sinful in the eyes of God Almighty." Several authors have written about these things, but this writer is doing what is long overdue – saying that it is time to talk about what this passing culture has cost so many. Ironically, a life-long pursuit of

God that usually ends when the searcher finally finds themselves. This is a book about overcoming terrible theological thinking from generations past, and finally accepting the beauty that is you.

A bold work. –
Ken Dahl, author of Honesty: The Final Frontier, *and other books*

I was privileged to read this autobiography by David having been Facebook friends for some years and was immediately drawn into a world long past of naked religious ambition and puritanical legalism. I am a nurse and having lived alongside a Christian Community from 1998 and observed the excesses that extreme religious beliefs create I was disquieted and not a little angry.

Following David's ups and downs as a child growing up into a man in a well-meaning but narrow environment echoed my own feelings as a child of knowing there was much more to life, but not being able to access it. It has produced in David an unquenchable thirst for knowledge and a mind that questions everything. His journey was in turns heartbreaking and triumphant as he pursued a successful career always striving to be accepted and enough.

I recommend this book by my honourable and wise friend and if you read it you will be educated both with knowledge and spiritually in a world that at once changes unrecognizably, and never changes.

Janice Gale; Chaumouth, UK

Preface

In writing this little note on my life, I purposely used the given names of most of the characters. I do not use dad, daddy, pop, mother, mom, or nana or nanny to write completely objectively. I had been so angry with Lester, my father, for so many years for his personal abuse that I could not speak of him as dad or daddy. To relieve the psychic energy, I began to use his given name, Lester. In writing about Dorothy Louise, my beloved wife and ever-faithful companion/soul mate, I usually address her as Dorothy Louise instead of the old family familiar, Louise. Of course, in the familiar, she addresses me darling, and I call her sweetheart or darling. She began to use her full name while we were in England during one of my many career moves, and it sort of stuck with her. She will answer, however, to either name you choose to use. I am still the same David or Dave. But, don't call me Sabbie.

Most of the poetry was written between 1965 and 1968, first at the behest of my psychiatrist who used it for therapeutic reasons, and after that, by my own volition. In 1985, I once again began to write. I finally pulled out of my chronic depression having completed a brutal two-year offshore contract in the North Sea, where I was put in charge of a thousand construction personnel on a large offshore petroleum project. I found the work intense. My depression became detached from my personality and when I returned to the States, the depression was gone.

Then I obtained an MBA from Pepperdine University while working on a similar project in the Gulf of Mexico. Four years later, I obtained a Ph.D. from Kennedy Western University all the while building a new biomedical company. Perhaps, academia crowded out my sense of loneliness.

Most religious people seem to live with a sense of divine expectation and the powerful force of nostalgia. As such, they find themselves between two conflicting passions. In my family, Jesus the Nazarene of the Bible was life's Savior sine qua non. Nothing was possible except the invocation of Him, as he was the pinnacle of experience. Almost equal was the fear of the Devil, the evil one, who relentlessly attempted to snare one's attention away from holiness and thus, in a moment, destroy the goodness of one's entire life. I grew up with that dichotomy of cyclic thought. Extreme good vs extreme bad was the lexicon.

This type of thought produces a continuous imprint upon the brain as a source of unresolved injury to the mind. These repetitive mini-memories begin to crosslink as emotional sensations as childhood evolves into maturity. Sensation is the root of all thought. These sensational imprints are called *memes*. Most of my religious male acquaintances were unable to cope. The imprint of conflicting memes was so extreme as a childhood developmental philosophy that the subsequent adulthood behavior of most of the male members of my religious sect became pathologically injured for life. They became depressed, developed bipolar disorder, eating disorders, or worse, developed various reality pathological escapisms such sexual fantasy, sexual masochism, sadomasochism, narcissism, alcohol/substance abuse, and more. And of course, as in nature, our biological evolution passed these pathologies on to their offspring.

I became one of those offspring.

I discuss memes further in my Forward.

The term myth I use in my religious discussions does not mean that the recount is not true. A myth is a traditional story, especially one concerning the early history of a people passed down orally over the centuries before becoming codified or explained as some natural or social phenomenon thought to evolve out of ancient history. Myths typically involve supernatural beings or events.

Warning: Do not read this book if adult language and blunt truth offend you.

Foreword

I use the term *memes* (rhymes with *teams*) throughout this book.

Memes are clusters of nerve cells that bring thoughts to the forefront of thinking.

They are our "tuned to" our minds and are a contextual nexus of our familial, religious, or cultural symbologies, and they have universal emotional and mental affects when stimulated. Biologically, a meme is an associated group of memories having ideation. Coined by scientist Richard Dawkins in 1976, who argued that memes are genetically passed down by cultures in a similar manner as genes are transferred from one generation to another. Memes are enhanced by another biological structure. Quoting an article in "The Scientist" journal; 04.2018, "Cellular wrappings call perineuronal nets (PNN) control brain plasticity and are woven into memory and psychiatric disorders. For a while after birth, the external environment has a profound effect on the wiring of neuronal circuits and, in turn, on the development of an organism's skills and behaviors, such as language, sensory processing, and emotional traits. But during childhood and adolescence, neuronal networks become more fixed, allowing the individual to retain the acquired functions. Once adulthood is reached, memes become fixed into the mind and by and large control all thinking.

Science has located a region of the brain called the posterior parietal cortex that merges synaptic signals from different sensory modalities that affect these memories and the history that they carry with them. PNNs, like genes, carry a controlling imprint and influence the way we view our lives. As the PNNs are stimulated, axons group to form new neural nexus of memory and emotions. PNNs stabilize synapses that carry the neural transmissions. When overstimulated, especially in early childhood, PNNs develop a constant negative charge in order to drain off the excitable activity of neural firing.

This theory is my basis for the formation of memes.

What this means is we all have a central nexus that can provoke neurological stimuli to various organ systems as it instantly brings forward to consciousness various emotions with their historical definitions. PNNs provide for the nervous transmissions of these networks of neurons. The perineural net covers the entire brain. Therefore, like the universe of electrons and protons, any perturbation will travel throughout the entire brain and at least obliquely, evoke a response, be it subtle or overt. Some refer to this development as "hard-wiring."

Memes start with the over-stimulated nervous response to arousal. If this arousal is sharp, excitable, and most of all, painful, the arousal will form a nexus of nerve clusters with nerve fibers leading to the "fight or flight" mechanism in the cerebellum, the primitive brain. Conversely, a pleasurable event will imprint in the same manner. This *de novo* nexus will then form neural memories and patterns that consist of more neural networks that recall the sight, sound, smell, feel or taste (one or more of the five senses) that holistically reinforce the occasion of these memories when any of the five senses are stimulated.

Progressing from simple experiences of life to painful trauma, for example, if the toddler has pulled the hot pot from the stove and it spills on and burns the child, the experience can cause a fearful reaction of hot utensils that will prevail throughout life. Other events like parental spankings, beatings, slaps, shoves, taunts, humiliations, and progressively, sexual molestations and abuse, cause similar memes to form that put the emotions on red alert when similar events are encountered later in life. The responses are reactive, far beyond ordinary adult reactions. The five senses are the alarm bells of life.

Incredibly, our thoughts are ruled by memes which are subliminal highways to what we think is our spontaneous consciousness. Most memes imprinted upon our naïve child world involve the acceptance of any parental figure. A lot are pre-verbal. It doesn't have to be a cruel, or even painful, experience, but memes imprint the neural nexus of nerve clusters that the brain builds by repetition, (most of it benign like, "uh-uh," "nono", "don't," "stop," "give it to me," with an occasional finger pointed to the face. Then there are the "please," "thank you," "aah, so cute!" "put it down," etc., which are instructive memes by parents, grandparents, siblings, nannies, teachers, and other gate-keepers of our childhood maturity. Memories are built from this. The more these memories are stimulated, the more emotions are brought into consciousness. Repetitions hardwire our memes.

Unless professional experts in the field of psychology, psychiatry, or psychotherapy apply intervention, memes are for a lifetime. For example, if a toddler is sitting on the kitchen floor, with the mother nonchalantly tending the stove for a meal, and suddenly a pot begins to boil over on the stove, the hyperactive attention to a boiling pot by a child's mom will forever imprint the sight, smell, and sound of the boiling liquid, the sound of mother voice, the rapid movement of grabbing the pot, all within a millisecond. The action is so uncommon to the young mind that the emotional experience is there for life. From that time forward, anytime a pot is set upon the stove, there is a cautionary nervous response in the brain which within a millisecond activates a series of memory nexus arousing the emotions for vigilance whether consciousness or not.

We don't need many of our primitive memes as adults. Fight or flight responses are now largely eliminated from our repertoire by familiarity, electric lights, portable electronics, radio, TV, newspapers, education, and other adaptive and/or artificial intelligent innovations. The comfort of these innovations has eliminated our need for constant vigilance. Yet, deep within our psyche, there remain primitive memes still, ever-controlling our innate emotional maturity. We still jump when something startles us. Ninety-nine times out a hundred, it is nothing to fight or flee from. Still, we jump, just like our primitive forbearers did hundreds of thousand years ago when he/she jumped to flee the sound of approaching danger.

But, memes, by and large, are essential for living life, day in and day out. If we didn't have such automatic memory mechanisms in our brains and emotions, we would be so overwhelmed with relentless nervous bombardment for instant action that rational thought would be impossible. Yet, primitive mankind lived only by memes. Only when civilization advanced beyond the hunter-gather groupings and consciousness emerged did primitive speech begin to replace guttural utterances. With the achievement of simple speech, man began to create symbols to designate his internal memes and, as such, began gradually to free up consciousness for comprehension and thought. There are a few positive memes that develop after birth, but most positive memes are already in the brain derived from embryonic development. These memes carry a lifelong need for warmth, comfort, security, satiety, and dependence. And of course, the need for love – the greatest positive meme.

Religious memes can be blamed for much of our cultural distress and unhappiness. Even non-religious people follow religious memes. Our legal system is full of laws that enforce religious memes and carry with them punishments for violation with fines, imprisonment, and civil judgments. Our work week is based upon a religious taboo (another word for meme) of working on the Sabbath. But most of all, religious memes are responsible for the pervasive beliefs in supernatural beings such as an archaic, ever-observant, punishing and/or rewarding God. Some religions play on a meme to create shame and guilt. When we displease or anger this God, we can be punished with perpetual shame and condemnation. Religious memes with feelings of self-reproach and guilt continue throughout life. This exemplifies memes – we try to avoid the negative ones all our life. They are difficult to overcome.

Finally, this book talks about religion and its control. For many people, their life after birth is high-jacked depriving them of any hope of natural happiness. Everything is in order. Early teaching of an all-seeing, punishing and rewarding "God" that is the core establishment of morality has left many in hopelessness and depression trying to live up to the standards set by religion. This guilt-bearing archetype requires retribution and service to maintain religious memes. Those remind us that we are not worthy of natural benefits such as self-acceptance and natural blessings such as satisfaction, creativity, and happiness.

Now that civilization has evolved out of its primitive beginnings, life should be largely a pleasant daily encounter with a clean slate of potential experiences arising from consciousness each day. Unfortunately, for many, it is not.

We *are* good, worthy beings, and we are naturally creative. Happiness, peace, contentment, and joyfulness memes were given to us by our mothers while we were still in the womb and therefore are a birthright. Habits and emotional hard-wiring that prevent this state of mind can be overcome by meditation, knowledge, and experience. This book is the story of how the author overcame the imprint of his own counterproductive memes and how he found a transformative and immanent God that completely opened his mind, heart and soul to a journey of infinite potential.

About the Author

Dr. David Paul Summers is the eldest son of a Pentecostal preacher in the Assembly of God Christian denomination and biopharmaceutical engineer. He is a prolific inventor with over 35 worldwide patents, scientifically cited over 4,000 times. He was raised in a deeply religious, Pentecostal holiness environment and, upon graduating high school, spent a year at what was then called Southwestern Bible Institute (SBI). His story tells how his marriage redirected his destiny and of his transition out of religion. Most of his career has involved medicine, especially in the treatment of heart disease. He engineered, designed and developed many devices and pharmaceuticals used in treatment. With over 50 years in his field, he is uniquely positioned to query the mechanics of religion and philosophy down to the molecular level.

Using his skills as a medical engineer, he takes his first dive into the effect of pre-verbal imprints into the brain and emotional systems of memes and their scientific correlations to physiology, psychology, philosophy, religion, and cultural behavior.

Dr. Summers' interest was piqued forty years ago when he first read the book by Julian Jaynes, *The Origin of Consciousness in the Breakdown of the Bicameral Mind*, first published by Houghton Mifflin Company of New York in 1976. Jaynes postulated then that consciousness was a property of matter – not an invisible and mysterious function of simply "knowing" or human behavior.

At that time, John Updike commented, "When Julian Jaynes speculates that until late in the second millennium B.C. men had no consciousness, but were automatically obeying the voices of gods, we are astounded but compelled to follow this remarkable thesis through all the corroborative evidence."

Dr. Summers has never been satisfied with popular explanations and the virtually total lack of understanding in the general population on what consciousness is and how we are driven to continually rise above the elemental concepts of perception, comprehension, thought, and consciousness.

Perhaps, he says, *it is something as simple as curiosity or obstinacy in purpose.* But obviously, there is something else at work beyond nature. His first book explains his thesis on the effects of religion and emotional imprints of neural memes on consciousness as he corroborates some of the evidence found prima facie in human nature and its successes and failures.

Chapter 1
The Leader of the Parade

Worlds of Mania

I awoke to madness in '37
To wars and the Great Depression

This: a time of tears
But mostly hate—
Just man against man.

An era of dead thoughts:
The ghastly vortex
Of fading images

An era of daily rites:
The gentle approach
Of faith and comfort

These were days
That dawn
Crept up
My body and
Caressed my tormented soul

What happened to those mirages That sprang up those days?

They died in the arms
Of the Mundane and Forgotten
And, It's still too cold
There's nothing new under the sun
(poem self-written at the start of psychotherapy in 1964)

A young, 21-year-old man furiously drove a shiny blue 1934 Chevrolet Cloth-Top Coupe down US 59 heading south toward Lufkin, Texas after a three-week circuitous journey of preaching in small East Texas churches. The Cloth Top Coupe had tears in the top and flapped continually in the wind as he drove. He was embarrassed, but he had been on a mission from God. The feeling of accomplishment filled his heart! God had blessed him. He wanted to look good for God, and the little Chevy had to be part of his best presentation. Right then, he subconsciously decided to take the little coupe to an upholsterer, take a little of his pithy "love offerings," the collection plate contribution from his preaching mission, and do just that. God would be pleased. He had been blessed.

He was obviously in a great hurry. He impatiently weaved in and out of the rural traffic, much of which was East Texas farmers taking late corn, fruit, and other vegetables like squash and potatoes to market. The highway was also crowded with truckers driving big oil field equipment or big log trucks pulling long logging trailers piled high with fresh-cut yellow pine on the way to a paper processing plant in a small town just south of Lufkin.

Approaching the outskirts of Lufkin, the young man made a sharp right turn onto US 69 Northwest and followed it out to the home of the Willmon family. The home was about five miles from the Lufkin business center and the Lufkin Foundry Works which produced steel for the other major industry in Lufkin, the Lufkin Trailer Company. Raymond Willmon worked for the foundry and held a good, steady job as an inspector—one of the highest paid hourly jobs in town.

The young man's wife, Mary, was in labor. Despite being in her last weeks of pregnancy, Mary had traveled with Lester, right up to her last weeks. Although Mary's mother was only a few miles away in Palestine, Texas, she was in poor health, unable to accommodate a birthing place for her daughter's first baby. Flora Lee, Mary's older sister, offered her home and a midwife in Lufkin, about 40 miles from Palestine.

As he approached the Willmon home, he noticed smoke rising from a house next door. Firetrucks blocked the street in front of the Willmon home, and fire hoses stretched between the pumpers and the fire. A fireman was standing in the middle of the street. As the young man drove closer, the fireman waved him away from entering the street, pointing him instead into a side street.

The young man ignored the fireman's directions, and as he entered the street, he began to drive over the water inflated hoses. The fireman standing in the street was the Fire Chief on the scene. He jumped on the running board of the Chevy.

"Stop!" he commanded. "Pull over! You're breaking the law!"

"I've got to get to that house next door to the fire!" The young driver shouted through the car's open window.

He kept driving, bumping over the firehoses as he approached his destination, the Willmon home.

As he finally pulled up in front of the house, the angry Fire Chief jumped from the car.

"Don't you know you're breaking the law?" he demanded. "So stop!" he ordered once again. "I'm writing you a ticket for not obeying a fire officer at the scene of a fire."

"I don't care," he shot back, "my wife is having a baby in that house!"

"In the Willmon's house?" yelled the chief.

"Yes," replied the young man, "Raymond Willmon is my brother-in-law."

"Oh!" the Chief said, now calming a bit, "Willmon…I know Raymond…you say your wife is having a baby in that house.?" he asked, pointing to the Willmon house.

"Yes, she called me."

The old Chief paused only for a moment. "What's your name?" he quickly asked.

"I'm Lester Summers…Raymond Willmon's brother-in-law," he responded emphasizing the Willmon name.

"So, you're Raymond's brother-in-law…?" he repeated.

"Yes, sir."

"Okay, Lester, I'll let you off this time. We got the fire out next door. But don't let this happen again!" he admonished. "You know you can't just drive over my fire hoses like that."

"No sir, I certainly won't," the young man called back as he ran to the front door of the house. "But I've got to get inside and be with her." He quickly disappeared inside.

Thus, begins this story, born in a moment of high anxiety, deficient of forethought, and scantiness of planning and contingency. This was my life. Bear with me on the below details.

First, let's get the vital statistics out of the way. I was born on October 24, 1937, in the home of my mother's older sister, Flora Lee Willmon, wife of Raymond Willmon, in Lufkin, Texas, first-born child to Lester Paul and Mary Imogene Summers. I was blessed with three siblings, Mary Helen, Donald Gene, and Robert Andrew. Lester was an itinerant, although extremely ambitious, evangelist, fervently preaching the strict religious Pentecostal doctrine of the fledgling Assemblies of God denomination. He had a vision. And he had a mission. And God told him to go preach it.

Now a little history, please:

The following is a summary of the religion that I was brought up in. I am providing it for reference.
The Assemblies of God (AG), officially the General Council of the Assemblies of God, is a Pentecostal Christian denomination founded in 1914 during a meeting of Pentecostal ministers at Hot Springs, Arkansas. Pentecostalism is a renewal movement within Protestant Christianity that places special emphasis on a direct personal experience of God through the baptism with the Holy Spirit. The denomination expects the experience of baptism of the Holy Spirit to be evidenced by "speaking in tongues" which is an unintelligible utterance known as glossolalia which is the fluid vocalizing of speech-like syllables that lack any readily comprehended meaning. The term Pentecostal is derived from Pentecost, the Greek name for the Jewish feast of "The Weeks" and goes back to the Azusa Street revival of 1901. The Assemblies of God sprung out of this revival. The Azusa Street Revival was a historic revival that took place in Los Angeles, California and is the origin of the Pentecostal religious movement.

Now back to the events of October 24, 1937:
Lester had been traveling and preaching on the road (evangelizing) when I came into the world. Mary's labor was hard. I didn't take my first breath until almost midnight that night. A midwife tapped my bottom, wiped me down, and tied my umbilical cord. Handing me to Mary, she exclaimed, "Why look, he's already a big boy!" Then she weighed me (8 ½ pounds), made a footprint, and signed my birth certificate, which she later duly filed with the Angelina County Courthouse.

Lester returned to his wife and newborn son twelve hours later.

As an infant, I went with my parents as they traveled "the evangelistic field" for the next two years, preaching and singing in various poverty-stricken churches around the East Texas oil fields during the heart of the Great Depression. Practically the only industry paying any real wages during that era was manual labor in the "oil patch." Those were the darkest days of the Depression, and no one had any money. People bartered for necessities. Those few fortunate laborers working in the oil fields could garner a few dollars a day for the usual 12-hour work day, six or seven days a week. These poor souls, eager for any kind of solace, were Lester's flock, and the "fleece" was always sparse.

The first pastorship Lester and Mary landed was in a small, white clapboard church deep in the heart of the oil fields in Arp, Texas. I have faint memories of Arp, mainly connected to primitive dreams that I recall to this day. I have vague memories of long trips down two-lane concrete highways (constructed by the Works Progress Administration (WPA) workers of the Roosevelt era), back and forth to Oak Cliff, Texas, the home of William and Mittie Summers, Lester's birth parents or to Palestine, Texas returning to Mary's family, Lee and Elizabeth Watts.

My sister Mary Helen (20 months younger than I) was born during this hazy period.

I remember the story Lester told of me, over and over, as a lesson in obedience at any cost. Even as I grew up, he couldn't help repeating this story from the pulpit whenever he thought it was appropriate. It went like this: He and Mary were holding a revival somewhere in Nebraska. It was during a particularly cold winter. Just as Lester began to preach, I began crying and could not be stopped by Mary.

I was crying in church.

Whatever the problem was, Mary could not alleviate it or soothe my discomfort. I persisted in my wailing. Finally, while the congregation sang a song, the exasperated Lester walked over to where Mary sat, grabbed me out of Mary's arms, took me outside and thrashed me soundly with a large switch he carried in his briefcase for occasions like this. When he finished punishing me for crying, he pulled me up to his face and commanded me never to cry again when he was preaching. I guess I was old enough to nod my head affirmatively, or otherwise understand because he brought me back into the service and handed me back to Mary. As he did, one of the stunned elders of the church asked him, "Brother Summers, why don't you use psychology on the little boy?"

Lester answered, "he doesn't know much about psychology brother, but he sure knows a lot about this switch." Still clutching the article of punishment in his right hand, he held his hand high. Then, he would turn to the audience and laugh, as would the audience on cue, and the service would continue. I have no recollection of this story, but he used this little example of brute force to teach indelible parental lessons very early in my life as a child. It was the beginning of a series of what I call "cruelty" memes.

Memes are preverbal and precognitive. They are emotional messages to the consciousness, made without words. In fact, they are "imprinted" mostly by overt external actions that result in internal trauma and autonomic nervous system reactions to protect our inner self that expresses "feeling-level" decisions that we make when we are young.

Memes are not actions made with words; they are pre-verbal, self-protective neural responses made by the emotions of our "fight or flight" reaction within the most primitive part of our brain. They continue to affect us throughout our lives. I will briefly describe how these subtle, emotional reactions prevent many of us from ever finding our true potential – neither in the physical realm nor in the spiritual realm.

The perineural network (PNN) – an actual delicate network of chondroitin sulfate fibers, facilitate "hardwiring" the brain. They condition every synaptic response that reminds the *naïve* mind where to find sustenance and comfort as well of what to fear and flee from to survive. Therefore, they are both a product of positive energy in which the self finds love and security as well avoidance of what one fears. Memes lie and wait outside of conscious awareness and arise out of the psyche to defeat any action taken that requires us to shed these primitive prejudices.

Lester had a profound, one-dimensional delivery when preaching. And that was fear of the Lord. But he was smart enough to tailor his delivery to his audience properly. He usually based his sermons on conflict/resolution – man and God eternally at odds with each other. But he preached there was always a way for the sinner to find forgiveness and thus avoid the awful wrath of God. It was by total surrender and submission to God's will.

Unfortunately, he was the only one who knew what God's will was.

Our family life was much the same. Lester "laid down rules," and even when they were childishly broken by his children, he used extreme punishment – just as he believed God did. At home, his belt or paddle was used to enforce his will around the house.

When he preached, he invariably used the fear of God and of eternal punishment in the lake of fire as fear behavior motivation. On the other hand, his motivation for reward was heaven. Streets of gold and a mansion for everyone who qualified. And this meant that any sacrifice was worth getting to heaven when you die. Obviously, he had no place in his belief system for reincarnation and second chances. It was this life or else. He tried to live it perfectly. But he almost entirely neglected to love his family because of his obsessive love for his congregation – his audience. He needed to stand before a group of people – to be a stage star – to be loved and admired by groups. It was his life.

With me, likely because of beatings he gave me as a small child, he instilled a pathological fear of future beatings, which broke the early psychological coupling of parent/child in need/want fulfillment and prevented us from bonding in a normal father/son relationship. Hell-fire and brimstone was my meme for guilt. The devil was to be found in any worldly action taken without his permission. My equivalent "lake of fire," was living with this imprimatur of life-long guilt and depression.

My memories become sharper as I recall the next church we moved to in Longview, Texas. This was right before the start of World War II, and I was now almost three years of age. My memories of that time were of seeing soldiers mobilizing to fight in foreign lands, and an ever-impatient Lester grumbling at having to pull the car to the side of the road for long periods as the motorized convoys of troops and military equipment sped by. His impatience finally caught up with him on a trip he took with a preacher-friend by the name of Guy Shields (deceased). Reverend Shields was one of the founders of Shield of Faith Bible School in Amarillo, Texas where Lester had attended a couple of years before he and Mary wed.

With Shields as his passenger, Lester tried to pass a convoy from the wrong lane when he was unfortunate enough to meet an oncoming car head-on at the top of a hill. Both Lester and his passenger Brother Shields were seriously injured. Maybe the memory was just the vague truth repeated so often, but it always was presented with a slight variance in Lester's favor. I heard the story over and over growing up as a kid. The subtle message was that Lester was obviously doing God's work and was more important than waiting for the U.S. Army to win a war and that the car they met at the top of the hill, well, should have waited until Lester had passed the convoy. Even if someone had heard the story before with a slightly different narrative, they still loved it. Lester was always forgiven to the point that his stories were taken as gospel.

The church in Longview had a small parsonage connected to the back of the building, and it was the first real home for the struggling Summers family. Donald Gene, named after the famous contemporary evangelist, Donald Gee, (deceased) soon came into this world, followed not long afterward by Robert Andrew (named after Lester's early spiritual mentor, Clifford Andrews who founded the Gospel Lighthouse Church in Dallas, Texas ca. 1933). Andrews pastored the church where Lester found his lasting relationship with God as a fledgling 16-year-old wannabe preacher. However, Lester was an equally incorrigible vainglorious seeker of appreciation and veneration from those he admired. Hence, my youngest sibling, Robert Andrew.

All of us lived in a two-bedroom, wood-framed bungalow that sat on cement blocks only a few feet behind the church.

One memory meme I will forever recall was that baby Helen was quite colicky at the time and could not drink cow's milk. Lester borrowed a milk goat from one of the parishioners. He tied it up in the backyard and milked her to supply Helen's colicky stomach with proper nourishment. One evening, after milking the goat, he left the nanny tied up next to his new 1938 Chevy with its newly repaired cloth top.

Unfortunately, Lester left far too much rope for the goat, and when he got up the next morning, the goat was standing on the roof-top of his prized little car. The new cloth top was ruined. Lester was beside himself over the incident. Of course, someone had to take the blame. He blamed Mary for not producing breast milk compatible with Mary Helen's colicky stomach.

The goat was soon found back in its original home. Helen soon developed a tolerance for cow's milk.

"I was raised on a church pew…" was a statement I heard over and over growing up. The sociology of my religion was my world. Early memories consisted of one religious grouping after another. Children were brought to church at every opportunity. Biblical teaching was repeatedly ingrained into their minds and emotions. I remember like yesterday my first lesson of sinful language. I had turned about four years of age and was playing in the alley behind the Longview parsonage. I had found a long strip of butcher paper and tore a hole in one end big enough to stick my small head through.

I was playing "Superman." Apparently one of the little church kids had covertly shown me color pictures from a "funny book" with Superman or Captain Marvel comics. (All caped marvels or any worldly captions representing worldly heroes as such were banned and forbidden in our sanctified family).

But, I was captivated by what I saw. Wearing a brightly colored costume, Superman had only to shout, "up, up, and away!" as he raised his arms and flew up into the air. I thought that if I ran fast enough that I would "fly" like Superman and Captain Marvel did. I was looking for a "miracle" like I had heard and seen in my Sunday School characterizations of Samson and the jawbone of an ass, David and Goliath, (of course) Elijah's swimming ax, and all those super miracles that Jesus did, like walking on water. I believed it! My whole family did.

I ran and ran. I tried and tried until I was exhausted. I could not fly! But, I tried one more time and tripped and fell ripping the paper "cape" apart. I got up crying. "Goddammit," I said, "Goddammit," just as Mary came out looking for me. I have no idea nor memory of where I had heard that sinful word.

She was horrified. "David," she said, "don't use those words. That's taking the Lord's name in vain. You can go to hell for that if you don't ask Jesus to forgive you right now!"

I had no idea that Jesus might be offended. I had no concept of the meaning of "taking the Lord's name in vain." And hell was a concept that I associated with fire and pain.

"Ask Jesus to forgive you, right now." She commanded once again.

"Jesus…please forgive me," four-year-old me responded, still not comprehending the gravity of my sin. But it was a start of a lifetime of thinking. It was the meme I still feel that I should ask God's forgiveness every time I cuss.

I had my first out-of-body experience (OBE) and first near-death experience (NDE) when I was around four. The family accompanied Lester to a small lake where he held a mass baptism. Apparently, no one was watching me as I waded around the edges of the lake. I had not learned to swim. Lester had the candidates for baptism wade out to about waist deep water so that he could completely submerge them in baptism just as Jesus had been.

Everyone had their eyes on Lester and the baptism candidates when I stepped into a hole over my head. My first reaction was one of surprise. I opened my eyes. All that I could see was the yellow East Texas lake water.

I did not know what to do other than struggle… to hold something… anything… I inhaled a big gulp of lake water and panicked. Water rushed into my lungs instead of air. I sank below the surface.

I was choking to death losing consciousness when suddenly I felt a hand grab me by the top of my head and jerk me out of the water. The next thing I saw was my body sitting on the bank of the lake. It seemed that I saw myself from thirty or forty yards away. Then instantly, there I was, completely okay, back in my body with no water in my lungs, breathing normally. And, as much as I recall, I brought back no lingering fear or panic.

As Lester continued to baptize, no one noticed my sudden absence from my near-death event. These are the sort of things that imprint a lifelong memory in a child, and this memory lingers throughout life. This is the definition of a meme.

As a three or four-year-old, I have a hazy recollection of church nights, lying on a church bench, looking toward Mary through the spaces between the back-boards of the old wooden benches. I intently watched the service, night after night as Lester preached repentance and salvation. Mary was always at the piano ready to strike a musical cord when Lester gave her a certain look to emphasize a certain phrase, comment, or ready to play the end-of-service hymns.

Most of the time I fell asleep on the bench. Usually, there was nothing else to occupy my mind except Alice, chosen as my twelve-year-old preadolescent babysitter. Or, when she couldn't make it, one of the church ladies sitting at my head or feet, keeping me in the pew. These childhood memories converted into memes of my life, forever embedded in my emotions that faithfully symbolized a mental scenario to any similar situation evoking the neural pathways in my brain.

And I loved Alice, forever.

I distinctly remember a dream I had about her after her family moved away from Longview and out of my life.

I dreamed that Alice was back, but that she had her legs cut off at her knees. She had been positioned upright up by the wall in the hall. I was so overcome and joyful at seeing her again that I ran over to her, hugging her legs and accidentally pushing her over. I tried to stand her up again but could not – she kept falling back to the floor. I awoke extremely saddened by the dream. I guess if you psychoanalyzed that dream you could have concluded that I took a guilt trip on Alice's' absence. Trying to stand her back up, again and again, represents my attempt to go back and find her. I have the meme of disappointed love vividly in my brain to this day when the name Alice comes to mind.

Lester preached about the Holy Ghost and its infilling for those who sought it. He "spoke in tongues" in almost every service. It symbolized a specific approach to communication with God in God's own language. Speaking in tongues was almost a standard practice for every Pentecostal service. An unspoken dictum was if you didn't have it you weren't Pentecostal! People would pray around the altar, some shouting praise to God, others weeping and wailing and seeking the Holy Ghost. You were to tarry until the Holy Ghost filled you with its divine spirit. They cited St. Paul's Acts: "And when Paul had laid his hands upon them, the Holy Ghost came on them; and they spoke with tongues and prophesied." (Acts 19:5-6 KLV).

Some would then begin to utter unintelligible words called *speaking in tongues*, as the Spirit fell upon them. Some would dance about on the floor in a trance, unaware of those around them. I distinctly remember those who became "slain in the Spirit," who would fall to the floor, also unconscious of their surroundings. If it was a woman, there was always some kindly little old lady who would step in to modestly cover her legs with a coat or barring that, with two or three of the church fans. It was my world. I knew no other.

These Pentecostal services would sometimes last into the late hours of the night. I groggily slept on a pew to be picked up by Lester and carried out of the church when the service finally ended, sometimes as late as 11:30 pm or midnight.

I had few friends because the church was a full-time preoccupation for Lester, and Mary had her hands full caring for three babies in diapers. Lester had a quick, fiery temper and began to physically beat me (he called it whippings) before I was even old enough to remember them. My grandmother Watts on Mary's side could not abide him for his abusive ways. When I was a little bit older, I recall Grandma Watts telling me that she witnessed one terrible beating of me when I was a two-year-old toddler. Lester had left his bible open on a small coffee table in her living room and had found a torn page.

There was but one guilty of the offense.

Since he fastidiously carried his bible with him and held on to it anywhere he went, it became an object of curiosity to me, being a curious two-year-old, she told me how I toddled up to the table and then reached for the open page and tore it from this holy treasure, his Bible. I vaguely remember the open Bible and the torn page, (maybe because he taped up the page and continued to use it) but would turn to it from time to time demonstrating my sinful deed.

But I have hidden the painful part of the beating out of my rational mind. It stays as a negative meme in my emotional mind.

On another occasion, I was left in charge of Mary Helen and Donald. That evening, leaving with Mary, Lester gave me (now a little less than four years old) complete charge of Mary Helen and Donald. It must have been a small wedding ceremony or something that only required both Lester and Mary being in the church sanctuary for a short time. Mary carried Robert out wrapped in a small blanket.

"We won't be gone long," he said. Take care of your sister and your little brother Donny, and we'll be back soon," he instructed. I nodded my head. I was secretly proud of the responsibility.

It was a cold winter evening, and a large open gas heater was warming a part of the house. Mary had put up some thin lace curtains in the living room windows. They were too close to the heater. The window was slightly open, and a cold, northern wind was blowing that evening. Occasionally, a gust was strong enough to blow the light curtains. Mary Helen, called "Sissie" by me, was playing with her little doll behind the curtains when a gust of wind caught the curtains that Helen had already pushed out.

They billowed out from the wall and somehow were blown over the top of the open gas-heater. One landed atop the rusty, old, grey heater and stayed. It never really caught fire, but it smoldered and produced a great deal of smoke. The accident was small and didn't do any damage to the room, but the heater slightly scorched the bottom of the nearest curtain. There was no hiding the accident.

Lester returned to the house fifteen minutes or so later smelling smoke, "Who did this?" he shouted, clearly ignoring any natural, accidental occurrence.

I looked at Helen. She looked at me. We were both terrified. "I'm going to whip both of you," Lester said, ripping off his leather belt from his trousers (which was a usual prelude to what was to be in store).

"Don't whip Sissie, Daddy. You can whip me," I said, "but please don't whip Sissie." Sissie was only 18 months old and barely able to talk. I was her constant protector and friend in those days. "Please Daddy," I begged. "I'm sorry."

Lester yanked off his belt, grabbed me by one arm and began to beat me. With my free hand, I tried to protect my backside. I was crying and trying to prevent the belt from further inflicting its intending pain. After five or six blows, Lester stopped. He did not speak further. But at least he didn't whip Mary Helen, not that time and I don't remember ever. It was just another harsh and painful experience that I remember receiving over and over as I grew up from childhood. I was terrified of his beatings. They hurt, but it was mainly the fear of it that hurt.

Consequently, I was terrified of an angry Lester whatever the situation. I was indelibly imprinted by my early childhood years in Longview and before. I began to withdraw from Lester. I was puzzled by my mother's apparent *obedience* to my father's demands, as well as her continuing affection for him. She was my best friend and always sympathetic to me, but she also answered Lester's beck and call.

I became friends with a few children my age who came to church. I could "go home with them" for Sunday dinner (really, Sunday lunch) and return with them for Sunday night services. I have many vivid memories of Lester preaching his standard sinner/salvation sermon and Mary holding up her end at the "altar call," holding forth on the piano with "Softly and Tenderly Jesus is Calling," or if Lester really got wound up, "Are You Ready for the Judgment Day?"

As I mentioned, in those days a church service lasting into the night past 10:00 pm or 11:00 pm was not at all unusual. He was in his element as a true believer and biblical literalist. His church was growing, and he was becoming rather well known as a "good preacher" in the Assemblies of God ecclesiastical circles.

But I began to develop a conflicting emotion to my love toward my father. On the one hand, it was obvious that he exemplified God or Jesus, the loving shepherd, sacrificing both himself and my mother for their "service to God," no matter the weather, the health of he or Mary, nor the health of the children… or just about anything short of death in the family. He was in the service of God! And he clearly loved it.

On the other hand, his need to control, to demand the strictest respect and obedience, and his total disregard for any excuse, coupled with a terrible temper, with a vengeance toward any infraction of his rules produced a conditional love between us that continued until his death.

But there was another side of him, the side that the church people saw. Handsome, witty, quick to demonstrate affection, a superb raconteur, he perpetually filled the church house with people who—after a few visits—either fell in love with this rough-hued young man and his preaching, seeing Lester as a true prophet of God or they went elsewhere.

Mary suffered most of all. We were told that she almost died at her birth, so she had been doted upon throughout her childhood by her deeply religious school-teacher mother, who told us that Mary had been born with her umbilical cord wrapped around her neck. According to Grandma Watts, she survived only after intercessory prayers by the Watts family and church. She subsequently grew up sheltered by her mother and her aunt, Flora Lee.

She was hardly equipped to handle the rough and tumble Summers family lifestyle of farmhands in a depression era, tenant-family with nine children of an uneducated tenant farmer. William G. Summers was himself a cruel patriarch, beating his boys with horsewhips and tying them to chains when he felt an example was needed for his five surviving (of six) sons. It left an indelible impression upon all the Summers boys. Lester was the fourth son.

Mary was the pretty, seventeen-year-old accomplished pianist in the little Assemblies of God church in Palestine, Texas when a young, dynamic, twenty-year-old, evangelist named Lester Summers showed up for a revival meeting and swept her off her feet. They were married a short time later. Married at eighteen and with four babies by the time she was twenty-four, the relentless strain of being a pastor's wife took its toll.

Lester preached twice on Sundays, once on Wednesday nights and, oftentimes, on Friday nights too. It was invariably necessary for Mary to be at Lester's side. There were periods when the pressure and burden were simply more than she could bear. With Mary Helen, Donald, and little Robert, she returned home to her mother's care, then living in Austin, Texas, on more occasions than I can recall. Frail and sickly, sometimes she would stay a month or more to recuperate. But she always came back. When she was gone, I was sent to stay with one or another church member. On a few occasions, I went with her and the rest of my siblings, usually back to her mother's home.

All my pre-public-school education was religious. I never attended any type of pre-school or kindergarten, though Mary enrolled me in piano lessons when I was four years old and we were still in Longview. She would walk with me the four or five blocks to the piano teacher, and as we walked, she taught me old songs that still carry powerful emotions. "Softly and Tenderly Jesus is calling," (Thompson, W. 1888 public domain) and "Are You Ready for the Judgment Day? (Filmore, F. 1893 public domain),

"Love Lifted Me," (Rowe, J 1912 public domain) and other tender songs about the love of Jesus that can still make my eyes well up with tears. (All written/or in the public domain before 1923)

One particular song always touched my heart and often brought tears to my eyes anytime I heard it: "Jesus Savior Pilot Me." "…Over life's tempestuous sea; Unknown waves before me roll, Hiding rock and treach'ous shoal. Chart and compass come from Thee. Jesus Savior, pilot me" (public domain) I didn't understand some of the words but was enraptured by singing along with Mary. Thus, began my enduring love affair with Jesus.

As a child, I never missed a Sunday-school lesson unless I was ill, or the family was traveling to some remote location. Even then, Lester would drive around town looking for an Assembly of God church to display us hoping for an invitation to perhaps "say a few words," and perhaps later secure a preaching engagement.

With a bit of flannel pasted on the back side, flannel-board images brought alive the cut-out biblical characters posted on a cloth-covered poster board. I learned about Jesus healing the lame, caring for the poor, and turning over the tables of the money changers in the temple.

I also learned about Adam and Eve in the Garden of Eden, with the talking snake and God's wrath over his envy and disappointment that the Devil had preempted God about their nakedness. I also learned about Lot's wife turning into a pillar of salt for glancing over her shoulder when she shouldn't have, and a guy named Jonah and the whale that swallowed him – for three days – duly acted out on the flannel board with a moralistic message from the teachers.

It was "true belief." I never doubted it. I remember my fourth Christmas. We didn't believe in Santa Claus and, strangely that year, we didn't observe Christmas as Lester didn't believe in "putting one day above another," according to Scripture. I recall getting nothing for Christmas, and the little "unsaved" lad across the street giving me one of his old toys as a Christmas present. That Spring Mary broke down again, and I was sent to stay with one of the congregation family. It was a miserable experience. It was made worse when I accidentally dropped a door-stop brick on the little boy who was supposed to be my playmate. The edge of the brick struck his big toe… which turned blue and began to fester. I was punished. I was made to stand on a bench for what seemed hours while the teenaged daughter made me sing while she played little children's songs on an ancient piano.

Finally, in a fit of desperation, I ran away. I knew no other place for refuge than the now empty church parsonage that I was so familiar. I began running…and running. A feeling of survival filled me with a strange excitement. I knew it was several miles down the main highway that ran in front of the church. I could find it! I just knew I could. I ran.

I must have been gone an hour or so before the family missed me. But they soon figured out where I might be headed, found me, and picked me up off the road about a mile or so from their home. I was taken back with them to live until Lester and Mary returned. I expected to be punished just as I would have at home, but I wasn't. I wasn't made to sing anymore, and my little, so-called playmate stopped playing with me, I was simply ignored until they returned for me.

I waited for the day when I could get even with the little boy who had betrayed my friendship. It was several weeks before I saw him again. When I did, all my anger had dissipated, and he was just another kid in my Dad's church. But we could never become friends again. To this day, the *meme* of betrayal is as vivid as the day I ran away.

As a true-believing, little boy of pre-school age, my life was a constant state of bewilderment. "God is love," I would recite, before Lester's audience, along with a few other scriptural standbys that I could memorize. And Mary had me learn some little songs like "Jesus loves me this I know…for the bible tells me so… ", (Warner, A ca. 1850 public domain) that I sang along with other songs before the entire congregation.

But I also heard of God's wrath and learned of his cruelty, especially the Old Testament stories of God striking people dead, sending plagues, or sending "fiery snakes" to bite people for complaining. I was distinctly split mentally between the wrath of God and the love of Jesus. It was almost as if Jesus had come to apologize for his angry and murderous God the-Father.

I began to disassociate God from Jesus. I could see a God of anger and wrath and a God of kindness and love as two different spirits.

One summer when I was about four and a half, I was told by some church people that my mother had had another nervous breakdown. I was going to stay with Lester's mother, Grandma Summers, who lived in Oak Cliff, Texas, a suburb of Dallas. Lester took me to the train station and bought a one-way ticket for my trip to Dallas.

It was fun, and I was away from the awful shame and beatings. World War II had begun, and I recall that the train was full of uniformed soldiers. Lester found one who promised to look out for me all the way to Dallas.

He paid the young serviceman $10, which was a lot of money in those days.

The trip from Longview to Dallas lasted about four or five hours with stops all along the way to pick up more soldiers on their way back to camp. When the train pulled into Dallas' Union Station, Grandma Summers and my Aunt Flora (who went by the affectionate name of "Baby Doll") met me at the station. We had two or three more visits before we all picked up stakes and moved to Ft. Worth, Texas in 1942. This is where Lester felt he was called again to minister.

Dr. David P. Summers

Chapter 2
The "Big Time!"

Oh, Tomorrow!

It's dawn.
I gather flecks of myself
To cloak against the chill.

The past is a price
Of a victorious life.
Joy sparks as wind
Beneath the leaves of memory

I was reborn from pain,
From the long lists of disgruntled hopes
Suddenly fulfilled—alive—vibrant
With laughter—glory—newness.

As I voyaged into the rambling memes of memories I
realize what was imagined.

I had crossed over.

(this poem was written at the height of a manic episode in 1965)

Hemphill Heights Assembly of God Church of Ft Worth, Texas was a brand-new, modern endeavor. I never heard talk of the former pastor, but it was far removed from the working class, racially-prejudiced, East Texas oil field congregation of Longview, Texas. The church building was an attractive, new, brick sanctuary, and the congregation was far more educated and affluent. I especially recall Sister Anderson, (fictitious) a beautiful lady with an operatic voice who became very attached to Lester's preaching and came to almost every service.

Her husband was an officer in the army, so she was left alone with her only son, Danny (fictitious), who was a little older than me. He also had a younger sister. Sister Anderson would bring them along to play with me when she came to church to practice her songs for the next Sunday morning. Mary, as ever, faithfully accompanied anyone who wanted to sing.

Sister Anderson lived some blocks away from us in a beautiful, brick home in an affluent neighborhood. The home was beautifully furnished with carpets and drapes, and in one corner of the living room, she had a small electric organ. I was raised with music, but it was entirely from pianos. I was amazed at the beautiful sounds that she made playing the organ. She often had us all over for either dinner or some other social occasion, such as prayer meetings at her home. One evening I was left alone with my little friend to spend the night. As the sun set and darkness gathered, we were having a lot of fun playing around the outside of the house. Suddenly, Danny began jumping up to the window and peeping into the bathroom as he did.

"Whatcha' doing?" I asked.

"C'mon David, you can look at my sister," he said.

Puzzled I went along with the fun.

"C'mon look at her!" he said, as he excitedly pulled me to the bathroom window.

I pulled my head up to the window. Inside, Danny's younger sister was undressing and preparing for her bath. I looked at her completely nude body with total indifference and without any excitement at all. After all, I had seen people almost nude. I had meandered around and watched as ladies changed clothes behind trees or in their cars after being baptized in a lake or pond. From time to time, I had observed Mary Helen as an infant, without clothes. Nudity did not interest my young state of emotional fantasy.

I was puzzled by Danny's fascination with sexual nudity. Sexuality didn't raise its head with me for another two or three years. But when it did, it was of monstrous effect. During my days, I found adventure by roaming the neighborhood, climbing my tree in the backyard, and dreaming of becoming a grown-up. I couldn't read yet, but Mary had taught me several little piano pieces that I played on an old upright parked in the living room.

Sex was simply never mentioned in any manner either at home or in my little church groups. Since I had no prior exposure to the topic, I had no curiosity about it. Sex was still a blank slate.

It was summer in Ft. Worth and a small, city park just a block or two away began setting up activities for kids in the neighborhood. Many families were fatherless as fathers, uncles, and other male relatives had left for war. As World War II became the national obsession, the town council set up city park entertainment during my first summer. The City assigned park counselors and coordinators to oversee activities such as supervised games and activities appropriate for small children such as myself. Two of my most vivid memories were from that summer. For some reason, Lester dropped me off to join a little group of children playing under the supervision of a counselor. I was left alone, playing in the sandbox with a group of neighborhood children.

I had never played in a sandbox, let alone built sand-castles, walls, and small mountains of sand. I was so preoccupied that I forgot my instruction to stay only for a short time and then to "come right home." I was in a state of nirvana. The long minutes turned into an hour or two, and now, way over my time limit, the sun was beginning to set. I was having so much fun that I became unconscious of time. I was living completely in the here and now.

As dusk crept upon us, a small screen was set up in the park, and the children gathered around, sitting on the ground with a few adults on chairs, as an old 8-mm projector was set up. I watched with fascination at the outdoor cartoons that started to play. I was captivated by "moving pictures." They fascinated me! How could those characters that were so very human appear on a flat screen set up in a small city park?

I had never seen such a display of light and sound. I had never seen moving pictures! Transfixed, I could not leave. I knew that I had overstayed my fun; nevertheless, I could not wait to run home and tell Lester or Mary what an unusual sight I witnessed in the park. I was sure that my discovery would be met with interest or, at least, curiosity, and that my tardiness would be excused.

Instead, after I arrived home late, an already irritated Lester told me that I could go to hell for watching "shows." He truly objected to me watching Donald Duck and Bugs Bunny on an outdoor movie screen with a dozen or so other little kids. My newly found nirvana quickly faded.

I was so taken back, that I never saw a Hollywood-made movie until I was in fifth grade, around thirteen years old.

That year had been a great time for me as I learned to swim that summer. That fall I entered the first grade and began making friends with little kids outside my church congregation. I was almost six years old. Mary enrolled me at five-years of age; the school made an exception to its six year-old enrollment requirement since I would be six in October.

On the first day of school, our first-grade teacher called all the class to the blackboards and instructed us to take the chalk and write our names on the blackboard. I had never been taught to spell my name. In fact, I was totally ignorant of the alphabet. When I was called to write my name, I could not. A little classmate stepped in to help and wrote my name based on the sound of the syllables he heard me pronounce. It didn't quite pass muster with my teacher.

After less than one year in Ft. Worth, Lester again felt the "call" to move on. This time it was to Brownwood, Texas. With tears in their eyes, Sister Anderson and my little friends told me good-bye.

Why would God call him away so quickly, I wondered?

The "call" to Brownwood was a non-sequitur; it just didn't make sense. We were leaving a politely-educated, rather intellectual, congregation in a beautiful two-story brick sanctuary with a big frame parsonage on South Adams street in a friendly neighborhood with good schools for an unknown "calling" to Central Texas. Lester was "called" to a "church" that consisted of an old run-down tin warehouse with the former pastor's family of seven or eight still living in some clap-board rooms thrown together at the back of the warehouse. The services were a mix of three or four families and a few G.I.s transitioning through Camp Bowie on their way to war.

In Brownwood, the former preacher and family father had abandoned the family, but some of the older children were still living there with the mother when we arrived (and there were rumors that two of the older daughters had temporarily taken "live-in" soldiers without the benefit of a marriage license. Suffice to say, their activities would hardly fall into the "sanctified" category for an acceptable Assembly of God lifestyle.

The meeting hall was the interior of an old warehouse interspaced with floor-to-ceiling, wooden beams. The seats were 1"x 6" wooden slats nailed to X-shaped boards of the same material and size that hopefully supported the weight of the attendees. The floor was heavy, wooden slats with red oiled, saw-dust sprinkled here and there to catch dirt from shoes and was easily swept when services were over.

With our worldly belongings packed into a little two-wheeled trailer borrowed from Mary's father, Lester and I made a couple of trips from Ft. Worth to Brownwood with our meager belongings tucked under a large tarpaulin, flapping in the wind behind Lester's '38 Chevy cloth-top coupe.

I was six years old, and the move to Brownwood became etched in my mind. The trip took us about five hours each way. And this was the first time that I was alone with Lester for such an extended period. I recall how emotional Lester would become at times on that trip. We would begin singing one of his favorite hymns. Then he would begin to pray aloud as he drove and occasionally he would speak in tongues, asking God to forgive him of his (unknown to me) sins. "I'm unworthy, Lord," he would repeat over and over as I sat beside him on the front seat. "Lord, I'm unworthy." I was puzzled that he felt "unworthy." To me, he was the ideal child of God. No one worked harder and deserved to be "worthy" more than Lester. I heard him use these words and phrases in his prayers throughout his entire life.

Other times during these trips, he would recount stories of his boyhood in Lancaster County and of his move to Oak Cliff when he was in his early teens. And many times, he would retell the story of his "hunting accident" at 16 years of age, when a boyhood friend was kidding around with a rifle. It accidentally went off and put a bullet into Lester's back and stomach. He told and retold of how he almost died and, in the hospital, and in his deliriums, he saw hell itself.

He told me that he saw himself standing at the edge of a steep, crumbling precipice. He looked out into a burning hell. As the precipice began to fall beneath his feet, he saw Jesus reach out to him, pulling him back, saving him from eternal perdition in the lake of fire beneath his feet. This vision was imprinted into my mind as a place of damnation and eternal punishment for any sin that I might commit. The story was repeated many, many times in church services as he used it to exemplify the need for salvation from damnation as a sinner. In his early years, he invariably made his call to sinners to come and be saved at the end of almost every sermon.

Mercifully, Lester did not attempt to integrate us into the shabby rooms at the back of the old warehouse and into what remained of the husbandless family that…well, had no place to go. He found a small track home at the foot of "Bangs Hill" (part of the Llano Estacado – a range of low cap-rock hills that separated Central Texas from West Texas), newly constructed on the outskirts of Brownwood. Lester miraculously swung a deal that put our little family into the brand-new, two-bedroom bungalow. Cute, perhaps, for a family with one kid, but, for a family of six, we were constantly stepping on and over each other. Poor Sissie had to make do sleeping in the same bed as Robert.

Lonely, scared, and dejected, I picked up my interrupted first-grade instruction and enrolled at Brownwood's J.R. Looney grammar school in the winter of 1944.

After a few months, I completed my first school year. That summer I began to make a few friends, and my loneliness and self-doubt began to lift. The rocky hill running almost into our backyard became my "secret garden" of imaginary adventure and exploration. I began to hike the thousand or so feet to the top of the outcrop just to be able to look out over the horizon and take in the beauty of the vista below. By the time school started again, I was eager to explore new worlds.

The city of Brownwood had an archaic little bus that served our edge of-town subdivision as municipal transportation. Each morning in the second grade, I walked three blocks from the house to wait for the creaky old bus to pick me up at 7:30 am that got me and the other kids to school by 8:15 am.

As I took my tin lunch box, my school books, and enough change for the fare, I would ride the bus to school and then around 3:30 pm, I rode it back. The school set on our side of town, about 3 or 4 miles away. However, my biggest adventure was walking home from school when the bus broke down.

Late one afternoon, on one of those occasions, I had walked home but had stopped to inspect the little garden I had planted at the back of the house. While I was looking at my small crop of tomatoes, I heard Mary call out from the kitchen window.

"Davey," she called, "Come on into the house – now!" There was a certain urgency in her voice.

"Why," I answered, "What is it?" as I began to walk towards the house. As I approached the back door, I smelled smoke. It was not the smell of something burning, but the smell of wet smoldering wood, the lingering odor of a snuffed-out fire. The ground was wet and tramped down, and it looked like a lot of people had walked around the backyard to the last window of the back bedroom where my two brothers and I slept. The fire department had left their distinct signature on the grounds. It dawned on me that the unbelievable had happened. There had been a fire…in my house!

"Oh my, momma, did the house catch on fire or something?" I yelled as I pulled open the screen door.

"Yes, she replied," but it's all out now. The fire department left about an hour ago. It started in the closet in your bedroom." That remark puzzled me.

As I entered the house, I noticed my four-year-old brother Donny sitting on a chair close to Mary. He had been crying. "What happened?" I asked.

"It was an accident," she said. "Donny and his little friend were in the closet with a candle looking at Daddy's new outboard motor."

Lester had just bought the little outboard motor from Montgomery Ward's and just couldn't wait to try it out. Much to our delight, he took us all for a quick outing one spring Saturday.

Donny was fascinated by the outboard motor. He brought a little neighbor boy into the house, and then into the closet to show him Lester's prize toy. They were in a closet full of clothes with lighted candles when one of them accidentally set the clothes in the closet on fire. No one ever knew which came first; the fire igniting a recital dress that Mary Helen had hung in the closet or…if Lester's outboard had a residue of gas from the fuel tank and wonders of wonders that there was not an explosion…a fire might have started just from the fumes from the tank itself.

Accidents happen. But this one came awfully close to becoming a disaster.

Mercifully, Donny and his little friend were able to exit the closet with only singed eyebrows and scorched faces. The fire burned the inside of the closet door and some of the bedroom walls before the volunteer firefighters arrived and quickly extinguished it. Mary contained the fire by the simple act of slamming the closet door behind the two boys. Lester was away on church business.

The next day Lester contacted Lee Watts to come to help repair the damage so that we boys had a place to sleep, except on the floor in the living room, which we did until the repairs were made. Grampa Watts was always there, willing to help when needed. Within a day or so, he arrived with his tools and big electric saw on the same trailer that we had used to move to Brownwood.

Working together, they quickly repaired the fire-damaged bedroom. While they were doing so, Lester had Lee build the garage into a third bedroom, so Mary Helen could have her own bed and would not have to sleep with one of her brothers. Donny, she complained, was a "kicker" and woke her up by thrashing around in his sleep. Certainly, she could not put up with baby Robert. He still regularly wet the bed. Since Mary only washed clothes once per week and bed linen was in short supply, Lester routinely came into the bedroom, sometimes late at night and awakened us all to rouse young Bobby from bed to take him to the bathroom to relieve his bladder, hoping to avoid another wet bed and bedsheet change. Sometimes it worked, but most of the time, it didn't. When it didn't, Lester would simply throw a towel over the wet spot for Robert to sleep through the night. It was a relief for Donny and me to have a bed in the garage.

The year my little church friends taught me to masturbate, I was an oversized, seven-year-old. They also taught me secrecy, shame, and guilt.

World War II was in full swing by then, and the new Camp Bowie with the 36th Armored Division located just outside of Brownwood brought tens of thousands of raw, young men for their final training. The 36th Armored Division was on its way to Europe to participate in the Allied landing at Anzio and were the first American troops to land in Europe. I was fascinated with the life of soldiers, many of whom would never return. These "worldly" young men, laughing and joking, seemingly without a care in the world, were so different from the stern, tight-lipped, guilt-tripping Pentecostals that dominated my earlier impressions of those childhood years.

I was amazed that they could be so happy and not be one of us: "the chosen few." When Lester preached a few "street services," I happily handed out gospel tracts to the little crowd that gathered around him. I hoped that they all would become "saved," so I could be one of them. They seemed so free! I was allowed to talk to a few as I handed them the little folded message from God, but that stopped when they accepted and asked me questions, which I usually could not answer. Otherwise, I was forbidden to develop a relationship.

Chapter 3

Build 'em and They Will Come!

Winter on Bang's Hill

*The old dog sniffs the wind
High nosed, Tail tucked
between his legs.*

*Vapour swirls up
From the ground
Then quickly disappears*

*The fall air is full of light
And wind scythes across the plains.*

*The scent of damp straw
And carefree laughter
Calms for another season.*

*And around the square
Men gabble About
hog-killing.
And "beef on the hoof."*

*And occasionally
About the war
That they missed
Winter is coming.
Get busy!*

(all poetry was written by me, 1966)

It was time to build!

Grandpa Lee Watts, a proficient carpenter and builder, soon joined Lester and a few church members to demolish the old, tin-framed, warehouse building in Brownwood called the Central Assembly of God by Lester. Even before the old building was demolished, Lester hired a professional sign maker and put up a 4' by 4' sign in front reading, "Future home of Central Assembly of God." He was proud of his sign as it was made of a "new metal material called magnesium." Why he was so giddy over magnesium, we never knew. Someone evidently did a good sales job on him!

Construction began on a brand-new, cement block building that could seat 200 or more.

The new church, made from cream-colored blocks, was completed within a few months, and Lester began holding services as soon as the roof and floor were laid. There were about fifty or so regular attendees for Sunday School and about the same number that attended the Sunday night services. He simultaneously began to promote the church to prospective attendees by lining up a series of weekly revivalists and singers.

Mary was an essential part of all Lester's services. She played piano and Lester would lead the singing. Occasionally, they sang together as a rather pleasing duet with Lester singing tenor. We always had one or two instrumentalists who sang, and they often played guitar and/or accordion. Mary installed a choir to sing regular, old and familiar hymns to brighten the services. "There's Power in Blood," (Public domain Jones, L.,1899) "Blessed Assurance, Jesus is Mine," (Public Domain, Crosby, F., 1873) "What a Friend We have in Jesus," (Public Domain, Scriven, J., 1855) and other mostly old Methodist hymns drifted up into the day or night, as the service went on and on.

Handing out lovely, little white bibles as prizes for highest attendance, Lester had Sunday School attendance and Sunday night services hitting about a hundred or so in no time.

I was then in the second grade and began to learn that I was not quite like the other kids in my school. Though my classmates did not know it, I knew that it was sinful to "go to shows" (movies) like they did, "take the Lord's name in vain," like I occasionally heard one of the "unsaved" boys do, play cards, smoke, drink alcohol, or dance, like their parents did, and I knew that you could go to hell if you forgot to ask for forgiveness for your sins every night at bedtime.

Some things are inevitable.

I suppose there was nothing unusual in the way Lester began to expose himself sexually to me, but it goes back earlier in my life than I can remember. In fact, it seemed a usual practice in my early life. He had absolutely no hesitation about urinating or defecating while I was in the bathtub or out in the woods somewhere, but his emphasis on nudity and teaching me how to clean my penis with instructions on how to make a habit of keeping the foreskin pulled back made a distinct impression on me.

On a regular basis, in order "to avoid circumcision," he would have me pull my foreskin back behind the head of my penis. I began to carry out his instructions. Invariably, when my attention was directed to this little bit of hygiene, but when I was alone, it usually resulted in an erection. The erection was nothing new in my young life, as more times than not, I would awaken with a full bladder accompanied by an annoying erection. The annoying part was that I couldn't pee until the erection went away.

But Lester also made it a habit of quizzing me on how well I assimilated his health details into my own life. "David, are you washing your peter (Lester's nomenclature for penis) and keeping it clean?" he would ask me when he would intrude on my bath time.

"Uh huh," I would duly answer. "Let me see it," he would order. When I stood up to show my clean penis, he would direct me to pull the foreskin back for examination. "Okay, you sure don't want to have to get it circumcised," he would say when exiting.

No, I didn't, and I made sure it was nice and clean!

But I never learned masturbation until Ronny showed me his fascination with penises.

Ronny Hudson (fictitious) was the little church boy who gave me my first lessons in masturbation. He was the son of a poor, large, retired preacher's family that attended Lester's church. I was maybe a little older than he, but he seemed to be the wisest, at least street-wise. He seemed to know more about the world than I, at least regarding sexual anatomy.

The preacher-father had retired to become a junk dealer selling used furniture and appliances, old car parts, and any other thing of minimal value that could be found in and around Brownwood. A lot of it was just given to him as friends and acquaintances replaced their own worn-out household items. The little boy had at least eight or nine brothers and sisters. His family lived on the edge of abject hunger and poverty. But they, like other impoverished members, came to church regularly, and occasionally, Lester would have the old preacher come up to the pulpit and

"say a few words."

One Sunday, he asked if I would like to go home with him for lunch and return that evening for Sunday night service. It was okay with Lester, so I went.

I was fascinated by the way they lived. Impoverished and primitive hardly described the lifestyle. Junk was everywhere. They were junk dealers. There were secret places out of sight that were a world of sheer fantasy to me.

We were privately playing amongst the junk and squalor inside the old wooden container when Ronny unbuttoned his pants and began to masturbate right in front of me. "Let's play with ourselves," he invited.

"Okay," I responded. But when I took my limp penis out of my pants, Ronny said, "Look, you have to play with it," he said, pointing to my penis. "Like this," he said.

He had a tiny erection which he was wagging up and down. "Look, go back and forth," he instructed, demonstrating with his own penis, "it feels good!"

Curious, I followed as he demonstrated, but nothing happened, and nothing seemed any more unusual to me than when I urinated in front of my two younger brothers. On occasions I had woken up with an erection in the past but thought nothing of it other than I would have to stand before the toilet and wait for it to go down. It was the massaging and stroking that intrigued me. But, nothing took place out of my ordinary bounds of experience.

It wasn't until I was alone in bed sometime later that I discovered the real purpose of an erect penis. Obviously, as a naïve, seven-year-old boy, I had no preconceptions about sex. I didn't achieve orgasm the first few times I tried to masturbate. It didn't feel bad, but it didn't do anything for me other than wear me out. I certainly did not know that there was a certain point when the sexual orgasm took over, and nothing would stop it.

But a few nights later I was in bed fondling my penis and doing the masturbation routine that Ronny had taught me. Suddenly, a strange sensation began to occur in my penis that I had never experienced before. It was a warm and pleasant sensation and felt better and better the more I stroked it. Finally, as the feeling intensified, something happened beyond any past experiences – the sensation peaked in an indescribable, pleasurable few moments of orgasm. It began deep down in my groin then moved up into my penis. It lasted only several seconds, then subsided just as quickly as it came. I was literally overwhelmed by the brief pleasure that I had discovered.

I didn't know what they called it but learned that in that orgasmic moment of pleasure, those feelings clouded all my sense of presence and surroundings. Those few moments soon became something of which I couldn't get enough. In that moment, I found pure freedom from sin and shame that I subconsciously carried with me every moment of the day.

And I also soon found out that it was something that most of my other little friends were already indulging in. It was called, "jacking off."

None of us had a clue that this practice was perfectly normal for sexually maturing, prepubescent boys, nor did any of us have a clue as to what homosexuality was, but, subjectively, it was innocent fun. It was jokingly called a "circle jerk" by the big boys. In my little group of friends, we called it "playing with yourself." Thus, a social group of three or four prepubescent boys was born in my neighborhood. We indulged freely and innocently in masturbation for a few years.

But, you "go to hell for it," I was told later by one of the church boys. *Go to hell for something that makes you feel good?* I wondered. *I thought you go to hell for the things that make you feel bad.*

I was about eight years of age. Like Adam and Eve in the Garden of Eden from the Bible stories I learned in Sunday School who told God little white lies about who ate the apple, I subliminally felt that I was disobeying some biblical commandment. I began fabricating a life of little white lies about where I was and what I was doing as masturbating became a nightly ritual, right after my bedside prayers to Jesus for forgiveness for what I had learned to do.

My mind was already split between God, the stern and unforgiving father and Jesus, the loving and forgiving son.

More and more, I opted for the loving Jesus.

Masturbation had split my personality between good and evil.

I was in a strange state of emotional dichotomy. I was good when I didn't allow myself the sexual pleasure, but evil when I did? Lester had not queried me on this new habit, but I subliminally knew that I was doing something that could come back to haunt me. I was hooked on this new pleasure that I had so recently learned.

About the same time, I began to slip out of church just before Lester preached. The restrooms were at the entrance of the church and had windows that would open outward when turned with a small crank. I was slender enough to slip through the opening and drop to ground a few feet below.

I would wait until Lester was about to begin his preaching and then during an opening prayer or song make my move to the restroom – like a normal kid needing to pee. Lester would become so preoccupied with preaching that he never noticed my absence. I learned that once I slipped through the restroom window, I was free to walk around the darkened streets alone. Sometimes, I would go and sit in our car with the radio playing softly, and other times I would simply roam the mostly empty street in front of the church in the dark of night, occasionally walking down to an ice house on the corner to buy a piece of candy or, if lucky enough, a soda. As the service ended, I would slip in with the exited crowd, mingling as if I too had just finished sitting through the service.

One night, I slipped out the restroom window, and noticed a car parked across the street with a man sitting in the front seat with the radio playing. I had seen him before. He was the man who always dropped off and picked up Sister Sanders (fictitious), one of Lester's regulars, and tonight she was attending the regular Sunday night meeting. I noticed that he was obviously quite early to be waiting for services to end.

I walked casually by the car parked under a street light, "Hey, where you are going?" he pleasantly asked.

"Uh, nowhere," I slowly replied. "I'm just waiting for church to be over."

"Well, me too," he said, "Come on over and listen to the radio with me!" He reached over and opened the passenger door.

"Get in," he said. "I'm waiting for my wife to come out."

I recognized who he was, so with little hesitation I got in. Then he said,

"yeah, I thought you were the preacher's boy." "Yes sir, I am," I said.

"What are you doing out here and not in church?" He queried.

"I dunno," I said, "I just wanted to come outside for a little while."

I didn't tell him how I had slipped out and gotten outside, or that slipping out was one of my regular routines. "Don't you get into trouble for slipping out?" he asked.

I didn't answer.

I could see his reflection in the windshield as he slowly puffed on his cigarette.

Finally, he said, "You know, Ronny comes out and talks to me sometimes."

"You mean Ronnie Hudson?" I asked.

"Yeah," said the man, "that's the one."

Ronny, my little junk dealer's preacher-son Sunday School playmate, was not at church that night. The man obviously had some agenda.

"He does?" I asked again.

"Yeah, sometimes we drive over to Pecan Bayou Park," said the man.

Pecan Park was a little truck-stop-layover built at the edge of town where Pecan Bayou intersected the main highway running southwest from Dallas/Ft. Worth to Brownwood. A lot of traffic coming in and out of Camp Bowie simply caught a few winks once the passenger was dropped off or picked up from the for the 36th Armored Division.

Wow! I thought. Riding around town at night in a car…what a break from just walking up and down the sidewalk. Then I said, "that would be fun."

You could hear through the open windows that Lester had just started preaching so it would still be about an hour or so before the service let out. We talked as the radio played softly in the background.

"Well, let's go see what's going on in the park," the man suddenly said.

"Okay," I said. He turned the ignition key on and stepped on the starter pedal. The car started, and he eased it out in low gear. He drove quietly away from the front of the church. Ten minutes later, we were at the park.

He stopped the car and lit up another cigarette. I sat in the dark silently, but I could still see his face because of the dim light of the radio. He said nothing for a long time. Finally, he said, "you know…Ronny played with me," he looked at me. It was sort of an inquisitive statement that left me to figure out the meaning. He looked closely at me for my reaction.

Played? Does that mean what I think it does? I wondered. Do little boys play that way with grown men? Apparently so.

I looked over in the dim light. Brother Sanders had opened his trousers and exposed his erect penis.

"Want to make fifty cents?" he asked. "I paid Ronny fifty cents to play with me."

"Um…" I hesitated, "what do I have to do?" I said slowly. I was pretty sure I knew what he was talking about.

"I bet you can do it better than Ronny…let's see" he urged, taking my hand and placing it on his penis.

I had never seen an adult man's erect penis and was intrigued more than anything else. I had made rather close, passing relationships with Lester's adult friends. Usually, it was through a revival or similar church gathering. But, never in my wildest dreams did I consider that anyone in my father's church carried an ulterior, much more sinful, motive for a boy-man friendship. This man was asking me to do to him what I had just been taught by another little boy in the church.

Ronny had already shown me how to do it. So, I slowly began the stroking the man's penis.

After no more than a few seconds Brother Sanders reached over to the glove box, opened it, and pulled out a handful of tissue. "I've got to put these over it," he said sheepishly as he ejaculated into the tissue.

At that time, however, I had no idea that anything was coming from his Kleenex-covered penis.

I was bemused, without any sense of erotic experience.

"Now, don't tell anyone," he instructed. "in fact, I'm going to give you a dollar, so promise you won't tell anybody about this," he said. "Now, I've got to go back and pick up my wife.

"Okay," I said. "I promise not to tell anyone." (Incidentally, I've never broken the promise until now). So much for the sanctity of promises to immoral churchgoers.

It was the first and last time I encountered Brother Sanders at the church. He would quickly arrive and drop Sister Sanders off, then quickly drive away. I never again saw him waiting for his wife an hour or so before church let out. He obviously feared that his deeds with Ronny and myself would get back to Lester and the churchmen. My little friend Ronny may have continued to rendezvous with him from time to time.

Even then, as a seven-year-old boy, I felt something was fundamentally wrong with the situation of a grown man having a child masturbate him.

With World-War II ending in 1945, Mary Helen (now simply called Helen), Donald (now just called Donny or Don), and Robert (now just called Bob by all his siblings and Bobby by Mary) had finally all grown up beyond babyhood. Now a tall, lanky eight-year-old, I was given the responsibility of watching over them on many church service nights. The perpetually exhausted Mary, sometimes unable to get herself and all of us dressed each time there was a service, entrusted me to "babysit" them at home, especially when a revival preacher came to hold nightly revival meetings lasting every night for two or three weeks.

This was the period when I was given the "big brother" image. The mental imprinting and emotional bonding into the minds of my younger siblings gave me a certain parent-like dominion over their lives with their wonderful respect that remains to this day. I recall our old black-dial, stand-up RCA radio that was parked in the living room. I would turn it on, and we would gather around listening as I tuned it to the Lone Ranger or the Shadow Knows and other long-running radio programs that we never listened to when Lester was home. I could see the excitement mingled with happiness in their eyes as they gathered about and sat cross-legged on the floor, listening intently.

I was a hero to them. Big brother.

The relief and joy of the Allied victory and the war's end brought a brief period of happy experiences to the Summers family. We began to take middle of the week holidays at Lake Brownwood, a few miles to the west. We would be joined by the B.J. Brumbel (deceased) family of De Leon, Texas. De Leon was about an hour's drive from Brownwood. The Brumbels pastored the Assembly of God church in that small Central Texas town. They were not as stern and strict as our family with Lester as the patriarch, because in the Brumbel family, the matriarch, Zannie Mary, (deceased) was the dominant authority and not B.J. Though she was as stern as Lester, she ruled the house in a kindlier, matriarchal manner. During those family get-togethers, the family's only son, Elton, and I developed a strong boyhood friendship.

During the summer vacation, the two families would often get together for a Friday and Saturday mini-holiday on Lake Brownwood. Lester and B.J. rented small boats from the rental guy who had his boats on the lake. He had them tied up in long floating docks near the dam. Lester locked his prized (still scorched from the house fire) 5-HP Sea King outboard motor onto the transom of the little aluminum boat and, careful not to tip the boat, we piled in. With the wind streaming by and our hands over the sides, we'd gleefully putter around Lake Brownwood for an hour or so of boating adventure and excitement.

In the afternoon, we strung long trotlines with hooks hanging down about three feet and about a foot apart. For bait, we used a long net sein trapping crayfish, minnows, and small perch, pulling the net along the small creeks and tributaries that ran along the lake. Sometimes, we even caught grasshoppers and small frogs for bait, or anything that would attract the catfish we were after. We then set the lines with the bait and waited overnight.

Mary and Zannie oversaw the meals. At night we all camped out on surplus army cots we set up by a log fire. I was filled with excitement and could hardly go to sleep! I looked up at the stars and occasionally a shooting star would streak across the dark sky. As the sun rose, we took our little boat across the lake and ran the lines. It was great fun. We usually caught six or seven catfish, weighing 5-10 pounds. Sometimes we caught a very large catfish. Once we caught a very large "yellow cat" that weighed about 60 pounds.

I became fast friends with Elton, (fictitious) the youngest of the two sibling family, (Mary Evelyn (deceased) was the older sister by several years). Elton was a year older than me. Sometimes, I could go visit him for a few days. I was like a bird out of its cage when at the Brumbels and, since Elton was almost a year older than me, all those big kid friends of his automatically liked me and accepted me as an equal.

I learned a lot from Elton. During the summer, I could spend a week or so with him. We would sometimes join a group of older boys at a beloved swimming hole on the Colorado River. We would shed our clothes gleefully to jump into the water buck-naked, splashing and yelling in boyhood delight.

Much of the boyhood conversations were about boy-girl sexual fantasies. Occasionally, there were some boys who masturbated together, seemingly without guilt, but Elton claimed to have what every boyhood dreamed of: a girlfriend who was having sex with him! I was enthralled. My imagination was captivated as he described how the sex act was carried out.

That summer the Brumbel family became a once-upon-a-summer escape from perpetual church and Sister Sanders' perverted husband. I forgot fear and guilt!

But not for long. Something began to bother Lester. He seemed torn by compulsion and restraint. It was a psychological enigma to me. The second shoe was still to drop.

Shortly after I entered the fourth grade, my music teacher began to audition us for a class musical. She was a wonderful, kind and gracious lady who asked us all to sing a little song for the program. The class presentation was a few songs based on the new hit Broadway stage and song debut, "Oklahoma!" which I knew absolutely nothing about. But always eager to please my teachers and grown-ups, I gave my little singing rendition and was selected immediately for the lead role. After confiding in Mary, she told me to keep it a little secret and not tell Lester. His obsession against any Hollywood or Broadway presentation to mankind – even reading the Sunday "funnies" before church was forbidden in the Summers household. So, I kept it to myself.

Luckily for me, the show was put on one Friday afternoon. Somehow, Mary was able to sneak away to attend my worldly song and stage debut presentation. She was never able to fully share my joy of playing the lead in the all-time hit.

But before the year could end, I was caught up in a net of "sin" once again. I was caught passing notes with another boy. We were giggling and kidding around about New Year's Resolutions as this was the class topic. We began to joke about our own New Year's Resolutions. He wrote something like he would quit playing hooky from school and passed the note to me. I made a similar promise and passed the note back.

He then wrote that he would be nice to girls and not kiss them. I agreed and then wrote that I would quit "jacking off" for the new year. He wrote back that he would not "corn-hole" anyone (adolescent expression for anal sex). We were having a good time with our New Year's Resolutions! But, the teacher eventually caught us and grabbed the note. I was petrified as she quickly read the note. Then she frowned and began walking out of the classroom.

"I'm taking this to Mr. Franklin" (fictitious) she said. *Oh no, not the principal*, I thought. I grimaced and sunk down in my seat awaiting my fate. Once again, I was caught during a "sinful" act and was terrified of the consequences. We'd simply been joking around – pre-adolescent boys mimicking grown-up adults in class. Any mature parent would have just instructed a kid that some words were inappropriate.

Not in my life.

That evening Lester called me to the living room to tell me that the principal had called him to his office and shown him the note. He said the principal "had never seen anything as bad as this," and "was in tears" when he showed Lester the note. "You and that boy were talking about sin," he shouted.

"No Daddy, no," I said. "We were just kidding around." "David. I'm going to whip you," he said.

"I'm sorry Daddy," I cried, "I didn't really mean it. Please don't whip me again," I pleaded. "I won't do it again."

But Lester was committed to letting this be a lesson to me. He once again whipped off his belt and administered a beating.

Strangely, Lester never attempted to sit down with me and discuss sex, much less lecture me on the "evils" of masturbation until a couple of years later. But he began coming into the bathroom and observing me while I took a bath. It was nothing unusual about it, but I wanted privacy. I tried locking the door, but he would pound on it and order me to unlock it and let him in, dripping wet I would climb out of the bathtub and flip the pushdown door latch, so he could enter the bathroom, and then try to get back into the tub before he entered. His standard saying always was that he had to "go to the bathroom."

One evening, I was alone in the bathtub taking my Saturday night bath. Suddenly, Lester burst in. "Stand up!" he commanded. Then pointing at my penis, "why is that thing so red?" he demanded. On some occasions, it was, as I sometimes overdid Lester's genital washing instructions and washing turned into masturbation. But most of the time it wasn't. I didn't want to get caught doing it. When it was red, I had an excuse, saying that a tick or chigger had bitten me on my penis (which happened once) and that chiggers did make my penis red and swollen.

I could tell that most of the time he didn't believe me. But oddly, at other times, he was indifferent. Additionally, it always seemed that Lester enjoyed undressing in front of me and exhibiting himself naked. And he liked that I always cleaned my penis when bathing. We were oddly like two naked men in a bathhouse, except that I was eight years old. The one time I remember Mary trying to intervene on my behalf to stop Lester from another beating was also associated with bath-time.

I had taken a long bath and left the water standing for the next in line (usually it would be one of the boys, either Don or Bob). Water was scarce, especially hot water. My big mistake was forgetting to take the bar of soap from the bathwater and placing it on the side of the tub as I had been instructed. It was the Saturday night bath ritual.

I had taken my bath in preparation for Sunday services. There was still water in the tub as I had left it for other children to bathe. Also, a custom. Lester entered the bathroom shortly after I left. "David, you come here," he commanded. Fear gripped my heart. I knew by the tone and delivery of his voice that I was in deep trouble for something, but I didn't know what.

Lester was holding a thoroughly softened bar of soap in his hand. "Look what you left in the bathtub," he loudly called me from the bathroom. "You're supposed to take the soap out of the water when you get out!" He began to unbuckle his belt. "I'm going to make you remember to take it out next time you bathe," he shouted.

"Oh please, Daddy, don't whip me," I pleaded. "I won't do it again."

But as Lester raised his belt, suddenly Mary seized his hand and yanked the belt away. "No Daddy," she said. "You are not going to whip David again." She stood defiantly between Lester and me. He again started to move his hand to strike me, but Mary raised the belt she had grabbed from his hand. Then, she slapped the thoroughly surprised Lester hard in the face with the belt she had grabbed from him. Lester stood bewildered.

Mary had never countermanded his divine, patriarchal authority in the family. "But he disobeyed me, Mary," Lester said.

"I don't care," Mary responded, "you're not whipping him again."

There was a momentary standoff. Finally, Mary handed him his belt. Lester turned and walked away.

"Go to your room, David," she instructed. This was the only time I ever witnessed Mary trying to protect one of us from our father's wrath.

It was almost biblical to me. Like the angel that stayed the hand of Abraham when he was about to sacrifice Isaac, his only son. But nothing much changed. Lester still exerted his patriarchal authority.

Since Lester never had any reluctance to urinate or defecate in front of me, and he was never shy about being naked in front of me, he also had me give him enemas because he was chronically constipated. Over my early years growing up, he constantly asked me to come into the bathroom with him when he was constipated and help him give himself an enema. He asked me to hold the enema tube in his rectum. I did as I was asked. It was almost a weekly occurrence for me in Brownwood.

Kneeling on the bathroom floor with the enema tube inserted in his rectum, he would ask me to hold the tube.

Then, when he was ready he would say, "turn it on." After a minute or so, he would order "now turn it off," and then, "take it out," as he quickly moved from the floor to the commode seat in a repulsive, explosive release.

Bits of feces sometimes clung to the tube as I held it away from me and waited for his next command. It was abhorrent to me psychologically, but I carried out his request as I always tried to do the many others, while mentally holding my nose and hiding in a cloud of mental darkness to try and forget the experiences. This practice lasted into my early adolescence.

It was male nudity in its most grotesque manifestation.

Sex was beginning to consume my life. I was masturbating almost every day and sometimes two or three times a day, taking any opportunity when alone to do it. I was also obsessed with the guilt that it produced. I was miserable and knew I was going to hell for it. But the sexual climax from masturbation was more than enough to overcome my inhibitions and my tormented thoughts of sinning and going to hell. At least, I could transcend these psychopathic thoughts in the few moments of orgasm. But my depression would come back relentlessly.

And Lester again had the itch to move on.

Unexplainably abandoning the three-year-old church, now with a solid growing congregation he had worked so hard to develop in Brownwood, he again told us that God had "called," and he "tried out" for pastorship of a rickety, old, two-story frame church in urban Houston called Glad Tidings Assembly of God.

I was yanked out of Brownwood's Central Ward School's fourth-grade class right before the school year ended. Then we all packed up and moved to Houston's Glad Tidings Assembly of God which was immediately found to be such a disappointment to Lester and hence to the rest of the family that we all referred to the church as "Sad Tidings Assembly."

Again, we were crammed into a small two-bedroom parsonage connected to the back of the church. When September rolled around, I again set out to make friends with another new group of classmates in Houston. But this was to be short-lived as well.

Right before Christmas, Lester decided he had enough of "Sad Tidings" and decided to go back to the evangelistic field. He had his older brother Milton (*deceased*), send down a large, open rack, flat-bed truck with its driver which we loaded up with all our belongings, and again moved. This time we moved to Irving, Texas. We moved into a small home on the edge of town which was rented out to him by Milton.

But this too was short-lived. Lester only managed to secure a couple of preaching engagements several hundred miles away. He took the train or bus and left Mary the car to drive us to school and pick us up, go to the grocery store, wash clothes and carry out any other errands that were needed. His preaching engagements kept him away while Mary tried her best to cope with the helplessness of the situation. Bob was still not in school. Don was in the first grade, Helen in third grade and I in fifth grade.

Just before Christmas that year, Lester was out on the road when a terribly unusual winter blizzard blew in and dumped about a foot or so of snow on the ground. It was a school day, but Mary had no idea that Irving had closed its schools due to the severe weather. So, as usual, she bundled us up, loaded us into the car and drove us three miles into town where the large elementary and junior high school sat.

I vividly recall Mary pulling up in front of the school, and as we opened the car door, telling us goodbye. This sort of traumatic mental scene will never go away.

Neither Helen nor Don noticed anything unusual, as Mary had a habit of being either right at the bell or a minute or two late. As she drove away, I felt that something was wrong. I walked to the front door, and it was locked.

"Oh my," I told Helen and Don, "I don't think there's school today."

"What are we going to do?" Helen asked. We hadn't been in the house long enough for a telephone to be installed. "I don't know Sis," I said. "I guess we'll walk back home."

"I'm cold," Don said, starting to cry.

"Me too, Davey," said Helen.

"Well, let's walk back home," I said. "It won't take us long."

It was frigid for North Texas with the temperature in the teens. The snow had stopped, but the wind was still blowing fiercely. There were deep snow-drifts along the sidewalks and street crossings. Holding Helen's and Don's hands, I began leading our little band of three back to our rental home at the edge of town. Sometimes the snow-drifts were up to little Donny's knees. Poor Helen was wearing a little dress with a pair of white, thin leggings that did little to block the wind.

We had walked about a mile and still had another mile to go. By now we were all numb, freezing, and relentlessly shivering. Helen and Don were crying. We crossed the highway that ran through Irving and in the next block I spied a car dealership with lights on, and miracles of miracles, they were open for customers and selling cars, even on a day like this. We made it inside, and I asked one of the salesmen if we could warm ourselves. He said yes. The show-room was deserted.

We were finally warmed enough to continue. About an hour later, we all walked through the front door of the house, much to Mary's total surprise. "The school was closed, Mom," I said, cold, but inwardly proud that I had safely brought my little sister and brother back to the warmth of home. "Oh, you must be freezing," Mary said. She grabbed some blankets and threw them around us. "I didn't know they closed the school," she said.

This was the sort of thing that Mary was left to cope with while Lester was on the road preaching revivals. But Lester was convinced that he was following the will of God and could not forsake his "calling."

By spring, Lester moved us again. This time to Austin, Texas and into the old home that was previously owned (or rented) by Mary's elderly family, the Lee and Elizabeth Watts family. I once again found myself in a new school with new acquaintances, but no real friends. And again, I was alone with myself. But, surprisingly, school in Austin gave me a lot more than it took from me. I learned to box in the sports class and was invited to sing in the school choir. Singing was nothing new to me as I always sang in church, but boxing gave me a sense of confidence that the beatings I received growing up had taken from me. I could out-box all the boys in the fifth grade.

Lester preached a few revivals but soon found that his ability to sell himself on his old friends had practically disappeared. Finally, he called on O.C. Bigham, (*deceased*) a successful preacher-friend since his brief Bible college days. O.C pastored a rather large church in Tyler, Texas. Lester secured a three-week revival.

But darkness was falling upon our little family.

Some lonely nights when I was left with Mary and my siblings, she would ask me if I would lie down in bed next to her, and I did, managing to find a strange, but warm solace next to my mother. She was fighting her own emotional devils, and I would comfort her. She would occasionally rub my back, sing with me, or tell me stories of her own childhood as I fell asleep. I was comforted in return, comfort that was so needed.

I began to skip school as Mary would invariably write an "excuse" for me. I would wander for hours unmissed, down to a small park four blocks away and while away the hours until sunset. Mary was alone with her three other children, encompassed in her own world, sometimes weeping, sometimes with Grandma Watts, sometimes with church people.

I never felt missed. But, embarrassed over my constant erections, I tried to tie my penis to my leg to avoid having the embarrassing lump in my pants noticed. As I walked around, my penis tied to my leg, I would fantasize that I was just a regular person, free from my demons and obsessional urges for orgasm. There was a vacant farm behind our house where I could walk endlessly, alone in the untended acreage, which represented the empty content of my emotional life as I lived it at that time.

One afternoon, I was alone in my bedroom fantasizing about sex. I was about to masturbate when I glanced up and caught Mary watching me. I quickly turned away from her stare, ashamed. That weekend Lester drove back for a short visit. On Saturday as he prepared to go back to Tyler, he asked me if I wanted to skip more school and spend the final week of the revival with him.

I hesitated at first. Then with a strange premonition, I decided to go with him. Little did I know what was in store, but I was compelled to face it. And Lester was ready to administer my sexual inquisition. I would stand before God Almighty and be condemned to my own hell.

At the service that night Lester preached on God and man's deception. His example was the two sowers, one who sows sin and the other who sows to please the spirit (Galatians 6 KJV). "A man reaps what he sows," he preached. "If you try to hide your sins, be sure that God will find you out."

That night, we got ready for bed and both got into the same bed. Lester began to interrogate me about sex.

"Do you play with your peter, David?" Lester asked me.

"Uh…sometimes," I meekly responded.

"Well, you know that it's a sin," he said.

"Yes, sir."

"And you can go to hell for that," he continued.

"Yes, sir."

"How often do you do it?" he asked.

"Every day."

Lester was quiet for a moment.

"That's sinning," he said, "yes sir, that's really sinning," he raised his voice slightly, becoming more relentless.

"God's not pleased with you," he said as he pressed on. "You could go crazy or even die! My cousin Leonard (*deceased*) went crazy from jacking off." Now, he had lapsed into the street vernacular. I could feel the hair raise on the back of my head. I was thoroughly frightened.

He then went into a long story about Leonard, and how, when out with the gang, he would playfully come up from behind and "hunch" all the boys like animals do when copulating. Lester told me the story over and over to make his vulgar point that that type of behavior was forbidden. He was especially explicit about Leonard's propensity to hunch something like a telephone pole.

Am I like Leonard? I wondered. *Yes*, my subconscious guilt responded.

Before the night was over, Lester had filled my head with stories of bad boys he had known when he was a boy. He even blamed the accidental shooting of himself on a boyhood friend who was also probably crazy over sex.

To be truthful, he scared the living crap out of me. I had no idea that I had become such a terrible young kid and a major sinner to boot. I began to cry and prayed with him for divine forgiveness. But he persisted in the death scenario.

"You could die or go crazy from this," he said.

Terrified I sobbed, "If I stop right now, will I still die or go crazy,"

"Well, if you stop tonight, you might not die, but it might be too late to stop from going crazy…you could still go crazy," he said. He was obsessed with the thought of losing one's mind to sexual addiction.

Then he somberly asked, "when you do it, does some white stuff come out?"

"No," I replied, now weeping. I was still too young to ejaculate.

"Well," he slowly said, "if you promise me to never play with yourself again, well…we'll just have to see."

"I do Daddy, I promise. When will I know?" I pleaded.

"Well, you might have to wait for a year or so, and if you don't go crazy by then…" his voice trailed off somberly, "we'll see." With that, he turned over and went to sleep.

"Please God, please don't make me die or go crazy, please God." I silently prayed, "please, please."

I lay trembling, awake beside him, sobbing quietly until I, too, fell into an unconscious sleep.

The days that came and went that next year were a nightmare combination of fear, loathing of my body, shame and high anxiety over the fears that Lester had implanted in my young mind. I was subliminally directed to act out this insanity.

I was consumed by long periods of surreal thoughts and feelings that separated me from reality. I hated my sexual urges. I hated my penis for leading me into such a loathsome state. My depression was so severe that all I wanted to do was sleep and never awaken. I lost my appetite and never fully regained my hunger to eat since that time. I was crazy!

I hardly touched my penis, and when I did it was only to urinate. My life and ability to experience fun and happiness went totally off the rails of life. But, like a prisoner on death row, I counted the days that that passed throughout the year.

One by one.

Lester had scared me to death. My childhood mind could not contain the idea of "going crazy." It was worse than the idea of death.

It was a curse.

I also began to question my own gender identity. I hated what my penis made me do. How much easier would it have been had I been born a girl? During that year, I began to fail at school. I lost all confidence in myself and began to visualize what death could be like. I began to practice self-destructive behavior that lasted well into my adulthood.

I was cursed.

There was a train track only a few blocks from our house. I began to hide in the ditch beside the track and then when the train was rapidly approaching I would climb out of the ditch and stand on the track while the engineer blasted his horn warning me to get off the track. Only when the train was almost upon me would I jump off and back into the ditch, adrenaline surging through my body…thrilled that I was alive! I was not dead! Such self-destructive behavior became integrated into my life. The feeling I had was a momentary triumph over death itself.

Then one day, almost a year to that earlier fateful day, I was alone in my bedroom and noticed my penis was erect once more. So, I curiously began to examine it and noticed some fluid on the orifice of my penis. I hoped that it was semen.

It was.

And I didn't die that year.

Nor did I go crazy.

Lester lied to me.

He had literally stolen a year out of my life.

He tried to steal my manhood, but God intervened. My depression turned to mania. That night I masturbated for the first time in over a year. I ejaculated for the first time. I was thrilled to still be alive. I was thrilled that I was now a man!

The curse was broken. I was alive, and not crazy as Lester had decreed that I would be. I could touch my penis again! I began to see that it was all a big lie. But, at that time, I didn't understand the emotional damage that had been done to my young mind.

Strangely, when it finally became obvious to me that Lester had convinced me of an awful lie, my depression did not go away. Like my life's experience, a small ray of hope was inevitably followed by the awful clap of thunder of despair. It was like getting a reprieve from death, but it could still be overturned by God's Court. I still feared life as I found it in Pentecostalism. God was always there to mete out judgment for some negligent sin and to re-impose the sentence of death.

I found no joy in knowing this God. Unfortunately, as I grew into an adult, this fear transformed itself into an intense hatred of Lester and his religion for what they both had done to me as a totally trusting child. Lester's lie had stolen my childhood innocence. I could not forgive him. His religion stole my joy.

Chapter 4

But Hope Springs eternal

From Out of Death

From ashes comes life.
As I died, The Spirit
grew from me.

Ah, the bitter-sweet sorrow
Of the bell toll.
I see the bewildered come to pray
At its mournful message.

Farwell, my cherished friend.
Tomorrow I must depart
For I am no longer
Of the same essence.

Darkness enclosed the Spirit
That was exhausted of all meaning.

I must follow this New Light.
Never again will I follow false angels.
Never again will darkness rob me
Of my sight.

(poetry written as I reflected on the death of a friend)

    I was almost eleven years old in the summer of 1947. After four or five months in Austin, Lester heard of a little church in South Texas that was looking for a pastor. He drove to the small south Texas town and preached before the First Assembly of God congregation on a Sunday night.

Immediately, that same night, he was voted in. We were "on the road again."

Life was pretty good for a while. We spent the first year without incident. I didn't dwell much on what Lester had done to me. But I continued to subliminally refuse to forgive him. All of us except Robert enrolled in the town's school. I began to make new friends and made it through the entire sixth grade without interruption. I was still afraid to let myself masturbate too often, but when I did, it didn't bother me; it was like that part of my life never existed. My flirtation with death and my self-destructive lifestyle continued. I began to conflate sexual emotions with danger. I tried to wall off all thoughts of sex, but when I would take chances with self-destructive actions and each time come out unscathed, it was an attempt for manhood recognition. I habitually walked the railroad tracks behind the parsonage. As the train came roaring through our little town, I stayed on the tracks. The engineer blasted away on the engine's airhorns until the last minute when I would jump off the tracks into the soft ditch that ran alongside the tracks as the train roared by. I wasn't just overcoming my sexual obsession; I was sticking my thumb in Lester's eye.

It was an unconscious demonstration to all that cared that I could overcome the curse and psychic damage to my mind. I was able to free myself from the subconscious fear of Lester's whippings and abusive sexual psychology, and, now, I had overcome a fear of death.

Free at last! Free at last!

But inevitably, things took a bad turn again. I remember that year because during late October we all had to flee a hurricane that came right up the coast toward a nearby shore. We all packed into Lester's 1946 Chevrolet and drove inland to Lufkin, Texas, my birthplace and home of Mary's oldest sister, Flora Lee.

The storm was a minimal hurricane that did little damage, so we returned home after two nights. All seemed okay, except that I had an unusual asthma attack while at Flora Lee's home. We were all packed into the car. This was the first time I had been so close to Lester since he pronounced his curse upon me. On the trip back to Angleton, the attack worsened. It got so bad I could not breathe. Lester ignored me, but Mary became quite concerned as my condition deteriorated.

About two a.m. that morning, I still couldn't breathe properly. Mary took me to the little town hospital where the town's sole physician was called in. He listened to my lungs and airway and quickly administered an injection of cortisone. Within minutes, it relieved my closed alveoli and provided relief. I took in a breath.

I could never be close to Lester again without having that strange smothering, out-of-breath feeling. So, I established an emotional space between Lester and myself and kept my distance. I never had another asthma attack. I guess it shows you how the sympathetic nervous system can act. I was still subconsciously playing out and overcoming a smothering effect in my young life when Lester pronounced his death curse on me. It's strange how the mind will hold these memes forever.

The storm blew out one or two of the parsonage bedroom windows, so the rain did a slight amount of damage. Much to Lester's chagrin, the 80-something-year-old matriarch of the church Lettie Fowler (*deceased*) became angry with him for not properly putting storm windows up to protect the parsonage – which she owned along with being the head of the Board of Deacons and title to the church – which she owned as well. They got into a heated argument. She told him that he had done a bad job protecting the parsonage from the wind and rain. Lester's pride hurt, and he shouted back that he had done the best he could. But Lester's "best" was not good enough for Mrs. Fowler and the honeymoon soured. What else she didn't like about Lester was never revealed to us, but within a few weeks, he was voted out of the church.

Lester fought the decision. In anger, he called all the members that had a telephone and pleaded with them to join him in a new church that he promised to build. He told them that he had been unjustly accused. His pleading was somewhat successful, and he was able to leave with about half the congregation in tow. He named his new church, Central Assembly of God. He began holding services in the Veterans of Foreign Wars (VFW) hall on the outskirts of town. We continued living in the old parsonage, but not for long. Mrs. Follett (her husband was one of the two attorneys in town) quickly evicted us. Formally.

With hardly any income from his meager congregation, and now evicted from our home, Lester panicked and moved us into the first shelter he could find. It was a disaster. Our entire family of six was crammed into a one-bedroom shanty behind the local grocery. It was a severe blow to the family's pride and self-esteem. We were horribly ashamed and embarrassed. With the whole family squeezed into a little one-bedroom shack, everyone became angry, agitated, and flustered. I became ever more fearless and antagonistic to Lester's authoritative rules. The old "smothering" feeling was with me constantly. I wanted to get away. Staying late at school was one way. When I tried out for the junior basketball team, Lester vehemently objected.

"You will miss Wednesday and Friday night services," he admonished. "You have a duty to God."

"But, but Dad, I just made the team…" I pleaded with him. "Let me play, please."

"No!" he responded. His mind was made up.

When I tried to continue the argument, he simply took away my tennis shoes and refused to let me use them to practice. I begged him for my tennis shoes, but he would not give them back to me. I was checkmated in life once again. He was demanding that I give up something as innocuous as junior high basketball for Wednesday night services and once again demonstrating his power over me.

"God demands your sacrifice," he said. He was obsessed with his new challenge

Who are you to speak for God? I thought. His selfish action truly hurt me. I was astounded that he would carry out such an unusually cruel act. But he did, and I was forced to abandon the team.

I again sank into an angry depression. It had been such an escape to play basketball after school and not have to come home to face Lester for two or three hours. I hated Lester, and I hated his stupid obsession with religion. It seemed everything in life that was fun was found sinful by him. Why couldn't I just die and get away from all this hell? Once again, I considered killing myself.

Even though I hated Lester and had awful thoughts of him alongside thoughts of what death would be like to me, I never considered killing or even hurting Lester.

Then, something miraculous happened. *This pain is not from Jesus*, I thought. I began to think of Jesus as God, not Yahweh nor Jehovah, Lester's Gods. *My God might love me*, I thought, not some awful, vengeful, and wrathful God just waiting to punish me.

After a few weeks, the ever-resourceful deal-maker, Lester, got us out of the shack behind the grocery. He persuaded the substituting Episcopal priest from out of town to rent us the vacant parish parsonage across the street from his church. It was so much nicer than the shanty we moved away from. As soon as he had an agreement, Lester borrowed a small trailer from someone, put our meager possessions in it and moved us into the Episcopal parsonage.

Oh my God. It had three bedrooms, a screened-in porch, and two bathrooms! We had never had such luxurious digs. I gratefully found that I had my own bed. I could masturbate at night. There was a sense of separation that had I so desperately longed for. I could avoid Lester and his interrogations. I even obtained a small radio that I placed on the open window sill. I gazed at the nighttime stars as I tuned in to soft music and finally fell into a deep slumber.

There were four, very tall sycamore trees in front of the Episcopal church. It was summer vacation. Each day, I would climb one of the trees, sometimes climbing a hundred feet above the ground. I climbed far beyond the limits of the big limbs of the tree, fearlessly to the very top. There I would gaze across the countryside and allow my imagination to soar out of its prison of pain and suffering. The imagination that had been jailed for so long by religious prohibitions was temporarily freed. I even began to sing to myself and contemplate Jesus' love. I was being healed unconsciously. I was 12 years old. The freedom it brought were my initial feelings of getting, well, high. Naturally.

Once again, Grampa Watts was persuaded to come and help Lester build a new church. Grampa Watts drove down and stayed with us while the building was being built. It didn't take long this time as the building's dimensions were the same as the Brownwood church, with a little one story chapel, a square meeting-room sanctuary, raised pulpit and choir loft. The little break-away congregation was soon moved out of the VFW hall and into his new church. Simultaneously, Grampa and Lester built a new house on the other side of town, near the new "Central Assembly" to become the church parsonage.

Lester returned my tennis shoes, but the season was over.

I had been given an old trumpet by one of Lester's acquaintances a couple of years before. Lester told me to learn to play, but I had no teacher. Finally, the son of the donor taught me the finger-positions that go with the musical scale. I taught myself from then on. I joined the 7th grade band playing First Trumpet. As I recall, there was no second trumpet player in the small band.

My depression slowly began to lift, and life was beginning to improve when I met and developed a quick friendship with a fellow classmate, Isaac Stevenson. (*fictitious*) Isaac was the eldest child in his family, and they called him "Bud." He too played in the band, and we began a young "Lewis and Clark" adventure and comradeship that has lasted to this day. He gave me stability, and I gave him adventure. In short, we bonded as "brothers."

Both of Bud's parents worked, so he spent hours on end away from his home. I joined him when I could. His uncle owned land on the edge of town. One end had been excavated for gravel for a new highway. The excavated land was several acres in size and soon filled with water, but it wasn't terribly deep. We could wade across it on one end. The other end was considerably deeper. The lake contained some fairly large catfish. Bud and I both built little tin canoes to paddle around in it and fish. They were one-man canoes made from a single sheet of tin. We paddled them with our hands.

Once we got out of them, we simply sank them in the lake in shallow out-of-the-way spots that only we knew about. We could wade out, grab them off the bottom, turn them over, and then raise them. Once we emptied the water from the canoes, we were ready to use them. Then, both naked as the day we were born, but safely in our canoes, we paddled out into the lake and away from shore. The lake seemed much smaller when we were out in the middle. When we were ready to return, we simply reversed the routine, retrieved our clothes (hidden in one of the trees) dressed, and walked back home. It was a good way for two fourteen-year-olds to spend a summer afternoon.

Other times, we explored old barns and deserted farmhouses around the property. On weekends, we were needed as deck-hands on Bud's wealthy grandfather's yacht. Mr. Stevenson was the old patriarch of the Stevenson (*deceased*) family. The problem was "Grandfather" Stevenson only took his yacht out on Sunday. I asked Lester for permission to go out on the yacht. Predictably, he objected, unless, he said, I made it back to Sunday night services. Thankfully, I was able to get home in time for services. Most of the time.

Bud and I both loved to fish and hunt. I had a job as a combination soda jerk and delivery boy for the local pharmacy. I cleaned the office of the other town's attorney at night twice a week, so I made enough to pay for a brand-new Remington 12-gauge shotgun. Bud didn't have to work.

His early life's job was to simply look after his two younger sisters while his parents were at work.

On the weekends, he would borrow his dad's antique 16-gauge gauge double barrel, and we both would wander around the woods with our guns and our fishing tackle fishing the small creeks and ponds around our small town. We made our own fishing lures and found old rods and reels that we re-furbished with new guides and lines.

Occasionally, we would shoot at a snake or into a cloud of blackbirds that rose from the dry fields we trod, and in duck or quail season, we would occasionally bring home enough fish or game for a meal. Bud's mother was an excellent cook and delighted in making our excursions to the lakes and woods productive for all. But, we weren't really serious about killing something for the table.

Bud had another uncle living on the edge of town who owned perhaps fifty or so acres and had several horses that he let us ride. We raced each other bare-back down the dusty roads behind his uncle's pastures as neither of could afford a saddle. Doing all the things that young boys do began to bring me out of depression and back to life. It provided a new fascination for living…as a dare-devil: depression's flip-side – mania.

As early teenagers, we were capable of mischief. It was summer, and everyone had open windows hoping to catch a small breeze. Bud's mother and father were big bridge players. They alternated playing cards at Bud's house one night and then another night at his uncle and aunt's house about five or six blocks up the street. This preoccupation left Bud free to do whatever he damned well pleased from about seven to ten at night. I would ride my bicycle over to his house and join him. Thus, it was the beginning of a nightly ritual of wandering across neighborhoods seeking excitement. Sometimes one of our female classmates would come out of her house for an hour or two, and we would simply get together and gossip. Few neighborhood yards had fences.

One night, we were we were ambling across backyards short-cutting our way back to Bud's house when we noticed an open window. Inside, it looked like a partially nude woman was in the act of totally undressing. Surprised, we stopped and began watching, standing several yards away; we eased ourselves behind the hedges and peered intently into the open window. As we continued watching, mesmerized by what we were seeing, a nude male joined the scene and began a romantic pantomime. We watched in abject amazement as the sex-act was carried out right before our very eyes. We were glued to our spots until the act was completed and the couple put on their night clothes.

We didn't consider the morality of invading their privacy. To us, it was an exploration of limits to our boyhood curiosity. Of course, our higher instincts told us that we were "peeping toms," but we laughed it off as antique and old fashion. If the couple did not want to be seen, then why leave the shades up for anyone to see?

Most of the time we would just see a neighbor woman partially undressing for bed, and other times we just walked around at night talking and joking with each other. There was something about summer nights and the excitement it produced. It was freedom and discovery. Our favorite couple had sex practically every night.

But hoping to catch a glimpse of nudity was all that Bud and I did. We were acting out our boyhood, heterosexual curiosities. These actions were not the acts of pathopsychological voyeuristic compulsion. We obviously found excitement from the graphic sexual displays, but neither of us masturbated or otherwise progressed to any act of sexual transference while watching. To me, just seeing the act of coitus for its first time at fourteen years old was far more titillating than my urge to masturbate. I had never seen sexual intercourse before.

Looking back, I see that I used it as an escape from the religious holiness prohibitions that I lived with in my everyday world, which were so extreme that sexuality was taught to be sinful. In our occasional evening prayers we had at home, we prayed that God would deliver us from evil thoughts. Nothing ever happened…evil thoughts (going to movies, dancing, drinking, smoking, and sex) came anyway. I was an escapist. I was still subliminally living out my childhood curse regarding sex. It lived with me every day of my life. So, to me, voyeurism was a perfect substitute. I didn't touch my penis, and I didn't have to tell Lester about it.

For the same reason I presume, Bud was content to simply make himself invisible. And like all teenage boys, watching people having sex was tremendously exciting. We both unconsciously concluded that masturbation was now a little boy's habit. Big boys got real sex from real girls! Neither of us had girlfriends who were willing to have sex. At fourteen and fifteen, you had to at least, be "going steady" with a girl. The voyeurism experience was like a free pass to watch a sex movie. I learned to enjoy sex without participating. It was simply sexual fantasy acted out with no consequences. It lasted only for that summer. We never got caught.

Lester purchased a used Chevy flat-bed that he used to carry work supplies. Central Assembly was not paying a livable wage. The congregation was mostly older, retired couples with not a lot of money for the offering plate. So, Lester began working for a lumber supplier doing flooring for both new and refurbished homes. He bought a large electric floor sander. He bought a big manual tile cutter that was used to trim tiles. He went whole-hog and contracted his services for painting and varnishing. My sibling Don and I were the "hired help."

Don and I basically worked for nothing while the local boys were racing their cars up and down the highway. But, when we were not on a job, Lester allowed me to take the old truck out. It was my pay, and I could use it for recreation. I would swing by, pick up Bud, and we would head for the beach to spend the day diving and spear-fishing at the end of the jetties. With our snorkels in our mouths and face masks pushed securely against our faces, we cruised the bottom of the ocean about fifteen feet below for a big sheep's head or occasionally a big red-fish, which we strung up to take back home for dinner. Or sometimes we just drove over to the next town that had a public swimming pool. It had both low and high diving boards, and we both learned to perform jackknifes, swan dives, and double flips. I continued to avoid contact with my own family. There was nothing fun at home. At the same time, I was growing quite popular in class, and I was certainly a leader in the junior high school band. I stayed after school and practiced for hours. Sometimes Bud joined me. He had learned to play a tenor saxophone that year. It was gifted to him by another wealthy uncle who lived nearby in the same town.

As ashamed as I was of my religion, I continued to attend church almost as often as my siblings who never missed a service. Some boyhood friends called the Pentecostals tongue-speaking, holy-rollers. But not Bud. He was always respectful of my religion. Bud's family was Methodist, but they rarely attended. I greatly envied the bigger, more sedate Methodist, Presbyterian, and Baptist churches that my classmates attended. Their religion was so much easier to live by than mine. They could go to movies, my church still believed that attending movies was sinful. They could attend school dances, but my church still found dancing illicit in God's eyes. Rather than argue for these idiosyncrasies, I mostly hid my religion from my classmates.

And learned to cope.

The eighth grade was easy for me. I made friends with almost all the students in the small school. One night, one of my classmates had a party at her home, which was only a couple blocks from Bud's house. We ambled over and were quickly integrated into the happy group. It was Wanda Huntington's (*fictitious*) birthday. She was a girl that I hardly noticed before, At the birthday party, she seemed especially attracted to me. As we talked, she introduced me to her mom. A little later during the party, her mom asked me if I would take Wanda to the 8th-grade prom. I said yes, as I almost always did when asked by a grown-up to do something for them. After all, Bud and I had crashed her party.

Wanda was kind of cute, but she'd been born with a walking disability. I was deeply sympathetic to her. One leg was deformed and about two or three inches shorter than the other. She wore a special shoe that enabled her to walk; without it she would have had a terrible limp. Still, she was attractive and intelligent enough to be my first girlfriend. We both loved to talk to each other, but that was all we did. I could not take her to a movie or to a real dance, but that was what the disability was to her. So, we just talked at recess, and I walked her home from school each day carrying her books.

At the end of the eighth grade was the Junior High School Banquet and Prom. I had found myself in a dilemma with Wanda whom I had agreed to take to the banquet and perhaps stay for the prom dance. I could not explain to Lester and Mary that a prom included a dance after the banquet. I couldn't even tell them that I secretly had a girlfriend… outside our Pentecostal church. So, I carefully told them that I was going to the "8th Grade Junior High Banquet." And that was it! I think Mary saw through my little lie, but Lester never got it. But, be sure your sins will find you out! Lester got his revenge by an act of fate.

I was confused as to how I should follow up on the invitation to the Banquet and Prom. So, on the evening of the festivities, I waited at the banquet door (the school gym) and Wanda waited at home. I was totally mixed up on Prom protocol. She was right of course, the boy always goes to the date's home to pick her up, invariably meeting one or both girl's parents, not wait at the door of the gym for his date to show up. I waited for what seemed hours until Wanda suddenly showed up with her mom who was determined that she would go to the prom – even if her mother should take her.

"Why didn't you come for Wanda," her mother asked. She was holding a pretty white corsage in an open box.

"I didn't know," I said. I had no answer as I was once again winging a "sinful" act as a pure novice. I had never been to a dance before and really did not know how to dance, and I had no idea of the prom-dating etiquette.

With that answer, Mrs. Huntington began pinning the corsage to Wanda's pretty prom dress.

"Come on with me," she ordered as we all entered the gymnasium all decorated with ribbons and flowers.

But it ended well. Wanda and I sat together and ate at the Banquet, and she (sort of) showed me a few clumsy dance steps. We left early with her mother, and I returned home with no one the wiser.

But over the months that followed, something happened to Lester. He began to turn the new congregation into a more sedate group of mostly tired old-timers who just enjoyed coming to church and each other's company. His attendance now was a little over one-hundred, so a Sunday and Wednesday night offering began to make ends meet and he gave up his "day job" of contracting floor covering. Life went on. He seemed to settle down. Our family life seemed to settle down with him. I was able to live at home with some degree of comfort. I was turning fifteen.

The highlight of my life that summer was the invitation to deck hand on Bud's grandfather's yacht for a three-week cruise. Bud and I helped him maneuver the big, clumsy, wooden-hulled yacht up the Intercoastal Canal of the Texas coast to Rockport, Texas, where we docked for a three-week excursion. We fished, swam, and sailed the small gaff-rigged sailboat we used for a tender in the waterway. We sailed and explored the tiny bays and estuaries around the little resort town. When night fell, we laid bedding out on the back deck, talked and gazed at the bright moon and stars before finally falling asleep. It was the most beautiful experience I had ever had in my entire lifetime. I was now almost fifteen and wanted so much to be in this family. But as time passed, I become content with just friendship with Bud and the stabilizing effect his family had on me. It kept my painful depression at bay.

I attended summer band practice that year, which began in August before September classes resumed. It was that summer that I met Molly (*fictitious*) which I will take up in the next chapter.

By then, the control that Lester so desperately tried to impose on me was cracking, never to be fully restored. As I entered high school in 1950, I found that any life out of the clutches of my religiously strict, puritanical life was an antidote to my depression and relentless feelings of guilt. However, it did not come without pain.

The love-hate relationship between father and son continued. But now, it was mainly through coercion and/or threat. I would come to church and play my trumpet during the song service from time to time. But, like before, I would slip out of the service as soon as I could. It seemed okay with Lester. During those years, my siblings, Helen, Donald and Robert never caught my rebelliousness and estrangement from religion. They continued to faithfully attend services, serving up their talent at Lester's bidding. I felt guilty and depressed for my refusal to.

Of course, there is always the exception to the rule. Donald, like me, eventually drifted away from attending any church. But, Mary Helen and Robert were both and are now, ever-faithful to the Assemblies of God ministries that they had become so attached to during adolescence. Robert continued in the footsteps of Lester, finishing his last church-building project, the Mountain Creek Church in Duncanville, Texas and upon it, building a successful preaching ministry. Mary Helen was so talented in music that she and her husband Paul opened and ran a music store in Kalispell, Montana while she directed the local Assemblies of God choir for over 20 years.

Paul Jones was a preacher's son who never rebelled. He volunteered for the U.S. Airforce through the Montana Air National Guard and became a pilot. When the F-100 jets began to replace the F-89 Scorpions, the Air National Guard was given the aging F-89 fighter jets. Paul's pilot career came to a bitter end when a malfunction on his F-89 Scorpion caused him to be ejected on the ground. The parachute attached to his seat also failed to open properly. He came down far too fast and hit the ground hard. It caused severe injury to his feet and ankles. Unable to fly again as a fighter pilot, he was medically discharged early in his military service.

After a long, slow recovery, Paul was finally able to walk again.

Paul never tried to preach.

And my sister ran the household of three daughters with exquisite perfection.

Robert took the preaching mantle bestowed upon him after helping Lester build his last church, an independent, non-denominational church called Mountain Creek Christian Church. He took over when Lester retired and has pastored it as its sole pastor. He learned some lessons on keeping oneself from becoming obsolete. He controls the Board of Directors who owns the title to the church. But I'm getting ahead of myself.

Dr. David P. Summers

Chapter 5

Busted Again!

The Parting

The hollow echo
Of softly uttered words
That once fell from tender lips
Gently brushes A lover's ear.

Those eyes I used to follow
Dim, as I wander into the desert.

Those joy-filled words
Are now just resonance, echoes
In the canyons of my mind.

(This was written as I tried to become the salesman of the year and failed my first year)

Now fourteen and at the end of my 9th grade in high school, I had found a girl who literally took my mind off guilt and depression and ended my obsession with masturbation. She was a cute little majorette for the band, especially attractive in the short, cut-off dresses and tights that was the uniform for the twirlers (majorettes) of the Junior High marching band.

Her name was Molly Martin. (*fictitious*) And she seduced me.

Rather, I should say, she needed me. Just as Mary had needed me when she had another nervous breakdown, and I was a 5-year old.

For the most part, I was totally unconcerned about girls. After my little fiasco with Wanda at the 8th-grade prom, I'd had few romantic feelings. But at the beginning of my Freshman year, someone told me that Molly would like to "go with me." It aroused my attention. Soon, we became acquainted.

Molly was cute and shy. We were both freshmen in high school. Since I was using Lester's old truck almost constantly, I began taking Molly home after school. She seemed kind of bewildered in the high school world of 1953, so going with her sort of made me feel heroic, the big brother who stood up for fairness and decency for my siblings, something I had lost when I abandoned my attachment to family. But I knew that I couldn't go back to that relationship.

As the band followed the football team from town to town in school buses for "Friday Night Lights" (the football games always played on Friday nights), we would board the bus, find a seat toward the back and sit tightly together, riding in the darkened bus taking us to and from the high school games. We didn't talk much as the roar of the bus made talking almost impossible. So, we cupped our hands and whispered in each other's ear. But there was no need for much talk. We were together, that was the main thing.

It was exhilarating. Molly would let me put my hand on her tights and massage her genitals over her panties. I was fascinated by the sexual touch of the opposite sex even though it was not really "touching," and Molly was my first. It was all dark on the bus with no sound except for the big wheels rolling along the pavement.

All the boys did it – at least those who had girlfriends. The petting game. The end-game was not just to produce an orgasm (though some did); it was the romantic touching, rubbing, and manual probing in the dark secrecy of teenage romance that made it so attractive and alluring. Most teenage boys on the bus couldn't even explain the anatomy of female genitalia, much less explain the orgasm, though everyone knew who was doing it. Yet, we all sat silently, upright in bus seats, as if we were just holding hands or just with an arm over the shoulder of our seat companion. Occasionally, a teacher or chaperone would wander down the aisles. But that was to be expected. The romantic activity in those late night, band-bus excursions was euphoric.

I talked to Molly for hours; she poured out her heart to me. She told me the sad story of her mother's death when she was only eight years old. I held her as she told me how her father tried to care for her and her little sister and brother but was forced to hire an older woman as a nanny to help raise his kids. After a couple of years, he married the nanny. The new step-mom not only fell in love with Molly's father but loved all the kids with a passion. But Molly, being the oldest, could never get over losing her real mom and the hurt lingered in her heart and mind. Like two wounded soldiers, we bonded over common childhood wounds.

As time went on, Molly and I acted out even more sexual pantomime. We would lie atop each other, holding and kissing each other, and mimicking sexual intercourse, but it never involved the genuine sex act. Neither of us ever undressed or exposed our genitals. We just held and acted out a fantasy as though we were having sex. It was a substitute for the real thing as we held each other and kissed for hours in the seat of the old work-truck that I had borrowed so often from Lester and fixed it up so that it had practically become mine. That was enough. It filled the hole in Molly's broken heart.

Disobeying my religious taboo, I did sneak off from time to time to take Molly to watch a drive-in movie, eat hot-dogs, and drink colas. We always returned to smooch in Molly's driveway, and I always got home early enough to not arouse Lester's suspicion. I never discussed Molly with Lester. He never even knew her name.

This went on through most of that school year. One day as we walked to class, Molly told me that her menstrual period had stopped. I knew what that meant. The unwanted announcement brought my life to a sudden standstill.

I knew that we had not had real sex. I was puzzled and frightened by her statement. What did she mean? My emotions began to rise.

"How can you be pregnant?" I asked.

"I don't know," she replied. "I'm just not having my period." She didn't seem as scared as I was.

The old sex curse tapes began to run through my mind once again. The oh so familiar waves of anxiety swept over and over me once more. My mind immediately went into the worst-case scenario. Stark fear. I just wanted to survive. What do I do? It wasn't fear that I couldn't handle the situation, rather it was fear of "what would Lester do?" Would he put another curse on me? Do I have to marry her? I worried and ran every worst-case scenario through my mind, over and over, and it became an obsession. I was only fifteen years old. Should I run away? Almost every day I would ask, or she would pass me a note in the hall telling me the continued bad news.

"How could she be pregnant," I asked her?

"Well," she said, "maybe some of your stuff soaked through your pants and into my vagina," she replied.

I couldn't believe it! And it was driving me insane.

Sex was such a curse. Every time I engaged in sex in any manner I met trouble. I lapsed into a state of perpetual bewilderment and deep depression. "Why am I so cursed with sex?" I asked myself over and over. Underneath it all, I was fearful that it was Lester's God that would haunt me all my life. I prayed to Jesus for deliverance.

Finally, going into her third month of not having a period, she confided in her mother who promptly took her to a kindly physician in another town who was known to perform the standard D&C (dilation and curettage) for first-trimester abortion. Even though we lived in the Bible Belt, the rabid stigma of abortion had not yet become politicized, much less stigmatized. So, for a mother to bring a fifteen-year-old daughter who might have become pregnant was no big deal in Texas circa, 1952.

After examining her, the doctor told her to get dressed. "She was still a virgin," he told her mother. "And she still has her hymen."

The doctor explained that occasionally young girls like Molly could miss several menstrual periods while maturing into womanhood. Nevertheless, the incident had psychologically killed me once again, as well as the little teenage romance. It was all over. I was a zombie by the time Molly informed me of the good news, and the good news didn't bring me back to life.

We never went out together again… until much later. But that's another story for another time.

At roughly the same time, the high school mechanics class purchased an old Model A Ford in great need of repair. The class set about repairing and reconditioning the old car and after a few weeks had it ready for the annual Mechanic's Class raffle. One of my classmates approached me.

"Hey Dave, buy one of my raffle tickets. I need to sell about three more, and I'm done!" he said. I knew that I couldn't give him the brush-off, so I reluctantly (though I knew it was a form of gambling) bought a raffle ticket for the total amount of one dollar.

I quickly forgot about it.

Until one week later.

The day of the raffle.

Much to my surprise and total astonishment, I won the car! One of the Mechanics Class boys brought the prize around. Of course, all my class buddies wanted to celebrate with me, and they pooled money for a case of beer. We piled into the bright, shining 1929 Model A Ford. Off we went!

I didn't particularly like the taste of beer, but my need for manhood prevailed. I drank a can or two before coming home around 10 pm. Two beers had put me into a state of bravado. I was so proud of myself; I could not wait to tell everyone about it.

As I pulled up into the yard, I was met by an irate Lester who quickly became beside himself over the smell of alcohol on my breath. Things got progressively uglier, and he finally lost any composure. As his temper erupted into a spew of name-calling, and as he approached me with his belt in hand, something clicked. I was not going to endure another hand on me.

He grabbed at me, and I shoved him backward. "Don't mess with me, Dad," I said.

He looked surprised. "I'm going to whip you boy," he responded.

And came at me once more. As he did, I doubled my fist and swung at him. I think I landed a light blow on his back. He spun around, anger boiling. I didn't expect him to try to hit me with his fist, but he doubled his fist, and we came to fisticuffs in the garage. I couldn't believe his anger…a man of God! I don't think either of us landed a punch that hurt as I skillfully bobbed and weaved out of his range. "Dad, don't try it," I said again. Since I had learned to box in the 5th-grade, I had never been beaten in the usual schoolyard skirmishes. What's more, I simply was not to be beaten by Lester ever again. After a minute or two, he caught himself and, dropping his head, walked away. I wasn't going to take another beating by him – a man of God.

And that was it!

My relationship with my father had finally reached its limits. It was the end of me having any feeling of wanting to belong in the Summers family. That night, Bud invited me to spend the night at his home. My stay with his family turned into not returning home for almost a year.

During that time, and on the move again, Lester, Mary, and the rest of the kids moved to another Assembly of God church near Houston. Lester had once more "heard the calling" and responded. I didn't move with them. I was invited to continue staying with Bud, at least until the end of the school year. I took the offer, but now having wheels, I could drive. And I did! That old Model A brought much freedom, fun, and joy to myself and my classmates.

Occasionally, to relieve Bud's family, I drove the old antique on a 70mile round trip to Houston for a short visit with my family over the weekend. It was probably for the best, as I had to share a bed with Don or Bob. The decrepit old church was directly adjacent to the Missouri-Pacific Railway. Everything stopped when the trains went by. All it could offer in the way of living quarters was the usual two-bedroom clapboard frame house on a muddy street. This one was called Myrtle Lane. I kid you not!

And not a myrtle tree to be found.

Lester, once again, set out to build a new church building.

School was out, and I said goodbye to Bud and his family leaving the small town that I came of age in forever. In Houston, I alternatively finagled a bed (usually a couch) with Elton Brumbel, (*fictitious*) the Runsford son, John Edward, (*fictitious*) or Sammy Smith, (*fictitious*) Rev. Hector Smith's (*fictitious*) son, who sold musical instruments to Lester's church as well as others in the area.

There was something about Hector Smith that I couldn't put my finger on. He seemed outright effeminate, and his son Sammy was even more so. I didn't know then that there was a real culture to homosexuality. But our churches were full of these effeminates who usually sang or played instruments in local Assemblies of God church choirs. Knowing what I know now, they were gay Christians, but then it just seemed so loving and natural that there was no animosity towards them. Like contraception, which no one except our Catholic friends had an issue with until later, the animosity toward loving, gay Christians was provoked, stirred up, and continually stoked by our (Republican) politicians.

Then there was my friend John Ed Runsford of the Runsford family from the East Texas town of Gladewater. I met John Ed as a child; his father was a preacher in the same district as Lester in Longview. The big Runsford family of five or six kids just reaching puberty was the same song, second verse, of what I have already recited. Their lives revolved around freedom and sex. John Ed, one of the older boys, had already left home and moved to the big town of Houston. We shared similar Pentecostal experiences, and both of us had become "heretics." John Ed always shared a place to sleep for a night. We attended our respective family churches on various occasions, but as far as integrating into the common belief and worship, neither of us cared to do so. No one knew or cared to know, the difference.

Like John Ed, Elton, and myself, most of the young men we hung out with were Assembly of God preacher's sons who had moved from the family religion and away from homes and in one way or another were all living on the edge, trying to fit the extremity of Pentecostal Holiness fundamentalism while growing into their teen years, torn between the constrictions of religiosity and modernity.

They all smoked Camels or Luckies, drank booze, went to movies and fornicated when possible.

Dr. David P. Summers

Chapter 6

The Meeting on the Beach

To Woman

From friend to lover
Our lives now one.

Our sensual magnetism
The long, bound,
symbiotic duality
As she lies beneath me.
After, she sighs,
Cursed and hounded
By the gods themselves
And travels lonely
Through a world of Strength and Cunning.

I shed tears of pride in our friendship
And love.

The base passion I desire,
Means I am ultimately cursed
With her curse.
Oh, woman!

(all poetry written on reflection of misogyny)

"Hey David, want to drive around with me?" Sammy asked one Sunday. "I'm stuck out here at your church until after the service tonight."

He and his dad had installed a new organ in the Green's Bayou church that could hardly afford it, but Lester guaranteed that it would be fully paid for out of offerings. Sammy and his dad Vic had installed it and came back on Sunday to give it a final okay. Mary, as well as the church, loved the new Hammond organ's deep, vibrant tones that accompanied the singing.

After that, there was no argument. It was a done deal! However, they decided to return for Sunday night services to be sure that the organ's performance continued to charm the blue-collar, conservative congregation.

"Yeah," I said, "where do you want to go?"

"Hmm, let's drive down to the beach, I'll bring you back before church tonight."

"Ok, let's do it," I said, not wanting to hang out with my family any more than I had to.

I especially didn't want to hang out at Lester and Mary's on a Sunday afternoon. We climbed into Sammy's big Oldsmobile 88 and headed down to Freeport, Texas' Surfside beach on the Gulf of Mexico. It was a beautiful summer day in Texas. Arriving an hour or so later we parked close to the jetties and began to stroll along the jetties watching the fishing and of course (for me, anyway) looking at the girls in swimsuits.

We had walked to the end of the jetties, and when we went back toward the car, we came upon two young girls, both 16 or 17 years old, laughing and chatting with each other as they too, walked back toward the beach. One of the teens wore a bright yellow suit. The other girl's bathing suit is a blur to me, as I barely paid attention to her.

Neither Sammy nor I tried to make conversation. Instead, I began whistling the theme song to the 1954 hit movie "The High and Mighty," starring the popular John Wayne. ("I was high and mighty, how I laughed at love…") The words and melody stuck in my mind. John Wayne was the hero I wanted to be.

As I continued to whistle the melody, the girl in the yellow stopped ahead of us and turned to look at me, and asked, "Did you like that movie?"

For a moment, I hesitated. She was a petite girl with blond hair and a figure that could stop a freight train.

"Why yes, it had John Wayne in it," I responded.

"I know," said the girl, "I saw it too," But that was the end of the conversation. Again, she and her tall friend turned and continued walking toward the beach.

Neither Sammy nor I attempted to make further conversation with the girls, I suppose that we were both too timid to make an approach.

The girls seemed so self-confident and *cityfied*. After all, we were both country boys and they were city girls! The girls kept walking until they were a few minutes ahead of us. We got into Sammy's Oldsmobile and cruised down toward the San Louis Pass.

Then, for some reason, after a few miles, we turned around. "Let's drive back to the jetties," Sammy said, "nothing down this road but sand dunes, sand dunes…and more sand dunes."

As we cruised back toward where the girls had parked, I sensed trouble. The car that they were driving was stuck in the light, wind-blown sand. They were spinning the wheels and going nowhere. We pulled up beside them.

"Hey," I shouted to the driver – the smaller petite one, "Don't spin the wheels, you'll never get out!" The tall girl was out of the car, pushing on one of the back fenders. The petite driver looked at me as if I had intruded into a personal conversation. But she stopped gunning the motor and spinning the wheels. I felt sorry for her. She would never get out of the sand without some help.

"Let me help you," I said, "I know how to get the car out of the sand." I got out of our car and walked around to the driver's side of her 1952 Studebaker coupe. That model of Studebaker those days had a unique design. The back of the car resembled the front so much that sometimes you could mistake which was which. I loved those Studebakers. But they were not built for speed, a negative for Elvis wannabes.

"Can you back up slowly," I asked, walking around to the front of the car.

She tried, but again spun the wheels and sank even deeper into the sand.

She just couldn't help it.

"Stop, stop, stop," I yelled.

She did, and I walked up to the door and said, "I can get you out, but you will have to let me get into the car and drive it." She hesitated.

"You're not going to drive off with my car, are you?" she asked.

I laughed.

"Of course not, but there is a special way to get wheel-traction and get unstuck. You're just going deeper and deeper." She hesitated once more.

"I'm not going to steal your car," I said.

Finally, she agreed. She opened the door, got out, and let me into the car.

I got into the driver's seat and moved the stick-shift into second gear and, without racing the motor, slowly stepped on the gas pedal. As the wheels started to turn, the car moved forward about a foot, then meeting more sand, stopped. I then reversed the car and slowly backed it up to its original position.

Again, I put the car in second gear and gently increased the pressure on the gas pedal. This time, the car gained enough momentum and traction to drive completely out of the deep rut it had made and gently roll onto firmer sand. I drove a few more feet and stopped.

"Okay, you're out, but don't spin your wheels when you get stuck. It only makes the wheels sink."

I knew how to get out of sand as I'd had numerous experiences with it. As an avid surfer and beach lover, I had learned early on that it takes both momentum and traction to get unstuck from the clutches of soft beach sand.

Everyone was happy.

"Oh, thank you so much," said the girl in the yellow bathing suit. "This is my mother's car, but she let me drive it today."

"No problem," I responded. "By the way, what's your name?"

"Louise. It's my middle name. My first name is Dorothy, but I go by Louise."

"Well, listen, Louise," I said, "there's a drive-in soda shop back up the road, and if you all will follow Sammy and me, we'll buy you a Coke!" I turned to Sammy, and he was nodding in agreement.

Louise and her tall friend got back into her car.

"Just follow us," I instructed. "It's only a little way." She nodded her head, and we sped off down the beach to the road with Sammy's big Oldsmobile leading the way.

The die was cast!

I had met the girl of my dreams, not at church, but on a Sunday afternoon at the beach. She was not dressed in "religious modesty," but in a cute one-piece swimsuit that complemented her alluring figure. At the soda shop, we laughed and joked for an hour or so, exchanged telephone numbers and said goodbye.

That night, we were on the phone for several hours.

We soon had our first date driving Lester's new Buick loaned to me for the date. I had never met such a vivacious, confident, and beautiful girl who thought I was an interesting, although somewhat shy, and handsome guy.

We fell in love.

There were problems, though. Dorothy Louise lived at home with her single, working mom. She had not been indoctrinated by any religion. She had attended a few meetings of Jehovah's Witnesses with her mom when she was still a kid. She enjoyed an occasional Sunday School meeting at the big Church of Christ just two blocks from her home. But she knew little about the Bible or religion. And of course, nothing about doctrine.

But at that time, it didn't seem to matter.

On our first date, Dorothy Louise and her girlfriend accepted a date to spend an evening on a swimming date at the giant Olympic-sized pool at the Shamrock Hotel built by the famous wildcat millionaire oilman, Glen McCarthy. It was a double-date that was arranged by Sammy Shaw. But it was Dorothy Louise who had obtained tickets to the upscale pool, courtesy of a little neighbor-girl friend whose father was a physician connected to the hotel. Sammy seemed awkward around Dorothy Louise's friend and confessed that he didn't date very often. It appeared he was trying to act as though he was having more fun than he was.

I didn't know it then, but Sammy was gay. It was the first time he had ever been with a girl on a date. It may have been his last. He was trying to overcome an attraction to boys like me. It was fun though, and I liked Sammy anyway. It was before radical right-wing Conservative politics had married Evangelistic Christianity, so homophobia had not immersed the culture in hatred for gays, even in the South. We had fun at the pool, and Dorothy Louise was intrigued by my swimming and diving acrobatics. Afterward, we all went over to the big theme park, Playland Park, with dozens of thrill rides a few miles from the hotel. We rode the roller-coaster, tilt-a-whirl, bumper cars, and other exciting rides until midnight. Finally, we dropped both girls off at Dorothy Louise' home and drove back to Lester and Mary's. I thanked Sammy for helping me make my first date with Dorothy Louise a success. He drove away in his big Oldsmobile.

I didn't fall in love as quickly and hard as Dorothy Louise did for me. I felt sympathy for her as she told me how her real father had left her mom when she was only three. She barely remembered him other than he would take her with him around to the bars when he was drinking. According to her and her mother, he was an alcoholic and left after he was divorced by her mother.

Since her mother worked every day, she practically raised herself.

After about a year of going together, she mentioned marriage, something like, "after we are married we can…" I don't remember what, but I was practically blown off my feet. I didn't feel that I was ready for marriage. After all, I was sixteen and had just freed myself from the bonds of my fundamentalist family. I didn't think that I was ready to wrap myself up in marriage.

But, I wasn't completely free. I did it in gradual steps. I was still looking for a church or religion that I liked. And Dorothy Louise was eager to help me find one, but she was interested in my church. And strangely, she got along famously with both Lester and Mary.

The first time I took her with me to church, she was both enthralled and bemused. I was somewhat embarrassed. Her hair was basic Hollywood, and she wore bright red lipstick and all the facial make up that the "church girls" did not.

To her, the strange dress, hair in buns, and pale, non-cosmetic faces of the young girls her age was a curiosity at best. She had never been exposed to Pentecostalism and its holiness emphases, and the enthusiastic testimonials, shouting, loud singing, swooning, weeping, and speaking in unknown tongues was not only strange and peculiar, it was also alien. She didn't fall prey to that automatic guilt trip and "sinner" identification that was the initial effect of attending a Pentecostal service. She was free! And I wanted to learn how I could be free! Our love was too strong to let religion get in the way or to stop it.

I never returned to Bud's house to live. And I never returned to live with Lester and Mary, but on occasions, I would stop in to spend the night. Instead, I got a good paying job at a popular Chevrolet dealership in Houston. It was close enough to Dorothy Louise's home to simply drive to her house after work; we would go somewhere for dinner and then take in a movie in downtown Houston. Her mother allowed me to "sleep over" as often as I wanted. The front room couch was always available. We had become almost inseparable. After a few months, we began to have sex.

Not real sex, but almost.

Although Dorothy Louise was a virgin when we met, the latent sexuality of an effervescent and vibrant sixteen-year-old quickly began to explode in her, and as it did, something was happening inside me. She learned naturally what turned me on sexually. I learned the same about her. She was totally her natural self and had no inhibitions at all. In fact, her working, single-mom had not yet had time (nor inclination) to teach her anything about sex nor to watch for its "evil" consequences as I had, so her naturally uninhibited and unpretentious instincts functioned as if we were already married.

All the sexual maneuvers in the book came as natural to her as breathing. In fact, that's where she learned about sexuality – from the public library. My built-in sexual inhibitions and guilt flew out the door as I became totally mesmerized by this innocent and totally guileless girl. This was a real romance!

Maybe I was hypnotized by her.

Our romance progressed to nightly kissing, holding each other, hugging, and sexual pantomime. We both were entranced by our romance and our mutual sexual attraction. But, it was not just the sex, we both wanted to put it off until we married. I was afraid of it, but she wanted it in the proper way. Marriage.

I developed a deep desire to take care of this beautiful, spiritual novice. Dorothy Louise had deep wounds of abandonment by her father who had left when she was only three. She clung to me like a vine.

And it was obvious that she had picked me for that relationship.

When Lester and Mary saw that there was no hope of breaking my romantic tie with Dorothy Louise, a beautiful though "worldly" girl in the eyes of Pentecostalism, nor was there now any hope of my following in the footsteps of my preacher-father like my younger brothers were trying to do, they offered me a deal. Leave town.

Bible school in Waxahachie, Texas – two hundred miles away. And I, for all effects, volunteered for a renewal of spiritual prison.

Dr. David P. Summers

Chapter 7

He Maketh Me to Lie Down in Green Pastures...

Memories Still

Four thousand years ago I met
the Lord from the past,
In some gaunt swamp-oak
Of memory.

From eternal doom I was handed
A promise of reprieve.
Another life, if you please,
As the meter man came and went as usual.

(*poem on my relentless seeking god ca. 1960*)

Here was the deal.

Lester and Mary would provide for me one year, all-expenses-paid, at "bible school," if I would "get out of Dodge" and relocate myself to Waxahachie, Texas, the headquarters of the Southwestern Seminary of the Assemblies of God.

"I've talked to Brother Collington, (*fictitious*) the Dean," Lester said. "They will let you finish your two or three remaining courses in high school and, at the same time, enter college.

Why not? I thought. It might be interesting. So, in the fall of 1954, I said goodbye to the weeping Dorothy Louise and hitched a ride with my Uncle Frank and Aunt "Baby Doll" (Lester's older sister and lifelong "term of endearment" for Florence, her birth name) out of Houston to the Southwestern Bible Institute (SBI) of Waxahachie, Texas, some 200 miles away.

I was dropped off in front of the ancient, medieval-styled building that had been purchased by the Assemblies of God about ten years earlier from the Lutheran Church. I stood in front of the gate and long walkway that led to steps of the old building as Uncle Frank and Aunt Baby Doll sped off. For a long while, I stood there wondering what I had gotten into.

I had imagined life at Southwestern (now called Southwestern Assemblies of God University or SAGU) to be like a monastery juxtaposed to a convent. Not so. Many of the boys and girls were sent there, like me, in hopes that some of the AG faith and doctrine would rub off on them and change their rebellious ways back to piety. Good luck! The mix was about fifty/fifty wild and wooly to deeply religious and impossibly sanctimonious. The wild ones would at every opportunity sneak off campus to town or hitch-hike to Dallas to enjoy the forbidden bright lights and social scenery. The sanctimonious ones stayed on campus, incessantly reading the bible and praying for the early return of Christ.

It was a convocation of extremes, and I drifted somewhere in the middle.

Looking back at those nine months of total immersion into the fundamentalist belief in Pentecostalism and holiness, I can say, it wasn't all that bad. We had to be in our beds by 10 pm at night, and the dorm guy would come by for a bed check compliance. And the next morning by 7:30 am, we all lined up for breakfast of unsatisfying dry cereal, oatmeal, powdered scrambled eggs, and sliced ham with loaves of bread laid out for toasting. It was the same thing, day after day. Lunch and dinner were much the same.

Attending chapel every day was mandatory.

Each morning, precisely at 9 am we all entered the large and musty old chapel converted to hold the entire attendance of the school. There was a religious song or two, then a dry sermon delivered by one of the more proficient preaching scholars and occasionally a postgraduate returning to his/her alma mater. Then came announcements and various instructions for the coming days and weeks. But on special occasions, the school would host a prominent traveling revivalist, preaching at the school for two or sometimes three weeks daily and nightly.

It was the real deal. One would have to experience one of these meetings to understand the spiritual psychodynamics of repentance and recommitting to the love of Christ. If one personifies Jesus Christ with love, the experience will work with any religion. The mass consciousness of worship produced a palatable state of spiritual congruence. The movement of the Spirit of Christ's love was unmistakable. After the third or fourth night, small praying groups of students and on occasion, faculty would begin intercessional prayers, praying for hours into the night, recommitting and rededicating their lives to the faith.

Here is my remembrance of my spiritual experiences in that year at Southwestern Bible Institute: Invariably, there would be three or four male leaders who stood out as instructors in the faith. Occasionally, one of the more "spiritually filled" females would also organize a group. Otherwise, the women were pretty much subjected to the school's patriarchal approval.

They always had the same two or three who would "speak in tongues" (technically called *glossolalia*) with an interpreter who thought he/she understood these strange utterances of Pentecostalism and delivered the divine messages "directly from the Holy Spirit" to the others in the group. Of course, no one ever disputed what they heard coming directly from God, but the message was usually a naïve and unsophisticated calling to the group back to deeper devotion to God; "Come my little children and hear my voice…etc.," the level of the message was childlike in syntax, delivery, and contextual meaning. But, to "true believers," it was God himself, speaking through his Holy Spirit, a gift greatly treasured by those who spoke in that strange glossolalist tongue.

Though less frequent nowadays, the validity of the Pentecostal experience is still accepted without doubt within the Pentecostal circles. Since it was, at least initially, brought on by a continuous mantra of praise words or the repetitious repeat of the name of Jesus over and over sometimes for hours, until a trance-like state is reached, and words begin to link together in a string of non-intelligible phrases. All rational control of the self is relinquished with a concurrent release of dopamine in the brain producing a natural high.

You tarried (prayed incessantly) until it came out like that! This was speaking in tongues.

To me, it's a bicameral mind phenomenon, perhaps because the right brain hemisphere, which is conceptual and holistic in nature, and does not communicate in left brain hemisphere in logical, spoken words, nor has rationality until the ecstatic state is reached. Then it begins to communicate with the left brain, in an unknown right brain holistic message telling the left brain that it too has found ecstasy and bliss of the Holy Spirit. It, therefore, is rapturous, though unintelligible, verbal expression of right brain "speech" crossing the corpus callosum carrying the message of divine intuitive euphoria, a nonverbal but conceptual understanding to the dry, rational but "spirit-seeking" left-brain. The hormonic congruence of the bi-cameral brain produces an essential "connection" with a higher emotional consciousness can then be verbally comprehended. Whether this is divine or not remains to be seen.

For the believer, and the phenomenon of believing in everything that happens in those services is called the "true believer" effect, as the believer's mentality cannot possibly contain an alternative explanation. I met no admitted skeptics at SAGU. But I met a few rowdies who didn't care. And a bunch of religious fanatics.

But I had seen it all before!

The message was repetitious each time. You knew what was coming when certain individuals stood up and began to shout religious praises.

The school had two traveling groups who would leave each weekend and travel around the state, witnessing, presenting music, and preaching in local Assembly of God churches who committed a Sunday morning and/or a night offering to hear these very talented singers and musicians. Since it was both an escape and an excuse to miss a class or two, I joined a traveling musical ensemble called The Crusaders.

It was a weekly dedicated trip to witness for Christ, with a motorcade of three or so cars, one of which was pulling a small two-wheeled trailer that contained our musical instruments and suitcases. As part of our commitment to Christ, we could spend the nights with a half-dozen or so church members at each stop who gave us bed and breakfast as needed.

I played lead-trumpet in the ensemble, combined with another trumpet player, as well as a clarinet, a saxophone, a trombone, and a piano player. Two of our traveling girls just sang. We presented a message in an instrumental song that lasted either an entire hour or as long as the service lasted, sometimes into the wee hours.

After we presented our program of music and song, leader and conductor, Brother Peters, passed an offering plate to the congregation, then preached a short sermon before closing with an altar call for sinners to repent and be saved.

The money collected by the group never went to us. Instead, it went to pay for new instruments, gas and oil for the autos, food and necessities of travel. The rest was (supposedly) given to the school.

Occasionally, one or two attendees did get saved.

On one trip, beds were scarce. I was to share a bed with the trombone player, a tall, lanky guy from Kansas named James. He was one of the more demonstrative prayers in the group, frequently speaking in tongues at our prayers before our performances.

I undressed down to my briefs and climbed into bed. Sleeping with a guy was nothing new; it was something that most religious boys encounter rather frequently growing up. I turned on my side, away from James, and drifted off to sleep. After a half hour or so, I was aroused when I felt his hand on my leg. Trying not to awaken me, he slowly and carefully moved his hand up to my crotch. Although I was in a drowsy state of half wakefulness, I was aware enough to know what was happening. For a moment, the sexual excitement overcame my spiritual piety that I had so recently given over to God. But simultaneously, in that moment, I felt the old familiar guilt cover me like a cold blanket. It didn't overcome my sexual desire to allow James to fondle my genitals. In spite of Jesus, it was decision time in a world of sexual desire.

Help me Lord, I prayed.

I turned away from his advance. But the sexual attraction that James had stimulated in me at that moment continued to haunt me. This was a male attraction that I had never experienced before. The rejection of my male gender that I felt during my periods of sexual abuse came back. I questioned myself. *Was I gay or bisexual? What am I?* I had often wondered how Jesus handled the sexual encounters he had in his life. Obviously, they are not recorded in the bible other than the unusual meetings. But Jesus encountered every temptation that man would encounter. That was his mission…to overcome, but how? What about the woman at the well (John 4)? Did she try to seduce Jesus for sex? Of course, she did. And what about his obvious love for Mary Magdalene (Luke 8 KJV)? And what about his intimate encounter with Zacchaeus (Luke 19 KJV)?

Of course, the scriptures conveniently omit any discussion of this vital component of life, leaving these experiential lessons to be learned by faith.

After a few months at SBI, a young fireball evangelist came to campus to hold a campus revival. Since I had become known as a bit of a rebel, I deliberately avoided the services and contact whenever I could but, late one night, I was approached by a dozen or so "on fire for Jesus" students, praying and speaking "in unknown tongues." They had been looking for me as it seems that every single male soul on the campus except me had either "gotten saved" or "recommitted" their life to God, publicly.

The prerequisite was that it had to be public. They cornered me outside my dorm room and lo, the preacher laid his hands upon me and commanded me to repent and come back to Jesus. I had no other choice.

I lifted my hands heavenward and began to ask Jesus for forgiveness. It was just like I did when I was four years old, and Mary caught me saying "Goddammit." I repented. And it was genuine. But, I would have never escaped an interminable all-night call to Jesus, had I not recommitted once again, for the umpteenth time. They were determined to save every single soul on the campus. And they did. Willing or unwilling.

The irony was that I had never left Jesus! And Jesus never left me.

Temptations come and go. Don't they? Do you become a sinner just because you contemplated a temptation? When you give in to the temptation but learn a valuable lesson…is it a sin? Or simply a good lesson in choosing the right decision down the long road of life. Would a loving (and of course, understanding) eternal God (who's obviously seen all this before) condemn an innocent first-timer to eternal fire and brimstone for mistakes that we all make learning our way through this life? A lot of folks still think so.

Yeah, I was a cut-up at times, but I can't recall ever doing any "bad" thing that would cause me to leave Jesus. Nevertheless, I wept and cried out for Him just as I had done many times in the past.

It would be untruthful to say that I was not affected by this new anointing. I purposefully changed my daily lifestyle of avoiding the daily chapel and prayer groups and began to attend services again and pray and meditate in the Spirit. I stayed up in the evening and went down to the gymnasium where an all-night prayer meeting was always in progress. And I prayed and prayed and prayed…until I too, spoke in tongues.

Dorothy Louise was coming of age in a much different environment. Her mom rejected fundamentalism and had become a Jehovah's Witness for a short time when Dorothy Louise was a kid but had left the movement after a few years. Dorothy Louise had had no religious exposure growing up other than occasionally attending a nearby Disciples of Christ Sunday School. Although only sixteen, she had never had a boyfriend. She basically raised herself and was a complete novice in religious matters.

Dorothy Louise loved to write of her experiences. She wrote to me practically every day. On one such occasion, she wrote me her usual 15- to

20-page letter of how she loved and missed me, but she began with a little recital of a recent experience with a night out with her mother and some friends. Without a trace of guilt or inborn inhibition, she told me about her first taste of hard liquor.

She had gone to dinner with her aunt and uncle together with mom and mom's boyfriend. Her mom's friend ordered drinks for all. Eager to impress, but not knowing the taste of liquor, she asked the man if she could taste his drink. He had ordered a scotch on the rocks.

"The taste of scotch is terrible. I couldn't stand its taste," she wrote.

As I read her letter, I was stunned. She expressed no guilt of tasting at all. She seemed, to me at least, to be bragging about doing things that my commitment would not allow me to do. I recalled how I had put "all the things of the world" on the altar after my recent re-commitment to Jesus. And that included liquor.

It was during that time I also suddenly began to realize that I was going with an "unsaved" girl. (Well, let's say I had a lot of input from my fellow brothers and sisters-in-Christ who daily brought me a "Word from God" about my asymmetrical relationship). One such word from God was from 2 Corinthians 6:14, KJV: "Be ye not unequally yoked together with unbelievers…" which they used to relentlessly warn me of falling for an "unsaved" girl. It stuck in my mind.

I was thoroughly confused by the situation. I thought that God brought Dorothy Louise and me together. I could accept that she came from a "worldly" family, but I had witnessed her coming to Lester's church and her praying with me from time to time when we had little prayers over this or that. I had never considered her a sinful person.

Although she saw no guilt in what she had done in putting liquor to her lips, I fell into a state of profound sorrow. It lasted for several days before I sat down and returned my feelings in a letter.

She was about to become a sacrificial lamb for the sake of religious purity.

I wrote her and told her that I could no longer go with her and was in that letter breaking off our relationship. I told her that she had sinned, and quoted Proverbs: "Wine is a mocker; strong drink is raging: and whosoever is deceived thereby is not wise." And that was that.

I thought that I was doing what God wanted me to do…to end our relationship. But in my heart of hearts, I couldn't get myself to believe that this was the end of our relationship.

I didn't hear from her for several days. I knew she would take a breakup hard. But I was doing the Lord's will, I thought.

But Dorothy Louise bounced back. She didn't capitulate like the average little churchy person her age I knew at SBI – caught in, say, the sin of slipping out of a revival meeting before the altar call. She simply wouldn't accept that she had done anything to deserve a break in our relationship. Deeply hurt, she didn't write for a few days.

The next time I came back for a weekend at Lester and Mary's home I telephoned her. She was angry.

"What do you mean I'm sinning?" she asked. "I am as saved as you. And now you're telling me that I am not saved, simply because I tasted some scotch whiskey?"

"Well…um," I said, groping for words, "the Bible says to shun the very appearance of evil." My only comeback to this precious love of my life was to recite the standard phraseology that went with the rules and the standard public commitment to salvation that I had been indoctrinated with. At first, she was incredulous, then…

"Okay then," she said, "I'll get saved again. We'll do it your way."

Her quick response astonished me, I had always been taught that "sinners" are initially reluctant to come to Jesus. They had to be cajoled and frightened by the prospect of hell. They were supposed to take a guilt trip first of all. But I intuitively knew that she was not going to do it that way. I knew she wanted to share my spiritual life and experiences but "standard operating procedures" of the Assemblies of God was, well, just not her way.

My intuition was right.

The next time "The Crusaders" performed in Houston, she came to the service. At the end of the service, we made the standard come to Jesus invitation (it is still called an invitation, but it was really more like a big plea). But, she was determined to hold on to something that was in her heart deeper than religion and that her love for me was sufficient motivation for her to accept my brand of salvation.

With tears streaming down her face and surrounded by the lady singers, she accepted the altar call and public commitment to become "born again" and pledged to live a life for Jesus. I was happy beyond description. Now she was officially saved!

I was thrilled that she had taken the religious step that I had needed to witness. I began to take Dorothy Louise with me to Sunday church when I would come back to Houston from another week at Bible school. Lester had now built another new church (his 4th or 5th) on the same grounds as the old, and his attendance was steadily increasing. Lester and I were on rare good terms. Dorothy Louise enjoyed the friendly folks of Greens Bayou Assembly of God who now accepted her as a born-again Christian. After church, the Summers family, alongside some visitors, often went to a local cafeteria for Sunday lunch. After we finished, I took Dorothy Louise back home and spent the rest of the day with her.

Sometime after her official salvation, she told me of a strange experience she'd had just as she turned sixteen. She saw an "illuminated angel" coming into her room. It was the night she had received my letter telling her that I could not marry a girl who was "unsaved."

"I was crying my heart out that night," she told me. "Just before midnight, there appeared a being, clothed in light that appeared to be "angelic," glowing with a strange light, standing at the entrance of the door to her room. She said it was as tall as the ceiling and sparkling like frost in an early sunrise. The being had the characteristics of both an angel and a man.

She said, "he stood looking at her for several long minutes, in sympathy to her undeserved wound. The being then slowly raised its arms toward her, and as it did, she began to levitate from her bed. She said she was so enthralled by the experience that she moved her hand to the mattress to confirm that she was still in bed. She could feel herself above the mattress. Suddenly, she became fearful that she would hit the ceiling fan. At that moment, she was back in bed but full of joy and fascination with her experience. Was she raised up with him? Was this being Jesus?" She didn't know, but all the hurt and pain she had was suddenly all gone.

The experience made an indelible impression on her.

She knew then that she was worthy of divine love and not

condemnation. She was convinced of the spiritual reality of her experience and its feeling of comfort and unity with God, saying that it proved that "Jesus loved her."

I began to realize that my cruel judgment of her over the silly incident of tasting liquor was just plain stupid.

She did not disclose the incident to me or anyone else for several months.

I did well at Southwestern Bible Institute that year, graduating high school and picking up a few college hours in English, History, and Old Testament courses. But I became bored with the daily chapel and began to hide from the room inspection by climbing atop my closet and closing the closet door. My little hiding place also gave me a couple more hours to sleep that my roommate did not have. But toward the end of the semester, I changed roommates, rooming with a tough ex-Marine who had been in the Korean conflict.

He had a car, so we began to drive into Dallas to a local skating rink and hang out with guys who smoked cigarettes and drank beer. Although I smoked a few cigarettes and drank a little beer (Not so, my ex-military roomy), I still held to my commitment to Jesus and continued to "go steady" with Dorothy Louise, but toward the end of the last semester, once again, I began to lose my dedication to the strict requirements of Pentecostal fundamentalism. I just couldn't live it and be true to myself. It was too artificial.

The Dean was told of my extracurricular activities and contacted Lester at the end of my year at Southwestern asking him to not send me back to SBI for the next school year. I was unjustly accused of selling drugs on the campus. But it was just me showing off once again. The so-called drugs were quinine, which I had taken since I was diagnosed with the malaria disease in childhood. I hung out with a group of four or five boys from Houston Heights Assembly who all claimed to be in a gang and for me to do, so-called drugs, automatically made me a member.

So, I left Southwestern for good that summer and took up a steady offshore job. I started as a lowly orderly and cook's helper. But I didn't care, I wanted to go to sea so badly that I would have taken just about any offered position. When I returned from my 21-day work duty, I didn't go home; I went over to see Dorothy Louise.

By then her mother would let me sleep-over on the couch in the front living room. On Sunday, I would get up and dress for church as would

Dorothy Louise and we would drive over to Lester's church for Sunday Services. Some of the religious practices of Pentecostalism were simply incomprehensible to Dorothy Louise. For example, the true religion forbad working on Sunday (unless your "ox was in the ditch"). But my new offshore job required that I work seven-days-per-week, three weeks at a time, which meant that my ox was always in the ditch. But it was accepted as necessary as several of the men in the church worked shiftwork at the steel mills or refineries in the local area.

As the little episode above demonstrated, in the 1950s, the AG congregations still maintained a hard prohibition against imbibing alcohol of any type (that's changed, as they all drink wine nowadays). However, the German heritage that Dorothy Louise was brought up under included an old ethic. Not only did this ethic allow drinking, but it also permitted the making of one's own liquor. This was perfectly natural and customary to do with her German grandfather, and he made some of the greatest beer I have ever drunk.

He fermented beer in his basement during Prohibition, and never dropped the habit even after Prohibition went away. Her mom had a drink almost every evening after coming home from work. Her mom also liked to play cards and gamble small amounts with her sister and brother-in-law when they visited. It was all social entertainment, which really put both of us in a dilemma.

The Assembly of God prohibition on these practices was too much for Dorothy Louise on minor issues such as above. She loved the people in the church but refused to conform to these beliefs. She especially refused to conform to the "pale-face" ideology of no makeup and wore bright red lipstick, eyeshadow, and other make-up. She ignored the "dress code" and wore the type of dress that sometimes put me ill at ease. The fact that the Church frowned upon open-toed shoes was comical to her. She simply refused to accept the doctrine.

Pentecostal fundamentalism was difficult for her because it was so illogical and anything in the religion that was put forward just because of church demanded such illogical acceptance, she did not accept it, and refused to argue about it if her logical mind did not see the virtue of it. But at other times, she made it work for her.

Take the case of her baptism in water. She made common-sense work for her.

Not long afterward, I brought up the topic of baptism by immersion as required by the AG's at that time for completion of scriptural adherence to the doctrine of Christian discipleship. She had witnessed several baptisms while visiting with me. Dorothy Louise was ready and willing to be "ducked" if that would further guarantee her acceptance into "God's family." Her fateful Sunday arrived on a beautiful clear spring day. Lester preached a rather brief, standard Sunday morning service, and then advised the congregation that there would be a baptism at the end of the service. I recall Dorothy bringing a change of clothes.

But nothing prepared neither me nor the entire church for what came next. Baptism in our church meant total immersion and the candidate is totally washed of their sins – clothes and all. The baptismal tank was filled with lukewarm water, and Dorothy Louise disappeared into an anti-room adjacent to the platform and the baptismal. Lester did the obligatory lesson of the significance of baptism by submersion then called out for Dorothy to come and be baptized.

No one I had ever seen (and I suspected no one Lester had ever seen) participated in a baptismal convert wearing a bathing-cap to keep their hair dry. When one is baptized that means the whole body! What would Jesus say? Oh my God!

Had Lester gently said, "sister, would you kindly remove your head covering for the baptism?" I am sure she would have. But it was the common-sense approach that Dorothy Louise brought to baptism. She was entirely innocent of any fundamental protocol.

"Shock and awe" was the collective reaction of the entire congregation. I could not believe my own eyes. Lester's jaw dropped, but he quickly recovered. Enter stage left, Dorothy Louise Harris, soon-to-be-wife of the eldest son of the pastor Lester dressed in a white flowing dress...

...and wearing an Esther Williams type white bathing cap with little flowers adorning the rubber. No one missed a beat and Lester proceeded to baptize Dorothy Louise in the name of the Father, Son, and the Holy Ghost!

I admired the nonplused reaction from Lester. He paused only for a split second, and I was for that moment afraid he would refuse to baptize her, but he took her by the hand and led her down into the baptismal. Putting a hand behind her head and the other over her mouth and nose he said, "I now baptize you in the name of the Father, the Son, and the Holy Ghost." And dunk her, he did.

With the congregation shouting "Amen," Dorothy Louise emerged from the water and gasped for air.

"Amen, Sister," he said again. "You are now a part of the body of Christ!"

Afterward, we were alone in the car and heading out to meet Lester and Mary and family at the usual Cafeteria on Federal Road. After recovering from my embarrassment over the head-covering with a bathing cap, I said,

"Honey, why did you wear that gaudy Esther Williams bathing cap?"

"What," she said, "why do you think?"

"Well…" I drawled out my response, "well, we just don't do that in my church."

"Why not?" she said as I tried to find the right words.

"Um…it's just not pure," I said. She just shook her head in disbelief.

"Is a wet head purer than a wet cap over dry hair?" I had no further words.

Dorothy Louise later explained the common-sense logic to her still disbelieving soon-to-be husband.

"Well," she said, "we always go out to eat Sunday dinner with your family and I had to keep my hair dry for that didn't I?" she matter-of-factly declared. Um, tradition died a little that day.

Now, how could one argue with that explanation?

We were engaged to be married a short time later.

Dr. David P. Summers

Chapter 8

Walking Between the (first) Raindrops

The Friend

"Hey Junior!"
Were his first words.
After I had lied
About my age With my faked
birth certificate!

At last, I was to be a man
On a ship!
He was painting the bulwark
When he casually glanced at me,
The seaman apprentice.

Smoking a pipe and sporting
A thin red mustache,
He was strikingly debonair.

He went by the name "Red."
But I called him Pat,
As only his close friends did.
We talked till dawn most days
Drinking whiskey from a single bottle.

Together,
We fought other seamen
In barrooms,
Whorehouses,
And even in jail.

We also fought each other.

But we were friends, such close friends.
He later married And so, did I.

Still, when he was drunk,
He would pound my door.
"Hey Junior, wake up!"
"Dammit, I'm sleeping."
"Have a drink with me"
"Ha ha, okay."
I was finally a man!

(written on love of my mentor of worldly indulgence, "Red" Patterson – deceased ca. 1960)

I had already begun to cast off from the shores of the familiar religiosity. My cook's helper job soon turned to a promotion to a job as an oiler on a giant lifting crane of an offshore constructions barge. The big seagoing barge was called the Herman B, named after one of the brothers who founded Brown and Root, Inc., Herman Brown, co-founder with his brother George.

As an oiler, I was responsible for lubrication of all the sheaves, bearings, fueling, and general maintenance of the huge heavy-lift crane. I loved the work. It was an all-day job. I would climb to the top of the crane's "A" frame every day with my lubrication gun just to enjoy the magnificent view of the ocean from a couple hundred feet above the sea. But I found a chance to do what I always dreamed of – go to sea.

Free at last.

There was a lot of turnover on the offshore projects. So, I quickly moved up in the trades to rigger, welder, pipefitter, then as a structural ironworker. I had acquired my merchant marine seaman's papers, so that put me even more in demand as every offshore construction required one or two Coast Guard registered seaman. Soon, I was relieving the operator on the giant 300-ton crane. The pay was excellent because we worked on average, twelve hours per day, seven days a week for three weeks at a time. It was the "time and a half" over-time that meant that I was paid my regular rate plus half. That made the big checks bigger! After working three weeks offshore, we were given ten days off for rest and recovery. More on the work in the next chapter.

And I was faithful in paying my tithe to Lester.

The next year, Dorothy Louise and I decided to marry.
Fast forward to June 1, 1956.

Dr. David P. Summers

Chapter 9

Here Comes the Bride (and Groom)

Someday Heaven

*Someday I think I'll check the Akashic records
And tidy up the details Because that's
how the Bible was written.*

*I used to brag with an old friend
About how Death was no longer chic.
I'd say,
"Get out of your body again,"
And he'd reply,
"you're so preoccupied, for Christ sake."*

*Well, from ten feet away
I couldn't see much difference
(except I could breathe the water—so what? So can fish?!)
Every other day I'd come back
To this aging vessel of clay.*

*And in time, I drove away the demons.
Strange how demons were always more attracted to me than angels.
Their talons have been torn from my back,
And the men I came to see have kept me waiting— much
too long to be gentlemanly.*

*Someone should do something.
Perhaps pass a law.*

*Damned if I can recall the last good times. 1942? 1952?
My, how time flies! I can't remember the year But the dichotomy grows.*

(poetry of depression written by me)

Lester read out the marriage vows, Mary played the wedding march and with David ("Bud") Stevens as my best man Dorothy Louise Harris became Mrs. David Summers on a beautiful June evening in 1956 in South Texas. I had entered a life that had no prior script.

The next six years were a hazy time, reminiscent of the "Father Knows Best!" popular radio show. The Lester Summers family became Dorothy's extended family. We bought a cute three-bedroom home in Green's Bayou. I continued to work in off-shore marine construction making decent money.

My relationship with Lester was split from my reality of work and family. On the positive side, I was still a church-going elder son and continued to give 10% to his church. On the negative side, when working away from home, I was totally one of the gang, in another world of hard drinkers, bar-room brawlers, gamblers, and women chasers that had no religious rules. I lived each side of life fully, a split personality that was hard to believe.

Our first child, Crystal Rae, was born a year and a fortnight after we married. Then came Marcia Louise and Sherry Rene, all born in Houston's Memorial Hermann Hospital. It was an idyllic life on Dorwayne Street. With Brown & Root, (now KBR-Halliburton) I was sent on jobs that took me to South America, Mexico, and Puerto Rico, and all over the Gulf of Mexico. It was tough and often dangerous macho work. But I loved the adventure of it. Climbing to the top of a 200-foot drilling platform and hooking it to swinging 3-inch cables so that it could be lifted by the monster crane from a barge rolling in 4-5-foot seas played into my psyche of flirting with death. One misstep or slip would send a person falling to instant death.

I became quite proficient at just about everything involved, but confidence has its downside.

Overconfidence.

It caught up with me one windy and cold night. As I climbed a metal ladder, my hands slipped on a greasy rung, and I suddenly fell backward some twenty-five feet. It could have cost me my life. As I fell I put my hands behind my back trying to break my fall, but instead fell against a large, upright steel beam, butt first. The beam propelled me forward instead of backward, and I hit the deck with my face forward. The foreman ran over. "Are you hurt?" he cried. I slowly got to my feet rubbing my face and nose. I was stunned, but I had sustained a relatively light injury to my hips. I was sent ashore on the next crew boat to be examined by the company doctor the next day. He too was amazed that such a fall could result in such a relatively light injury. Nevertheless, he recommended that I do "light duty" for several weeks. I considered it a miracle that I didn't break my back from the fall.

The company arranged my light-duty as the time-keeper and radio operator. But, for the first time, I began to feel that I might be better at using my mind as well as my skill with my hands and my brawn. In addition, it was hard on Dorothy Louise, because in the days when there were no cell-phones, not only was I away from home, I was simply out of touch for weeks.

After a long job in Venezuela, leaving Dorothy Louise alone with my daughters, Crystal, Marcia, and Sherry, I knew it was more than she should bear. She became desperately lonely. I decided to quit. I left offshore work in 1960 never intending to return.

My uncle Joe Summers (*deceased*), Lester's older brother, was starting a new business in Dallas. He asked me to become a partner with him selling funeral coaches and ambulances for his dealership in Duncanville, Texas. This was quite a jump in occupation! But, I was ready to leave Greens Bayou and move on. I moved the family to Dallas in June of that year, and I become Joe's partner.

My duties required that I wear a suit and tie, drive a black (usually) demo-hearse around Texas and Oklahoma, and call on funeral homes to show it and establish a customer relationship. Funeral directors were just like any other new car buyer; they became downright giddy over the prospect of a new hearse or ambulance. They loved to get in, enjoy the "new" smell, and drive my demonstrator around awhile while I set beside them and sold them on the advantages of buying a new hearse. My self-imposed requirement of making eight sales calls per day served me well as I quickly become Joe's top salesman.

I sort of liked the job, but again, I was on the road constantly and leaving Dorothy Louise behind in Dallas was hard on both of us. And things did not work out with Uncle Joe and me. We couldn't agree on what I was paid, so I decided to part company and after a year, I resigned.

The next year, we were in Charlotte, North Carolina where I obtained my own dealership with a premier coach company. Like what I had been selling for Joe, they were a custom-maker of funeral coaches and ambulances. I did well for a year or so, and both Dorothy Louise and I enjoyed living in North Carolina.

I couldn't have done it without Lester's financial assistance. On Lester and Mary's visit to Charlotte, he signed a guarantee for me in one of Charlotte's biggest banks.

From Charlotte, we moved further south to Atlanta, Georgia when after two years of running my own company selling new and used coaches, I hit a low spot. I began to be depressed again. My bank financing dried up and with it, my commissions. I began to look for something steadier.

Like a salary.

But not quite yet.

I had dropped my dealership with the funeral coach and ambulance company and moved to Atlanta to represent a funeral coach dealer from Columbia, South Carolina. So, I continued traveling away from home, selling funeral coaches and ambulances.

Troy Martin (*fictitious*) owned the Shell gas station where I serviced my vehicles. He was basically an uneducated "good ole Southern boy" who liked to get away from his wife and drink. She was even less educated than Troy but immediately latched on to Dorothy Louise. It made Dorothy Louise a little embarrassed over the friendship, but she went along with her anyway when I would stop and talk to Troy.

I would drop off my vehicle for service and Troy would leave one of the service guys to run the station.

At first, Troy and I would disappear for a few hours and drink beer in one of his good old Southern drinking establishments. But Troy had a deep psychological problem, typical with many men. As he drank, he relieved himself of his religious prohibitions. As did I. When we both got together, we fed off each other's need for psychological freedom from our common demons.

Within a few weeks, I began to tell Dorothy Louise that I needed to go out of town on business. Instead, Troy and I were spending several days and nights away from our respective occupations. As was my usual custom, I would park my demo in Troy's service station garage, and we would go out on all night drinking sprees. My model was one of my heroes from the early days with marine construction jobs with an ex-WWII GI named Red Patterson. Unfortunately, I wanted to be just like Red.

Red was a great guy when sober. But when he was drinking, he would completely drop off the world, sometimes for as long as a week or two.

Then he would return as though nothing happened. I envied his freedom to come and go, work or not work. This time, I began to play out Red's role in my life. Troy accompanied me.

One evening I again parked one of my vehicles on Troy's lot. "Let's get a beer while your boy washes and greases my demo coach," I said.

"Hey, damn right…thought you'd never ask," he ribbed. We were soon in his car headed for our favorite beer joint. It was not long until we were both intoxicated. That evening we were both drunk, but still driving around Atlanta. Around ten o'clock or so I was getting tired. "Troy," I mumbled, "I need to put my head down for a little while." Troy was not sleepy like I was; in fact, he seemed to talk and drive perfectly safe.

"Ok," he said, "I know where we can go. It's an old friend of mine."

We soon wound up with an old girlfriend of Troy, three more ladies, and a couple of guys. The night passed, and I fell into a deep drunken slumber on a couch. Just before daylight, I awoke needing to urinate asap. After all, partially metabolized warm beer has got to go somewhere. I got up and walked around. The sun was streaming in through the blinds. All three ladies were in various stages of undress and sleeping soundly.

Not knowing where the bathroom was, I decided to go outside and urinate on the grounds somewhere like when I was a child; I had been brought up to do when the bathroom was full. I walked through the kitchen and out through the back door toward a fence. But apparently, I made enough noise to awaken one of the guys. Just as I was going back up the back-door steps the door suddenly swung open. I had hardly enough time to pull up my zipper when a pistol was in my face. "I'll shoot you… you son of a bitch!" he said.

"Hey…hold on, it's me…Dave," I quickly replied. He looked at me again. Apparently Troy never introduced me, and we were all so drunk that no one cared when we arrived. He didn't seem to recognize me.

"Hey buddy, put the gun down…please," I said, as I slowly moved his arm away from my face. "I was just outside taking a piss," I said.

He continued looking at me. Finally, he did recognize me. "I thought you were robbing us," he slowly said, wiping his eyes. "Okay, come on back in," he said, sticking the snub-38 pistol revolver back in his pants.

This was not the only "near miss" I had with Troy. There were others as we continued a down-hill slide together.

One day we were talking about guns. "Hey, I carry," he said, "you can't be too careful. Some black dude could come by with robbing on his mind.

The remark was typical Southern racism at that time, but that was the consciousness. "How 'bout you, you carry?"

"No," I said, "I've never felt the need." (I always assumed that machomen could take care of themselves without resorting to guns and knives.)

"That's stupid," Troy replied. "You can never know what you are going to meet up with." After my scare with Troy's friends, I decided to buy a gun to carry. I bought a small .38 caliber Smith and Wesson pistol that I could carry in my pocket or waistband. The gun was really bought for Dorothy Louise – for protection when she was left alone when I was on one of my many sales trips. But I soon began to carry it with me.

I was still driving my sales territories in Georgia and South Carolina, but was losing my enthusiasm and with it, losing income. I began to drink and drive. Still trying to find Jesus, Dorothy Louise and I had joined the Episcopal church. We had all three of our kids confirmed in the faith. I kept trying to get back my enthusiasm and with it, get out of my depression, but I was again, rapidly going downhill. But the mania side of my manic/depressive sickness was craving excitement and danger.

I had made friends with another young man who worked for Troy. His name was Jack. He was a rather small guy who, for some unexplained reason to me, also carried a gun. Sometimes when we got together for a couple of beers, we would take our weapons out, cock and uncock them and joke about Russian Roulette. I was in such psychic pain that I considered the possibility. I was so depressed that Dorothy Louise finally insisted that I see our family physician.

After resisting for a few days, I knew she was right and made an appointment. After talking to me and asking me a few questions, he wrote out a prescription for tranquilizers and gave me the name of the most prestigious psychiatrist in Atlanta. They were at the Atlanta Psychiatric Clinic. "You really need to make an appointment," he said. "I think your depression is getting you into a very bad mental state." After a few days brooding over the diagnosis, I did.

When I called, I talked to one of the staff-members at the clinic who screen incoming patients. She told me that the psychiatrist would only see me if I brought Dorothy Louise in with me. "We try to practice couples' therapy here when the patient is married," she said.

Two weeks later, I showed up with Dorothy Louise for our first appointment. We met a kind, gentle, and understanding psychiatric physician named Dr. Thomas Lann (*fictitious*), who interviewed both of us separately. We thus began our couples-therapy that day. But, the relief I sought would be slow to come. Dr. Lann began, "So David, tell me a little about your childhood," he encouraged both of us to feel free to say anything that came into our minds.

"I didn't get along with dad, but other than that I think I had a pretty good childhood, Dr. Lann," I lied.

"Me too," piped Dorothy Louise, "I was an only kid…with a single mom, but I had a great childhood!"

"Okay, let's talk about it, and just call me Tom," replied Dr. Lann. He then opened up to us about how he had completed his post-doctorate fellowship training at Topeka, Kansas' Menninger School of Psychiatry. "We treat the entire milieu of experiences," he said. "Everything matters. That's why we want you both involved in the therapy." Thus, began a therapeutic dialog that spanned a decade.

We talked for about an hour with my anxiety rising toward the end. I had never been to a psychiatrist and had no idea how "talk-therapy" worked. The more I talked, the more it seemed I needed to talk. I thought it was sort of crazy that Dr. Lann just listened to me. When he did talk, he simply asked me how certain experiences I related to him made me feel. It was the first time in my life that I had sat for an hour and poured out my feelings. Finally, it was over.

"I will talk to my supervisors and see if you are a candidate for our treatment," he said.

"What?" I said, "I thought you were going to try to figure out if anything is wrong with me or if I even needed to see you." My anxiety was clearly rising. I had clearly already made an emotional attachment to him.

"Well, we don't try to treat everyone," he said, "and I will talk to Dr. Cramer (*fictitious*), my superior, and get his opinion."

A bizarre feeling of abandonment hit me in the gut. I knew subliminally that I desperately needed his help. What if they turn us down I thought?

Dr. Lann was really establishing my level of need, coupled with my commitment to the protracted treatment. "Our treatment is for a minimum of six weeks," he said. I simply stared at him.

"OK, I'm ready," I replied.

"Good, we'll see you next week."

With Dorothy Louise at my side, we walked out. Thus, began the most life-saving (literally) medical procedure of my life. I was so depressed that I was suicidal. But rather than think about taking my life, which was explicitly against my religious teachings, I was, in fact, engaging in dangerous and self-destructive behavior that could likely substitute for suicide. I felt more distressed leaving than when I went in. Hell, I was ready to begin the same day. But with the real therapy commencing the next week, I hardly knew what to expect. I acted out one more self-destructive behavior the next week. It could have been my last one, as I told my psychiatrist, I "chickened out." He said my rational mind overrode the macho man and rescued me.

"Hey Dave," Jack called out. "Are you as broke as I am?" He was sitting alone at Troy's gas station. I still had the nozzle of the gas hose stuck in the gas tank of Uncle Joe's shiny-black funeral hearse.

"Pretty much," I replied. "Why?"

"Um… you packing?" he said. "I mean, got your piece?"

"No, it's in the car," I replied…why, where's Troy?"

"He's with Margaret. They went back down to Macon to see Maggie's mama."

"Oh," I said. "How long?" I handed Jack a credit card and followed him inside the station. "I dunno," Jack replied. "Couple of days, I guess." Jack kept staring at me.

"Gotcha piece?" he pressed me to answer his original question. "Go get it," he commanded. "I've got a job staked out."

I didn't like being commanded by anyone. And I always sought to be the bravest guy in any situation. I had always overcome thoughts that brought fear. But, I was broke and therefore willing to hear more.

"What'cha got in mind, Jack?" I said, slightly lowering voice on the last word, then, sitting down beside him. I lapsed into street language, "and gimme a beer," dude.

"Okay," he said, handing me an unopened can. "Look, there is a little store around the corner, and there is only an old lady in there running it most of the time. It would be a piece of cake."

"What?" I said. "You want to rob a store?"

"Yeah…easy. We could pull it off in five minutes," he said excitedly. "I've knocked off little stores like that before." Clearly, he expected this little scenario to whet my appetite for an experience of petty criminality. It didn't.

I looked at Jack while I ran the thought through my mind. *Yes, it might be that easy. Dare I go where I've never gone before?* With bravado rising, I thought, "but how could a dare-devil-macho-guy-like-me back down now?

"I'll be back in two minutes," I said, going toward my car. I quickly returned with my little .38 caliber Smith and Wesson tucked inside my pants under my shirt. It was becoming evening. "You're really serious?" I questioned.

"God damn right, I'm serious," he replied. There was some tightening in his voice.

"Hmm," I said, "how much money do you think we can get out of her?"

"I dunno," Jack said, "maybe two-to-three hundred?"

"Okay, let's do it!" I said. We laid out a simple plan. I would go in and hold-up the old lady and rob the cash box. Jack would stand outside and act as the look-out. I pulled the black demo I was driving into Troy's garage and locked it. Jack locked the station

We got into the car, drove over to the little store and parked a little down the street from it. I was both excited and calm. It was the same emotion I used to have right before I would have to stand before Lester to explain some goofy fuck-up on my part…like the little episode of nasty note passing in the fourth grade. We parked, and I got out. Now I was really in the "big time." My heart was pounding.

"Okay, I'm going in," I said. I stuffed my gun under my shirt and entered the store. I saw the little old lady out of the corner of my eye. At the same time, I got a glimpse of someone else standing in a small office behind the counter. I pretended that I was looking for something.

"Can I help you?" the little old lady asked. I could see that the man in the background was now eyeing me.

"No," I said, "I don't see what I was looking for." I turned and walked out of the store.

At the psychiatric clinic, the next week, I recounted my story. I was truly embarrassed and ashamed, I told Dr. Tom. Not at what I had done, but what I hadn't done.

"Just because there was someone in the back of the store I shouldn't have lost my nerve," I said to Dr. Lann. "I guess I am nothing more than a punk-assed sissy," I said.

Both Dorothy Louise and Dr. Tom Lann listened intently to my account of the past week.

"I chickened out, Dr. Tom," I told him, after going through the story. "I didn't have the guts to do it."

Dr. Lann looked at me over his glasses in surprise and said slowly, "no, that wasn't chickening out. Think about it… that was using your head, David. You could have been easily killed. You wisely used your mind," he repeated… "This was no hero decision. It was the right decision."

I was truly stunned and confounded. I had always pushed myself to be a real-macho man partly for the admiration and partly for my own ego. No one had ever given me a rational alternative to my macho-man egomania that was so desperate for emotional compensation. I sat and looked over at Dorothy Louise, she was nodding her head. "Yes," she said, "I agree with Dr. Tom."

"Don't you see?" he gently asked again. "You didn't chicken out. You used the better part of your consciousness, your rational mind. Your emotions were telling your ego what to do." He said.

What is my consciousness? I thought that consciousness was simply being awake and not asleep. It was strange, I thought. I never even thought whether I was right or wrong. Strong men like Sampson or King David never worried about whether they should use their strength – they just did it!

"Why didn't my religion stop me?" I asked the doctor. "Where was Jesus when I needed him?"

"You're trying to fit religion into your dysfunctional emotional needs," he said, "I don't know where Jesus was, perhaps Jesus let you do this to show you a lesson for a bad decision…" His voice trailed off leaving me to ponder. He continued, "It could have been really bad."

Dr. Lann then began to explain how we live in different levels of consciousness. It was mostly Freudian concepts explained as best as I could comprehend. "You let your Ego become overwhelmed by the Id," he explained.

Toward the end of the session, he said, "I've got a book for you to read." He handed me a copy of Joseph Campbell's Hero with a Thousand Faces. "I'm loaning it to you, David. Bring it back when you finish it."

I read the book. It was Campbell's exhaustive account of worldwide religions and sects. He related how all great religions of the world had basically the same story to tell. There was the miraculous birth, the adoption of the savior-child, the teachings, crucifixion, death, and resurrection. And all required one to believe the stories as "true."

But I didn't really understand what I was reading at that time. It didn't fit my own religious paradigm of simple fundamentalism. Do the right thing. My subconscious mind was steeped in Pentecostal Christianity, wobbling from mania to deep despair, seeking some part of that I could incorporate into my own life and carry with me - anything but total conformity to a preacher's message. Campbell's book was Leland's initial attempt to get me to see that my religion was at the source of my mental psychosis.

The next week we checked in at ten o'clock for our hour appointment. We sat down in big comfortable chairs, and then Dr. Lann came into the room. "Someone broke into our offices."

"Did they catch him?" asked Dorothy Louise. "No," replied Dr. Lann, then paused for a minute. "But we first suspected that it might be one of our patients, and David's name came up first," he said, still smiling.

"What?" I thought. "I didn't get the joke." I was appalled, how could they consider me a common thief who would steal from someone who was trying to help me? I was confused. But I can see why I was at the top of consideration.

"Oh no," Dorothy Louise replied without hesitation, "He was home with me all weekend!"

"Well, the staff decided that it was likely another patient," He said.

Dorothy Louise and I entered Dr. Lann's initial course of psychotherapy and for the next six weeks and I worked my way out of depression into the inevitable "flight into health." At last, I began to find and explore a world of non-religious based life that I had never knew existed. I began to find something called congruency.

Dr. David P. Summers

Chapter 10

Something Old, Something Borrowed

When the West was Won

The courthouse clock strikes high noon,
as a lone rider comes to town.

There's a murmur in the crowd
And a cowboy whispers, "that's Big Bart,
He'll be looking for a cowardly rustler."

There's a fire
Thriving in his eyes
As he slowly walks to Fate.
Sure, one will die
But also, one will live.

(poem of extreme pessimism or suicide ca.1965)

In 1965, I abandoned my little company and was hired by a major manufacturer of pharmaceuticals and medical supplies headquartered in New Jersey. They moved me to Lubbock, Texas to represent their products in hospitals and doctor's offices. I was given the vast, mostly flat expanses of West Texas, New Mexico, and Northern Mexico as my territory. It was probably the worst territory in the company, but I went to work and made it pay off. It became the top territory in the division. As usual, Dorothy Louise went to work as a data processing specialist. We put the girls into a private Episcopal school and regularly attended the All Saints Episcopal church. I sang in the choir.

I spent three years on the road, leaving on Monday and returning late Friday night. I relentlessly drove the vast differences in miles between calls, trying to make the Company's standard – eight calls per day. It's not easy to do when each town was 50 to 100 miles between.

I still drank heavily while traveling. Not while driving, but as soon as I wrote my daily call reports, I headed to the nearest bar. Friendly pharmacist or nurse acquaintances supplied me "uppers" and "downers," which kept my eyes open driving from town to town during the day, and, after I had my last drink, put me to sleep at night. I was in a perpetual battle with my manic-depressiveness. Mania was my goal, for in the state of mania – well, I could do anything! I drove myself relentlessly. And I loved the job, which continually nullified both extremes of disease manifestations!

Then, after winning "Salesman of the Year" two years in a row and almost three years in the loneliest, most desolate territory the company had, the company moved us to Houston where I was given a much more lucrative, albeit smaller, territory. We bought a new home, enrolled the kids in a new modern school near Sharpstown, and with a new company car I now not only looked but felt like I had hit the jackpot. It looked like I had money, but it was really the company's American Express credit card; my earlier learned lessons on how to cheat on my expense account was my escape.

I was selected to work alongside the famed heart surgeon Michael E. DeBakey, MD (*deceased*) who was at that time working with my company to develop the famous DeBakey arterial prosthesis for arterial aneurysms. An aneurysm is a blown-out tire in the vital aorta. It was a woven Dacron or nylon tube, the same size as the patient's blown artery. To not have such a replacement usually meant certain death.

My company was the sole manufacturer of the life-saving device. I was instructed to not only call upon but to entertain my clients as often as possible, which I did with enthusiasm. There was drinking, dining, and entertainment almost every night while on the road. I quickly rose in the ranks to become the Midwest Divisional Manager. The company asked us to move to Kansas. We did. We took the kids out of school again and moved, this time to a swanky home in Overland Park, Kansas, a suburb of Kansas City, Missouri. Once again, I was on a flight into a giddy mental mania with visions of loyal sales representatives in my own self-image.

Chapter 11

Making the Cut

Sell it, They'll Buy it

I hope
That in being born
I did gain at least
Some glimpse
Of life's beauty.

I've observed a lot
Through these jaundiced eyes.

We laymen
Draw on our soul
For the picture of existence.

The Holy Ghost descended alright:
I saw tongues thrashing All over the world.

But from the vantage of the Seventh Heaven,
It didn't look much different
Than it did five thousand years ago.

Men spoke back then too,
Through the locked-in syllables
Of grunts and groans.

(Self-written mania/depressive period)

Becoming an executive for a large New England pharmaceutical company was once again an adventure into a world I hardly knew. I was not prepared for it. But I treated it like the religious genre that I grew up in – I took orders, studied, and tried to do what management asked me to do. I continued to receive treatment for chronic depression, so I was always taking the latest pharmaceutical anti-depressant. I began taking other drugs as well. It was a life of constant social interactions with the medical world that mainly consisted of dinners and entertainment with every customer I could take out (really a form of bribery) to use our products.

Pharmaceutical contraceptives had just hit the market and my clientele of mostly nurses was now empowered to have sex anywhere, anytime.

The annual convention of nurses such as the American Nursing Association (ANA), the American Association of Operating Room Nurses (AORN), the American Association of Nurses (ANA), and the Society of Urology Nurses and Associates (SUNA) was one big sex party. My management, a couple of research people, and a Vice President of two would fly in and help man the display booth. At night we would have at least two or three hospitality rooms at the hotels that roomed us and the other convention-goers. It was 1968, and birth control was legal; everyone was horny, and we hit all the conventions.

But, I had an ongoing problem with my own peers. I had picked up only a few academic hours of college (while at SBI), and I could not help but feel rather inadequate. When the managers got together at various sales and marketing meetings, the chatter drifted to fraternities, college sports, and who you knew at the company headquarters in Murray Hill, New Jersey. They all had college degrees from Rutgers, Princeton, Columbia, or other prestigious New England universities. Invariably, I was asked about my college credentials, which I grossly lied about. I would say something like I had almost finished college and was working on completing my degree by correspondence. It was usually good enough.

My macho-man, redneck, past-expertise at marine rigging, pipe-fitting, and heavy crane operations and deep-sea diving gave me nothing in common with the fast-talking guys from New York or New Jersey. But knowing when to talk and when to shut up and my ability to out-drink all of them, a tolerance I had acquired, do or die, from the raft of roughnecks and riggers who worked in off-shore trades with me, gave me an edge that leveled the playing field.

So, I if I could hold my own with alcohol I could hold my own selling the doctors and nurses. But it was hard to get to the front of the line as a manager because of my lack of university credentials. So, it looked like I would be stuck in my middle-management role for a long time.

As time went on, the luster of the job began to wear off. I could handle the demands of the job – flying out to Minneapolis, St. Louis or Des Moines on Monday or Tuesday and working with the salesman in the territory for a couple of days and then returning to Kansas City on Thursday or Friday, week after week. I began to smoke pot to relax on a regular basis. The example of the polished, uptight Mr. Executive wasn't nearly as attractive as it used to be. When I smoked pot, I discovered a freedom from the driving tension that produced so much depression. Maybe marijuana was blocking my depression caused by the overdominance of my linear, logic-processing left-brain? A few other managers were also using various drugs, but, like me, they all kept it secret.

The company was growing exponentially and making more and more demands for higher and higher sales from my division. My regional manager was a young man from Chicago who had a mannerism that strained my ability to maintain a good relationship. He came down to Kansas City on a regular basis, and his dropping reviews of my performance caused me considerable anguish. He was simply all business. One beer and dinner. Then he went to his room.

I was a perfectionist and wanted to be acknowledged for it. I kept up my pace, and when one of my salesmen quit, I would go out and work his territory until a replacement was found. This was not a requirement, but it got me some recognition that I craved. I put more and more pressure on myself, but it was a losing proposition. I should have been putting pressure on my salesmen. But it was my manager's demand that I fire and replace several of my salesmen and reorganize the division that was getting me down. That was the straw that broke the camel's back. It was like a knife to my heart. I hated firing men with families just like mine.

I had one salesman living in Omaha, Nebraska named Edwin (*fictitious*). He was a friendly guy. I fired him simply because he was late on his reporting for three months in the year. Yet, I had another salesman in Des Moines, Iowa named John who had been in his territory longer than I had worked for the company. He was a good sales representative, but he was the worst on getting his weekly and monthly reports to me, required by upper-management of the company. My own manager – the little one beer guy from Chicago -- was late in each of the 12 months of the first year that I was his manager, and I was showing dereliction of my duty to manage him. I was on the phone constantly pleading with him to send me his reports so I could make my own reports to my manager. He never mended his ways. To make matters worse, I was prevented from even filing my own negative report on him as he was such a good friend of my boss. I covered for him by making false reports on his behalf. I despised the double standard of management.

I began to lose interest in my job. Yet, I was becoming freer spiritually. Something was happening. I began to actually *see* another side of life. I embraced the philosophies of Carl Jung, Sigmund Freud, and, especially, Carl Rogers on the theory of congruency. Congruency required genuineness, transparency, authenticity, and realness – all terms used to convey Rogers' concept of harmonic relationships. Obviously, these traits did not apply in business.

In the meantime, I had signed up to attend Psychiatrist Eric Bern's transactional analysis (TA) program in Kansas City. His emphasis was growing a mature consciousness into the 'adult" level on understanding and communication. I attended every meeting and discussion on every treatment that I could find, yet I was in unrelenting psychic pain.

One August day it came time for me to work with one of my Kansas City-based salesmen, David Northberg (*fictitious*). I called him and told him to show up with a change of casual clothes and to bring his fishing tackle. "We should take a week off," I said, "and drive my company car to Mexico to go fishing."

The only resemblance this trip had to a fishing trip was that we took our fishing tackle with us. We intended to drive on down to Yucatan but never got past Matamoras, Mexico just over the border. "Papagayo's Cantina" captured us on the first night of a week of continuous imbibing and trying to improve our crude Spanish language capabilities. Suffice to say, the week in Mexico ended prematurely the second day of drinking with the local senoritas, when Northberg driving my company car cut short a corner and careened into a gas pump.

Our next stop was the Matamoras Jail which also served as the penitentiary for the state of Nuevo Leon, Mexico.

Strangely, I felt quite at home with inmates, sort of like Daniel socializing in the lion's den. It was a calm feeling that I'd had many times in the past when faced with overwhelming imminent danger. It was the familiar feeling of excitement played out on the stage of male bravado and leadership. We had emptied our pockets for the guard who checked us for weapons and contraband. All we had was cash; surprisingly, we were given a receipt for it. Northberg was moved to a different location so we were not able to communicate for the few days we were locked up.

Sleeping on the ground on the prison yard was not all that bad. It was decidedly better than being crammed into a cell with a dozen drug dealers, murderers, and thieves occupying a 10x10 bare cell. I tried to socialize. But I kept my back up against the prison wall.

The next day, a guard showed up and told us in broken English that we could get out if we paid our fine. To no surprise to either of us, the fine was the total amount of cash that we were receipted. I signed, and the guard gave me a "thumbs up" and pointed to a door that had SALIDA written above. With no money and only the company credit card, Dave and I agreed to fish another day at another place. "Northberg," I said, "let's get the hell out of here," We can fish another day.

"Yeah, let's go."

We headed to our car parked across the street from the prison entrance.

Leaving Matamoras, we headed north by northwest back up Highway 59 through Houston. Somewhere on the northern outskirts of Houston, we picked up a youthful hitch-hiker heading our way. He said little as he got in the car other than "he had been to some sort of spiritual meeting and was heading back to Chicago." He looked like a hippy with long hair and old clothes. He also carried the slight fragrance of cannabis. I was not interested in hearing details of his "spiritual meeting" because our adventures in the Matamoras penitentiary were still too fresh in both Dave's and my mind. We drove mainly in silence until we were almost to Oklahoma City.

Finally, Northberg (an ex-Mormon) broke the ice.

"So, tell us about the meeting," he said.

Dr. David P. Summers

Chapter 12

Stranger in a Strange Land

Hope

I hope that
In being born
I find the other side of Hell,
and see the vision of Heaven,
The untellable glory
And beauty of life
For life's sake.

Yes, I've read the encyclopedia of living
While becoming a man,
I've boxed the memes of experience
In my brain.

Unfortunately,
It is only our own creation that we see.
The illusion is in Pogo's words:
"We have met the enemy
And it is we."
(self-poem written in a state of depression ca. 1968)

We never got his name, but when the young hitchhiker began speaking, he opened up like a condemned man given one last chance to confess or die. It was the sort of stuff I had never heard of.

He spoke with deep conviction of his profound experiences in other spiritual dimensions, like the "Third Heaven" that St. John of Patmos spoke of. He discussed supernatural discernment, of spiritual gifts of being in two places at one time, and the spiritual states that made him invisible to the material world. To use the contemporary saying of the times, Northberg and I were both "blown away."

The hitchhiker also talked about how he could consciously transfer his consciousness to his earthly states of consciousness (calling them the physical, astral, mental, and causal) and finally to the state of consciousness that contained his soul, the soul state of consciousness.

Eventually, my own skepticism set in. "How do you do this," I asked?

"It is something that I learned from my spirit guide," he replied, "but I learned most of it in a past life."

"You mean that you believe in reincarnation?" I laughed. "And just how do you get out of your own body and travel these universes?"

"That's easy, man, once you learn it," he said. "Let me ask you, how can East be West and West be East, and where does East end and West begin or end?"

"What? That's crazy." I responded.

"You can't answer that, can you? It depends on where you are."

I was dumbfounded. *This man is senseless*, I thought. I looked over at Northberg; he seemed to be in a trance.

"It's relative," the hitchhiker said. "There is no up or down; there is no east or west; those concepts are products of a finite mind," he paused for a long period of time. "In the infinite mind there is only one reality, and that is that reality finally boils down to the present moment, the here and now; nothing else is real."

Both Northberg and I became silent for a while. Finally, I said, "tell me about being in your soul-consciousness. Is it like being in your normal mind?"

"Of course," he answered, "you see, you feel, and you can smell the roses." He grinned.

"But there are no earthly limits on where you are, you can be anywhere in the universe while your body is still, well, right here… in this car!"

"You are out of your mind," I said. "Can you see God?"

"Ah, I see that I have you in a dilemma," he replied. "What is God? A morphological, but spiritual embodiment of a man?" he asked. "A universal spirit? A cosmic consciousness? Could I be God? Is there any definition of God?"

I shook my head in disbelief and drove on without speaking. My *true belief* had never given me any *definition* of God other than biblical pictorials in the Old and New Testament. And, frankly, I had never even considered this question. I again looked over at Northberg. He still had a blank look on his face and was staring at something far off in the distance.

Finally, we entered the outskirts of Kansas City. Once we were on the freeway, the road split. One road led north to Omaha and Minneapolis, and the other led toward St. Louis. We turned toward St. Louis. As we drove into Kansas City, our rider began to be more down to earth.

"You know, three weeks ago, I was in Vietnam," he said.

Northberg looked at his hippie clothing and long hair. "Man, you sure don't look like you just got back from Vietnam," he said.

"Well, that's just my earthly appearance," replied the young man. "I happen to be more comfortable with the hippie vibrations. I got really bummed out by the war."

That was about all I could take.

"Hey, we are going to turn off up here, where do you want out?" I asked.

"Oh, it really doesn't matter. Let me out anywhere," he responded softly.

We let him out at the next cross-over.

"Weird guy," I said.

"Yeah, I think he was an angel," Northberg asked.

"What? An angel?"

"Oh yeah," said Northberg. "I've seen angels before."

Weary from the long drive, feeling somewhat dishonest that the fishing trip had turned out to be something so different, and internally embarrassed over the stupid incidents in Mexico, I dumped Northberg at his home and slipped into our beautiful three-story home on 151st Terrace in Overland Park, Kansas. I quietly slipped into bed with Dorothy Louise and fell into a deep, dreamless sleep.

Dr. David P. Summers

Chapter 13

Will Someone Pinch Me?

Wise Verdict

*Wise men counseled
And went away.*

*With arms around one another
They nodded their heads
In total agreement
With each other*

*They did return
But we all laughed at them
Because they seemed so sure
That nothing changed.
"It is what is to be," they said.*

*Ah, I see it now:
Wise men
Plodding the course
For lesser men.*

(poem on thoughts of suicide ca. 1969)

    The next day I was up and about early. Since Dorothy Louise was also up dressing for work, we had a little time to talk. I told her that we had not have much luck fishing and had decided to come home a day or two early.
    I did not tell her about the real experiences in Mexico.
    The next day I was driving along the Plaza listening to a call-in talk show on the radio when I heard a caller discussing an unusual lecture he had attended recently. He described the speaker as a "soul traveler."

The conversation sounded eerily like what I had heard from the hitchhiker the night before. The caller described the man's book and said the theory was explained in his book, *In My Soul, I Am Free*, which was a biography of an American prophet named Paul Twitchell (*deceased*), and written by the popular science writer, Brad Steiger.

Driving down the street, I saw a bookstore and decided to buy the book just to satisfy my curiosity.

"Yes, we have that book," said the clerk. Waving toward the shop window, he said, "we had a sign someone stuck on the window that tells about a meeting being held to discuss the book. I just took it down, and you just bought the last book!"

He pulled the black and white Xerox copy announcing the meeting out from under the counter and showed it to me. I wrote down the time and place. It was to be that very night!

Coincidence?

Now, filled with more curiosity over the coincidence of hearing the discussion on the radio, seeing the bookstore down the street and having the store clerk tell me about a meeting being held, and then pulling out a sign that he had just taken down seemed a bit of a stretch for coincidence. I handed my money over.

The discussion meeting was to be held that evening in the First National Bank building, downtown Kansas City. I wrote the time and place on the back of the book. That evening, I asked Dorothy Louise to join me to simply see what all this so-called "higher spirituality" was all about. She agreed to accompany me.

That evening we drove downtown and parked near the bank. The revolving door was open, and a guard directed us to the floor where the meeting was about to begin. There were about thirty or so people finding seats and talking in hushed tones. Not one person looked like the ragged hippie I had picked up. All looked affluent, professional, and quite normal. We took our seats and waited for the meeting to begin.

It was all very organized. An attractive, well-dressed woman opened the meeting by telling the group that Professor Frederic Foster (*fictitious*) of Wichita, Kansas would be delivering the lecture. She advised us to wait until the lecture was over for any questions we might have. Soon a rather heavy, but neatly dressed bearded man approached the lectern.

"Good evening and thank you for coming," he said pleasantly. "This evening I am going to discuss the ancient religion of Eckankar, the oldest spiritual teaching in the world."

What? I thought. *Doesn't the Old Testament go all the way back to God creating the world? Didn't God write it?! How much older can you get than that?*

Professor Foster's next statement put my rational mind into such a quandary that I hardly remember the rest of the meeting. He said nonchalantly: "Let me begin by saying, first, I am God."

I could not believe what I had just heard. Never in my life could I imagine that someone would stand before a group of otherwise sane people and utter such a phrase. What was even more astounding was that God did not immediately strike him dead for such blasphemy! All my life I had believed that anyone daring to make such a declaration would be in mortal danger of God's immediate wrath.

But nothing happened to him! He smiled and continued.

I sat stunned as the Professor nonchalantly went on to explain his basis for the claim as having enlightenment through something called "soul travel" to incomprehensibly spiritual states of conscious existence. He related the human consciousness to the "physical state," which was the physical body and its innate mechanisms. The body has its own mode of operation communicating to its organs and systems primarily via its neural system directed by the brain. He then describes other levels of consciousness beyond the physical that were readily available to anyone who was open to the Spirit beyond our conventional belief and wisdom.

It was almost more than I could take. It was a tug-a-war between my emotions fiercely resisting the information and my intellect eagerly desiring to hear more of it.

Just beyond the physical, he described the "astral" state of consciousness, consisting of the "consciousness" of the five senses which is, for the most part, the vehicle that reality is experienced throughout life, via the emotions.

"The emotions," he said, "provide the vehicle for communication and thought-consciousness for that state of being. Most of the beings on this earth live and die in this state of consciousness. This is also where most Western religions to teach and make sense of life and one's attempt to find God."

He went on to describe the "mental" state as pure reason detached from the "astral." Above that level of consciousness was called the "causal" where the power to change reality existed. As I listened, something was taking place in my own consciousness.

He explained that, on each "plane," there are initiations that require the loss of "attachment" to the lower levels of reality.

"It's like learning math," he said, smiling, "you've got to learn each grade one step at a time."

The goal, he said, was to reach the "soul plane" where one becomes completely free from the earthly (physical) world of matter and in that temporary state, one becomes unified with one's soul and one experiences incredible union with "Pure Spirit."

Here, guided via mediation and solely by one's thoughts, one can come face-to-face with God and/or the highest spiritual prophets and seers who have gone on before us. So, beyond our paltry ideation of God or "It" (he explained that God is genderless) through soul travel, one becomes inexorably transformed into a new being, a being who knew all things and could be in two places at one time!

Lordy me! I was intrigued! Who wouldn't be?

Over the days and weeks that followed, I devoured more of these ancient teachings that far predated the Bible, such as the Bhagavad Gita, Tao, Egyptian Book of the Dead, and other ancient scriptures from the Torah.

I had read *The Hero with a Thousand Faces, Creative Myths,* and *The Mask of God*, and other writings by Joseph Campbell years earlier and had already begun to understand that every age and civilization has its own hero (savior) and the similarities of the historical accounts were eerily similar.

And that understanding flew into the face of Pentecostal fundamentalism.

I found that almost all great religions had a divine immaculate conception, a virgin birth, the death of the savior and the inevitable resurrection. All appeared on the scene suddenly (the exception being Buddha) claiming either to be God or to have the power of God on earth. I began reading Paul Twitchell's books on the process of spiritual transformation. I read *In my Soul I am Free, The Tiger's Fang, The Far Country, The Shariyat-Ki Sudmad*, (The Eckankar bible) and all the rest.

And I began to meditate.

Dorothy Louise also became interested in Eckankar's teachings. She wanted to attend the annual, worldwide, three-night convocation coming up in Chicago. Paul Twitchell had died the year before, and Eckankar was to announce its new leader. I was still skeptical, but we drove up from

KC to Chicago to attend. On the first night, I was seated on the end of an aisle.

Darwin Gross (*deceased*), a musician from Portland, Oregon who later married the wife of Paul Twitchell after he died was to be Eckankar's new leader.

When Gross was announced, he came down the aisle walking toward the stage as we all stood and clapped. As he passed by me, he stopped momentarily, held out his hand to mine, and we shook hands. He said, "Thank you for your support!" I was both stunned and amused. I smiled back, shook his hand, and nodded my head-- as if I were "one of the twelve," so to speak. *Why did he pick me out of the crowd to stop*, I wondered?

I had personally met Gross, called the "Living Eck Master" (the word "Eck" was synonymous with Spirit or Holy Spirit) at that Chicago WorldWide meeting! Like it or not, I instantly changed from skeptic to intensely curious follower as the title implied that the Eck Master was, as Jesus was, in control of the Holy Spirit of God. Is that truthful audacity or just outright P.T. Barnum?

He was there that evening to take over spiritual control of the world as we know it. I kid you not!

However, there were many at the Chicago meeting who were against the installation of Darwin as the "Living Eck Master." You could literally feel the tension. Dorothy Louise, my teenaged daughters Crystal, Marcia, and Sherry, and I stood close to Mr. Gross and unconsciously formed a loose human ring around him the first night when he sat and introduced himself to all who wanted to question him.

The more I contemplated on the insights of what I was, the more I was beginning to see that Jesus had come teaching the same transformational truth. Jesus came saying the same thing to a Middle Eastern Semitic culture of monotheistic Hebrews who were also and profoundly taught that they had the exclusive right and control of access to God. That's why their holy scriptures called them "the Chosen People," and here it was, the same scenario being acted out right before my very eyes. And to a thousand or so people in the audience.

The profundity of this insight began to open my mind to deeply exploring these truths. I was under deep pressure to take what I saw before my eyes as valid and to turn my back on my Christian teachings and my belief that Jesus was the Savior of the world, not some former

Xylophone player who had a band in Portland. Holy Moly!

I was determined to find "truth" at any cost.

I knew I could choose any of the great teachings to follow, but once the choice was made, as Jesus said, (Luke 9:62 KJV) "once one puts the hand to the plow there would be no turning back," I knew the commitment was forever. I had already chosen to follow the hidden message of Jesus.

I began to meditate in earnest. There was something about taking my dog and driving out to Crystal Springs Reservoir and finding a solitary place to meditate that helped. Sometimes I rolled a blunt and took a few hits to relax while my big German Shepherd, Aquarius, happily explored the spectacular surroundings around the banks of the reservoir.

I would sit and meditate not only on his outer truths that all Christians believe and express, but also on his secret truths for hours on end.

Where did Jesus learn his spiritual wisdom? Certainly not from the Hebrew Pharisees.

I asked myself, *why did Jesus bother?*

The thing that kept coming back to me was that if God was everything, and "God created man," then there could be no separation between God and man. That the "God in heaven" had to be the same God that was in me. And Jesus knew that.

It wasn't that he simply decided to come to establish a new religion with himself as the top guy, organize a group, and collect tithes. Any fool could do that and there were plenty of them running around Israel during the time of the Roman occupation. Jesus had a compulsion to tell his message to an unbelieving Jewish Nation.

As St. Paul said, (1 Timothy 2:5 KJV), "the mediator between God and man was the Christ" that Jesus became. What did Paul mean by "mediator?" What if through Christ, I might become a mediator? All my life I had been exposed to people who had tried to play out this role: the role of mediator, arbitrator, negotiator, conciliator, etc., between God and me. The more I accepted this truth, the more I saw that the Christ "out there" was transcendent to us and to all men. But it was more: Wasn't the Christ out there the same Christ as the Christ in me? Christ represented the unlimited, unconditional love of the immanent God.

All of these questions came back to me in the affirmative.

I was also a mediator between man and God when I "came out" as Him. This realization brought on long periods of ecstatic meditations when even this distinction finally merged into the atonement (or *at-onement*) experience of total unity with the Christ. This is the stage of meditation where the idea of personal identification and becoming evolved into being.

The magnetic pull of this truth pulled me ever more so into the last great insight. I could no longer live outside, with God "out there" and me "in here." I accepted the truth.

And I became Jesus.

There was no other experience left for me to become.

I saw that once I had totally torn myself from all the pre-conceived ideas, beliefs, mythologies, stories, religious enslavement, and, of course, my own early religious doctrinal memes taught to me could I become transformed. Even before I could verbalize the concept. Then and only then could Christ totally enter my consciousness and replace that which had been religiously ingrained, allowing me to become transformed and unified with Christ's divine unconditional love. Then, and finally then, the separation from my old life was forever severed. And I became free.

I don't believe that Christ realization is a misnomer.

There is a moment when one unifies with that which is sought. In this moment, you become one with the same eternal spirit and eternal life of Jesus Christ. This is what some called the *at-one-ment* experience, coined by Twitchell. But it is not a one-way ticket to eternal bliss. Yes, these moments are rapturous and ecstatic, but they were just the beginning of my experiences of *at-one-ment* with Christ.

It was, however, a total surrender of will, of the linear stream of thought that identifies reality with the Newtonian physical world, the world of cause and effect introduced to mankind back in the 17th century. According to Isaac Newton, for every action, there is an equal and opposite reaction. I surrendered my attachment to cause and effect.

Once this part of your consciousness is finally disengaged, the conceptual, holistic consciousness takes over. In me, the Christ realization journey brought with it all the same spiritual temptations, test, and trials that Jesus had had in his life. But with each experience, there is a concurrent and incomprehensible level of insight, incorporating new dimensions of existence into your life in the present realm. In other words, I had to live the temptations of Christ to know what Jesus encountered on earth. I sought out the temptations of Christ and, in doing so, lost the concept of "sin." One then finds a new awareness in being your new "made whole" experiences. This comes with the total surrender to God.

This experience is perhaps the most exhilarating of one's life. There were occasions when I didn't know where I stopped, and God started. Once this surrender takes place, nothing is ever the same. You see yourself in everyone, for we are all "One." And for me, I had to experience everything.

Breakthroughs always come in "twos" for me. It's sort of funny how my brain's two hemispheres compete for experiences of reality. One idea that's often heard in popular discussions of psychology is that the left brain is the seat of language which comes with rational, linear, sequential thought, while the right brain is more creative and more holistic and sees conceptually. Regardless, they are separate thinking entities, and each sees the world in a different perspective.

But there are obvious differences in the concept of reality between the two neural sets of comprehension. It's also obvious that the big bundle of nerves that goes across the right and left hemispheres called the corpus callosum carries messages to and from these two "thinking" components of the brain. My long-dominant left brain began to surrender to a right brain concept of a now entirely different world. My alternative world of a Separate Reality (described by Carlos Castaneda in his conversations with Don Juan, (Simon and Schuster, 1971) was on specific occasions magnified by marijuana. I began living in two different worlds.

I began discovering a new dimension of spirituality. I became *at-one-ment* with God continually. But I carried an overpowering urge to live, work and get the job done, never quit and most of all, never drop out. The straight part of my dual world remained attached to Dorothy Louise and the kids. It would not let me do that. My left-brain husband and paternal instinct would not let me do that.

When I turned off my left logical brain and gave my right holistic brain permission to create a reality without the interference of logic and rationality, a whole new world appeared. It was full of spontaneous revelations, seeing the connection of all things spiritual and material, and most of all, it was full of love.

This is not an endorsement for pot, but I found marijuana easily turned off the relentless and tyrannical drive I inherited to keep on keeping on and allowed my right brain (for the first time) to take control of reality. It also broke my cycle of mania and depression. But there were initiations here too. Giving my right brain free reign opened a vast vista of de novo experiences that were mostly positive. I don't think that I ever had a negative reaction to smoking pot, but I had many, many beautiful experiences with Jesus while passing a joint around with loving friends. And I began to realize that if I were to find *at-one-ment* with Christ, I would have to open myself to the world as He did. I had to experience every temptation that he experienced. And through the total surrender of my life, I would become one with him. I said yes!

Dr. David P. Summers

Chapter 14

First, One Journey's the Dark Night of the Soul

Someday

Is now
And tomorrow Today?
Just one thought away?
Or is reality yesterday
In front of my eyes?

Am I to be this moment
Which is eternal?
Or am I to bought and sold
By fleeting days of enchantment

(poetry of my surrender. 1971)

It was 1971, and I had been a Midwest Division manager for two and a half years. My initial inspiration and joy of my fantastic promotion with all the perks I could ever want had now eroded into hard, cold-eyed business. But I could not shake the experience of what I had heard and seen in Eckankar. I went through something like the five stages of coping with a death.

First, there is denial. At first, I didn't believe a word of the book that I had read by Paul Twitchell nor the teachings in the "Satsangs" (consisting of more readings of books by Twitchell) that I attended. Then I felt anger. Who the hell does this guy think he is?

"It's just bull-shit," I told Dorothy Louise early on, often refusing to attend meetings.

Then began the bargaining phase.

"Well, I'm a pretty good person, so I don't need to believe any of that out-of-body stuff.".

Then came acceptance. Was all this out-of-body just another way to begin to describe a death of consciousness? Then finally, I relented. But still with extreme skepticism because his followers were all upper income, real professional people.

Okay, like Superman Jesus of spirituality?

If he could do it, then I had to do it. It was mano a mano.

Determined to live a new life, I wrote my letter of resignation on Christmas eve, 1971.

More of this, much more, later. I will describe what it is like to die.

Chapter 15

Looking for Truth in All the Wrong Places

From Here We Start

We must begin
In the recesses of consciousness
To understand that what exists
Is neither good nor bad.

It's Passion's often restless desire
And how life is bought
Through payments of pain.

The receipts of joy
Become a birthright
Of the sublime
And my consciousness must decline

(poetry of my journey ca. 1973)

Let me go back to the "real" world and pick up the chronology of the years that followed. I will leave the spiritual details that I experienced and continue to experience to a later writing. But the "mythic-described biblical-Jesus-God" I previously tried to know and desperately tried to serve is not the god of my reality today. The God of my life today is far beyond any pathetic attempt to describe in mythological concepts of materiality or spirituality, or of gain and loss. But again, that is another life and another story. Let me continue.

I had an offer from another large pharmaceutical company to take over the entire Western U.S. as their regional manager with a move to San Francisco, California. Moving to California intrigued me and moving to San Francisco—the liberal center of gravity in the country—allured me.

I decided to drive out there and just look around. After all, the offering company would pay for the trip.

So, I packed a bag and hit the road. And I made sure I took enough weed to make the round trip, if necessary.

I had been contemplating what "truth" was. Jesus said, "know the truth, and the truth shall set you free." But what was truth -- a life of complete honesty? Yes, I thought, that's a start…live in a complete, brutally honest state-of-being.

Then follow the results wherever it leads you.

Before I could claim my Christ-in-me, my first test was to come out of the closet as a marijuana user. I was determined to start the employment off by simply telling my new the company that yes, I use pot.

I determined that I was going to be brutally truthful in all things from here on out, just as Jesus did when he could have easily escaped the cross and crucifixion had he just told Pontius Pilot a little white lie about himself being God. I could see how it might play out in some dusty courtyard rather than the royal-robed Pontius I saw as a child in the family bible:

Pontius Pilot: "Are you King of the Jews as some say?"
Jesus: "Well, that's what some of my followers say."
Pontius Pilot: "Are you or are you not?"
Jesus: "Well Pontius, you can see that I am a man just like you, can't you?"
Pontius: "Final answer?"
Jesus: "Final answer, oh mighty Governor." (with that Jesus gives a royal bow)
Pontius: "Case dismissed."

That was not me. Brutal truth to me would be the real truth even if it might hurt me in the eyes of the asker.

As I drove I thought more about it, not considering that I might NOT control the situation as the old TV game show, *Who Wants to be a Millionaire?*

I took I-10 through New Mexico and Arizona. I had my old 8-track playing some Elton John tunes, and, before I knew it, I came upon the Arizona border way-station where the State of Arizona still maintained checkpoints on each end of I-10 to see if you were bringing any forbidden citrus and contraband veggies in that great state.

Ostensively, it was to protect their growers from contamination from New Mexico or California.

I never figured out why they gave a shit about what you took to California or New Mexico. But they did.

So, I dutifully pulled up under the canopy and waited on a little inspector of at least 70 years of age to hobble out to the car.

"Bringing any fruits or vegetables into Arizona?" he asked.

In that instant, I had to decide.

"Ah…um, no sir."

Then it hit me. "Know the truth, and the truth shall set you free." Truth my son, the truth, a voice commanded from inside my head. This was the first experience of my emotions and my intellect coming together into one, unified experience.

"Uh…just this," and I pulled open my glove box, clearly displaying a baggie of dope.

The old man looked at it in astonishment, then not believing what he was seeing, squinted once more at the open display of illegal evidence. It wasn't what he was looking for. For a moment he couldn't believe his eyes.

It was marijuana.

Finally, he said, "Well…er…ok…go on through."

"Thank you very much…and have a nice day," I said and sped off down I-10 West.

I'll cut to the chase; I took the job.

I left Kansas City in 1972 and with the entire family moved to San Francisco. I took a couple of sales positions that put me back into direct sales in a territory of the Western U.S. Without trying to describe the agony of living between faith and works, I found that I could not satisfy God and Caesar. Let me explain: on the one hand, I was intently attentive to my spiritual feedback on every action I took. As Jesus, I refused to live in any other mode than the experience of the "here and now." If it did not feel right, I didn't do it. If it felt right, I did it with gusto – religious prohibition or not!

As one of my literary heroes, the famous author Joseph Campbell says,

"follow your bliss."

I suddenly found myself in a painful dilemma.

I was in a sales meeting in Los Angeles for a prestigious job working for a German endoscopic firm from Tuttlingen, Germany that had just developed introduced a new break-through technology in endoscopic instrumentation. I had only taken the job of Regional Manager for the West Coast a few months before.

The new fiber-optic medical instruments were so far improved over what was currently available on the market, the interest and request for demonstrations was almost overwhelming. I sold a set of very expensive German instruments on almost every call I made. Although I was working on a straight commission, I was making a ton of money. I felt that I was doing something right! I had a real job again. Dorothy Louise was relieved as I was almost guaranteed to make some indescribable income for a least a couple of years or so.

Dorothy Louise and the girls had all moved (en toto) out to Daly City. She enrolled them in the rather chic Seramonte School System. I thoroughly worked the territory, but I simply followed where I thought the spirit led me. No advanced call agenda sent to the office, no travel schedule. I was very successful as almost every call resulted in an order. Then I was informed that the company had hired a new Vice President of Sales manager. A month later he called a sales meeting of all sales representatives in the U.S.

The new Sales VP opened the meeting with a litany of clerical reporting demands on how he intended to upgrade the sales operation by observing each of the Regional Managers. Up until that time, all of us were simply going where our leads took us and making a few "cold call" demonstrations as convenient. This was no longer good enough.

Our new VP informed us that, henceforth, we would all be required to submit a monthly agenda a month in advance of where we planned to make sales calls and why. When he asked the group if anyone had any comments, I stood up and responded that up until that day my methodology of "going with the flow" and following up on my leads as I felt best had put me to the head of the class and top producer in sales.

"No more," he dryly responded, then with something to the effect of "it's my way or the highway."

"Following my bliss," my faith that "the Spirit" had heretofore led me successfully to where the sales were, now came into conflict with an authoritarian, smartassed VP of Sales determined to show that he had brass gonads. Rather than argue the finer points of my "inner leading" to (futilely) justify my prior success, I arose and left the meeting.

Soon after, I was recruited by a big pharmaceutical firm headquartered in New York as the Sales Manager of the entire Western U.S. After a few months, it was deja vu all over again. Following my "inner leading," I showed up at a major meeting in New York with my wife Dorothy Louise in tow. She had never been to the Big Apple until then, and I wanted to show her a good time. I figured the cost to the company was negligible since we shared the same room and paid for our meals out of pocket just as any other minor expense on the trip. The problem was, I had failed to discuss taking her with me with…this…Vice President of Sales.

He was livid, and I was livid about even having to consider that I had such an obligation. In my mind, I had already shown how to be successful, so I should be left alone. I truly expected to do this, after all, "what would Jesus do?" (WWJD). I was fired as soon as we arrived back home; the company car was repossessed the next week, and I was again on foot.

To add salt to my wounds, the next week, my oldest daughter Crystal was out driving one day and totaled the little Ford Falcon that I had bought before coming to California. Miraculously, she came out of the wreck without a scratch. And this was before seat belts! I took it to be a sign of spiritual protection from the Spirit.

Now I needed a new car.

Without looking back, I jumped into my next test. I used the Eckankar method. Simply build your "mold" (use the mind to conceptualize what you want or need) then project energy into the thought simply by "seeing" it in your imaginary mind. This is also the secret of quantum mechanics. Then presto, there it was.

I kid you not. Somehow or other, I was able to swing a deal with the Daley City Nissan dealer for a brand-new little hatchback coupe, with no job, no down payment, and no apparent way to make payments. Hmm. Simple faith combined with truth. It worked. If you are a religionist, then praying to God "believing, ye shall receive" also works.

Now they call this meditation.

Despite it all, my belief in following my "bliss" grew stronger, and my ability to obey "authority" over my inner leading continued to diminish. The so-called "light" was leading me on to discovery after discovery. As a little footnote, the little Nissan that I so miraculously brought into being was immediately used by Dorothy Louise to find a good job within a few days sufficient to pay the rent.

But as much as bliss meant to me, I could not leave it to Dorothy Louise to create the life's sustenance for our family. The more right-brained, *bring it on*, "peace brother," and hippie I became, the more left-brained, "hey stop it, please get a job" manifested in Dorothy Louise to bring home the bacon for everyone. I applied for job after job to no avail. It seemed that the little question on the employment form inevitable did me in… "do you use drugs in any form other than alcohol?" This gave me lots of time on my hands.

One bright sunny afternoon I drove over to the Daly City Cliffs. The valley between the Serramonte Mountains and the Pacific Ocean abruptly ends with cliffs running north and south that plunge several hundred feet into to the sea.

There was a brisk wind blowing out of the west meeting the cliffs rising right up from the beach and producing a giant uplift of air. Several hang gliders were gently sailing back and forth along the uplift diving, then gently rising again and again like puppets on a string. I was mesmerized by the effortless piloting required to maintain aloft. It was all too natural. The guys on the gliders became a part of the craft accurately maintaining speed, lift, and distance out over the ocean, then arching back, never going too far out that they lost the effect of the wind meeting landfall.

I begin to think again about the man who said he was above my God.

How could he replace Jesus Christ, the man who I had always believed in, prayed to and religiously tried to worship? And why shouldn't my relationship be as effortless as gliding atop the wind as the hang gliders?

I decided then and there that someone had to step up and oppose this new "god" on earth. I decided to take over the role. If he could be something called The Living Eck Master, the Mahanta, the Vi-Guru or any other noun that makes folks believe that he has the golden keys to the kingdom, then I could become my own Jesus and use my life in opposition.

The downward spiral continued. I was kicked out of Eckankar.

Soon, to make ends meet, I found myself driving a Veteran's Taxicab on the night shift in downtown San Francisco. The drug question was conveniently not on the employment form. That was during a time when a crazy killer was in the process of hailing cabs and then killing the cabby simply to steal what meager cash he might have on hand. Many of the cabbies during that time refused to pick up a single male hailing a cab.

All I had was my faith in Jesus for protection as we were not allowed to carry weapons in the cab while on duty. The killer originated the name "Zodiac" in a series of taunting letters sent to the local Bay Area press. These letters included four cryptograms. Of the four cryptograms sent, only one has been definitively solved.

I think I picked up this weird Zodiac killer up one foggy San Francisco night. It was just one of those feelings.

When he got into my cab, something told me that this was no ordinary fare. He directed me to take him down to the beach below Golden Gate Park. Full of the strange confidence of spiritual invincibility, I turned the cab around, and I drove him to the beach. With the cab enshrouded in fog, he asked me to stop on the beach. We sat in the dark with neither of us speaking, he in the backseat smoking a cigarette, me awaiting the next move. We sat for at least ten long and suspenseful minutes. Silent. The only sound was the pounding roar of the surf.

Then the guy casually opened the door and walked down the beach away from the cab. He never returned. I decided not to look for him. I smoked a joint and waited about ten more minutes, and then drove away, high as a kite, and, obviously, never collecting my fare. Strangely, I did not care. I was shaking like a leaf, but I had never felt so triumphant! I felt that I had been protected by something magical, an invisible being. The "Zodiac killer" was never apprehended, but the killings never resumed while we lived in San Francisco.

Perhaps, Northberg's angel was sitting in the front seat with me.

Most of the cabbies on the night-shift were old timers who picked up regular Joes and Janes and delivered them to their favorite pubs, hotels/motels, or other places of vice. It was an exclusive relationship, and they were requested by name. Most of the time I hardly made enough money to pay for the gas the cab used. Again, it was more a job of activity rather than financial gain.

Dorothy Louise became the sole income producer. She never gave up on me. Nor did the Summers family. Robert kept calling me, urging me to come back to Texas, thinking perhaps that living with the "Philistines" of San Francisco might have caused to me to begin worshiping false Gods. Whatever.

On the other hand, I kept sending Robert audio tapes trying to explain (the good news?) my mystifying spirituality. Totally out of viable options, I finally decided to visit "home," to Texas.

The first time I drove to Dallas. I spent a few nights with my youngest brother, Robert. But to the dismay of all, I brought all my bad habits openly with me. Like the consternation of the Sadducees had toward the Jesus who came "eating and drinking," suffice to say, I came "smoking, drinking, and…cussing" And I was letting my hair grow.

But I also brought the "good news" of what Jesus really came to do.

My open and unconditional love for all included my estranged birth family. The effusive joy my *at-one-ment* with Christ brought helped me to overcame endless attempts by others to explain my strange faith and encounter with Jesus that overpowered the taboos of my family's Pentecostal history.

So, as with the biblical custom, I was welcomed at my first stop, at a distance, ("please go outside to smoke!") as the returning prodigal son. Robert was surprisingly attentive and helpful. He suggested that I drive down to Canyon Lake and stay for a while with Lester and Mary and maybe write about my experiences. A couple of days later, I took his advice. Overcoming years of estrangement, I drove my little Nissan down to get re-acquainted with Lester and Mary.

To them, the prodigal son had returned. No questions asked.

Lester and Mary were now semi-retired, as Lester had never completely quit preaching and opened a little evergreen nursery in Sattler, Texas. Basically, to supplement his now meager collection plate, he was selling young trees, ornamental hedges, flowers, and other plants picked up by buyers of new homes and businesses in the increasingly popular Sattler Canyon Lake retirement area. He made quite an issue that he had now put Mary on payroll and was deducting first-time, social security payments for her eventual retirement. He also was acquainted with the local "newspaper lady" whom they said knew about publishing and invited me to talk to her. Cool!

The newspaper lady owned a little paper that served the small communities that dotted Central Texas around the major industry, Canyon

Lake – a large man-made impoundment on the Guadalupe River. Ostensibly built for flood control during Lyndon Johnson's presidency, it soon became the home to a large residency of hippies and military retirees from San Antonio.

Everybody seemed to get along. Meanwhile, always the opportunist, Lester was building a small church a few miles from Sattler called "Church in the Wildwood." It was really Mary's little dream church, laid out on a couple of large lots among the heavily wooded acreage of "live oak" that grew around that part of Central Texas. It was all very lovely. And he had opened its doors to the few potential believers around the lake.

The newspaper lady lived in Blanco, Texas an old Central Texas town that likely goes back to Spanish Colonial times with a total population of about 1000. That week turned out to be one of the strangest of my life.

It started out with me trying to tell Lester how Jesus and I had become "one." My experiences were met with outright amazement and incredulity. Whichever way I tried to turn my story; it did not work. To him, a saved, holy ghost-filled, ordained Assembly of God preacher of over 50 years, there was no way a Johnny-come-lately prodigal son who had become involved in a California cult could conceivably know more about Jesus that he did…why, he did Jesus for a living! Gulp!

The second evening, I once again tried to talk to Lester. He was adamant about his disdain of any path to God except his.

He asked me, "How did you get to this prideful position of being Jesus?"

"I'm Christian, Dad. I'm only following the example of Jesus, when he said 'I and the father are one.'"

"Yes, but you're not Jesus," he responded. "He was God's son."

"He was first just a boy, then a man, then he stepped out and proclaimed himself as "God," when John the Baptist baptized him," I answered. "Don't you see?"

"No, I don't see, Dave, "I have never in my life heard a Christian make some of the absurd remarks you have made since you came here."

"Well they should, Dad," I said. "Maybe if they got their noses out of the Bible and began to live…the life that Jesus lived…just as Jesus did… trusting totally in the Spirit, then they would drop some of their religious dogma and start living in truth." I could see that this remark stunned Lester.

I could see that Lester was getting more and more irritated. Even in the dim lights of evening, the setting sun coming through the kitchen window, I could see that his face was red. I flashed to a childhood meme of his red facial glow when he got wound-up, preaching from the pulpit, calling out sinners to be saved (or else). Or worse, he was ready to punish me once more for some silly infraction of his will.

"So, who was this so-called guru you studied under in Kansas City?" he asked, his voice rising.

"Dad, I didn't study under him," I replied, "I just attended some of the meetings."

"What's his name?"

Lester was now beginning to key in on me, going for a verdict of guilty. "His name was Gross, Dad, Darwin Gross," I answered.

"Let me ask you something…did he say he was God?" I knew now the trap was about to be sprung, but there was no turning back. At first, the remark, "did he say he was God?" took me completely by surprise. I immediately thought where did he ever hear someone in his Pentecostal circles claim to be God? I remembered all those old tales of God striking folks dead for less – like those Amenite prophets who built a bonfire to compete with Elisha, etc. My meme of this fearful response of God's wrath was the flannel board Sunday School lessons imprinted when I was just four and five years old.

I thought I'd had enough religion in my time to know a thing or two, but I had never heard anyone make sane, serious, outright claim to rational folks that they "were God" other than the professor at my first Eckankar meeting in Kansas City, ca. 1969.

I never heard it again.

Where did Lester pick that up?

I had only one way to answer; it was the way I had been answering since that day in KC when I decided that the brutal truth was to be my new bible, the only way I was going to answer from then on out…about anything…was truth!

The question, "did he say he was God?" lingered. "Yes Dad, he did." I replied, "even more than Jesus." "Do you believe he is God?" He was relentless now.

"No…" I said. Then after a long period of silence, I had to finish my thought. I said, "because I am God…"

I was shaking and began to weep. I was weeping because I had lived up to the truth that I had promised to do, and I was weeping because I knew, in that moment, I had lost my father forever.

Lester was unable to speak for a minute. He simply looked at me in disbelief for a long minute then said, "well, that's all for tonight. I'm going to bed."

I had blasphemed in his face about all that *at-one-ment* with Christ stuff. We both tried to keep our cool, but I knew him well enough to read his unbelief. He was now older and wiser than in my young, more impressionable days. He had finally learned to control his volatile temper, but now his anger would not dissipate. He could barely contain it. He had cut off any further discussion about Jesus and dismissed himself.

He got up and walked to his bedroom and closed the door. But I wasn't through. I needed to further explain, to demonstrate, to do something to show him the love that *at-one-ment* with Christ really was. Being *at-one-ment* with Jesus didn't make him go away, it just enlarged him.

But I couldn't.

I knocked on the bedroom door, "Dad…Dad…please let me in," I begged. He refused to answer. I had no idea what I could say to him to assuage his absolute denial of the validity of my idea of truth. Whatever I could say, I knew would be rejected by him with his true-believer psychology in his Pentecostal Holiness religion.

His estranged attitude lasted through the next day, which was Saturday. He had to preach Sunday but could barely contain the anger of my imagined challenge to his whole life and career.

That day I wisely withdrew and began thinking about his reaction. I was bewildered. I thought that I would be met with joy and fellowship in my return to Jesus. Instead, I was met with anger, denial, and rejection.

Paranoia surfaced and began to make itself known. It was fear that I had not felt since childhood. I had challenged him to the supreme test, to the point that Jesus had challenged his Father in heaven. The more I thought, the more I could see a not good scenario working out.

He would put me to the test.

To Lester, that would be the only way to prove it one way or the other. I read his mind.

The thought of crucifixion came to mind and could not be dislodged. Would he kill me to see if I would rise again? I observed him talking quietly to a couple of his close church friends who just happened to drop by. Then another came by, and they too talked alone as I sat in a little guest house and tried to think of something to write. But paranoia was consuming me. Were they scheming like Judas did with the Pharisees?

When we met for dinner that evening, even Mary was acting strangely. It was almost like she was acting a part in a play. Mary set the plates in silence as we set down to eat.

"Are you coming to church with us tomorrow, Sabbie?" he asked.

"Why sure…I guess so, Dad." I said. I didn't think there would be much to the service; after all, Lester had had just finished the little chapel, and since he just started holding services, he couldn't have more than a dozen or so attendees.

But it was strange, calling me Sabbie, my earliest childhood nickname. Sabbie? I thought I'm not Sabbie, that 2 or 3-year-old apple of Lester's eye, who would proudly answer the following:

(Question) "What's your name, little boy?" (Answer) "Name's Sabbie!" (Question) "What's your moto, Sabbie?" (Answer) "tay outta tweet!" (Stay out of street) This little scenario of remembrance had been in the family humor all of my life.

Why would he call me that? Is he going to act out an attempted sacrifice of me like Abraham was ready to sacrifice Isaac…or worse, like Jehovah who really did sacrifice his only son? Was Lester so tenaciously caught up in his religion – his true belief – that he would sacrifice me to preserve the memory of that little boy Sabbie?

Yes! I thought. Yes, he would!

I became more paranoid as the day wore on. This is his faith against mine, I thought. Yes, of course, he would die for his belief…but I'm not ready for this test. Nor should I be.

The next morning was Sunday church. But I got up early and quietly slipped out of the guest house, leaving without saying goodbye to either Lester or Mary. I was still caught up in the psychosis of what I envisioned Lester was about to do to me. But I had nowhere to go.

I left a note thanking Lester and Mary for the guest house and drove away.

"Lead the way, Lord," I prayed.

I drove about 10 miles to New Braunfels and then stopped at an IHOP to eat breakfast. I couldn't eat much. I was still in total post-traumatic shock. Then the thought hit me to go over to see the newspaper lady. Have something real to do, I thought.

It was still too early to try to see her, so I just drove around the lake for a few hours to kill time. The obsessive thought refused to go away. Finally, that afternoon I drove over to Blanco, Texas, a town so small that everyone knew where everybody else lived. I had no problem finding the "newspaper lady."

I drove up to the newspaper lady's drive. It was rather warm that summer day, and she and her husband were sitting outside in the shade of one of those giant old trees called live-oaks (called "live" because they kept their leaves year-round) After greeting again, we talked writing and publishing for several hours. She had previously been a reporter for the Blanco County News but since had started her own little gossipy "newspaper." Nice, but not much help. As evening came, I asked if she knew a place where I might spend the night in that tiny town.

"Sure, you can stay at the old Masonic Lodge." She said. "I hear that there is a couple living there and you can stay for five dollars a night if you have your own bedding. It's right on Main Street."

Well, I didn't have bedding, but it didn't seem to matter. It was the warm time of year.

It wasn't hard to find; there was only one traffic light in town, and Main Street was the highway that ran down the center of town.

As I pulled up in front of the old lodge building, a Texas State Trooper pulled in behind me as I stopped. I got out and walked around to the little sidewalk in front of the building.

I had just smoked a joint on my way over, and the car was full of marijuana smoke.

Oh no, I thought, I'm about to be busted.

Two men got out. One wearing the recognizable tan, red and blue state trooper uniform, and the other in civilian clothes.

"Howdy Stranger." (I kid you not: his words.)

"Howdy," trying to stay calm I answered. He walked toward me.

"Can I help you?" the officer in uniform asked. "You seem to be looking for somebody."

"Um… (I was trying to put my mind in gear, having just smoked) … Uh…I was looking for the Masonic Lodge," I said.

"You a Mason?" he asked.

"Why yes," (I hoped that he didn't ask to see my lodge card…I hadn't paid my Masonic dues for 15 years or so). "I understand the Lodge is closed, but I can stay here for $5 a night." "You know the folks?" he asked.

Funny, I thought, am I supposed to be acquainted with the management to stay here?

"Why no, but Mrs. Clements, (*fictitious*) the newspaper lady said that the owner rented it out at night."

I could see him visibly relax. "You know her?"

"Yes, I'm a writer," I said, "and she's helping me find a publisher." (I hoped that he would not interrogate me further…like, "can I see your manuscript?")

But he didn't.

Instead, he asked, "Hey, I see you got California plates. You got Texas road insurance on the little Nissan?"

"No," I said, "I mean…California insurance doesn't work in Texas?"

"I mean road insurance…you know like AAA." He paused and walked to the front of the little Nissan and peered down at the left side of the windshield. "Nope, you don't seem to have any," he said.

"If you're going to drive in Texas, you better have road insurance," he said. "Pretty soon you will have to get Texas license plates."

I had immediate spiritual discernment. I knew that I had better buy Texas road insurance, right there, on the spot.

"You know, if you get pulled over and taken into custody, you need to call a wrecker to store your car." He continued merrily.

A shiver went up my spine. Are these guys serious, I thought? The thought of being pulled over on some lonely highway, being busted by some red-neck Texas cop, then having my car towed to some unknown, crooked, wrecker-storage yard while I tried to get out of jail was…just…well, unacceptable.

It all flashed in front of me.

"You know someone who sells that type of insurance…?" I didn't quite finish my question.

"Why yes, my brother here sells road insurance."

The brother who had been silent until now looked at me. "You need Texas auto insurance?"

"Yes, I believe I do," I answered. And with that came a transaction that relieved me of all but about $100 of my cash.

"Take care, partner," the Trooper said, as they both got into his state trooper car and left me standing bewildered outside the Lodge. It was evening.

Hmm, the salesman inside me thought as I walked toward the entrance, I'll bet they close every sale.

Welcome to Texas!

Welcome to Blanco!

I was greeted at the door by a nice-looking black man.

"Hello," I said. "I was looking for a room for the night."

"Well come in," he said. "We don't have rooms to rent, but we have the big room upstairs that you can sleep in. It's five dollars for the night."

"Ok," I said, as we walked in.

"Uh, this is my girlfriend Donna. She's from the UK." A frail-looking, white woman walked up to us.

"Hello Donna," I said.

This is weird, I thought. A black man and a white woman apparently shacked up in this tiny Central Texas town. And living in the Masonic

Lodge! Could you be more malapropos in this tiny Texas town? Shades of

KKK!

"You all live here?" I asked. They nodded.

No wonder the cop showed up at the same time as I did. Intuitively, I knew something was wrong with this picture. I knew that there was not a liberal-thinking Democrat within a hundred-mile radius of Blanco. The cop and his brother were not just being nice. There was something going down with the black dude and his white girlfriend.

"Are you guys buying the building?" I asked," I couldn't think of another reason in the world why a black man and white woman would be shacking up in the old Masonic Lodge building.

"Oh no," said Donna. "They let us stay here if we would fix it up, but we haven't been able to pay for electricity."

Strange reason, I thought, *probably finagled by some shyster real estate guy who left town*. Well, this is really and truly a flop-house. "Okay," I said, "here's five dollars."

With that, I grabbed my bag from the car and went inside.

The black guy led me to the stairs.

"Anywhere you want up there," he said. "Here's a candle. No lights, you know."

I took the candle and walked up the long stairway. It was still light enough to see my way around. At the top, I stopped and surveyed the scene. My old Masonic experience came back. This was the place of the holy of holies in Masonry...this is where I first stepped out of Pentecostalism. It was the main lodge room. Being a Mason myself, (though being delinquent on my dues for years) I felt strangely protected by being in the old lodge.

This was where the Masonic initiations took place. I knew I was here for a reason. But what? The first question an apprentice in Masonry is asked is, "Whence came you…"

That night I was joined by a friendly hippie. "Just lookin' for a place to crash dude?" he asked.

"Well, I guess," I responded. "I'm a writer."

"Me too," he said. We both laughed at the absurdity of our situation. He was friendly, but not too close, like if someone had hired him to be my bodyguard for the night. It felt good having another person sharing the big room. We talked for a few hours then both of us drifted off to sleep on the floor of Masonry. The dim light of the candle continued burning at the end of the room.

I had intuitively known that Lester would rather have me dead than to disdain his religion. Perhaps subconsciously, but he would rather see one of his other children dead than to see them backslide. What was worse, I knew he thought he was doing God's will. I was afraid my spiritual power was not adequate to survive his abandonment. Just as Jesus must have felt on the cross. His love for the father could not overcome the abandonment of his father's love. That night, I had hidden from my father's angry wrath.

Maybe it was just my paranoia. Or maybe I really did deserve death for being Jesus.

I awoke a little after sunrise. The friendly hippie had already left. I quietly gathered my bag and was ready to leave, but something made me stop. I walked over to the east wall and put my hand to the stucco and drew the outline of it. In the palm of the hand I drew I wrote the words "I Am." Something was supposed to happen last night that was prevented from happening by my being here, I thought. The "I Am" protected me.

I drove to Ft. Worth that day and met Robert. He took me over to meet his friend, the publisher. "David I've got a biographical outline of Johnny Barnes. He wants someone to write his biography from this," he said. I took the one-pager and told the publisher that I would "write" the "autobiography." I got a $100 advance and returned to Canyon Lake to write. I was welcomed as though nothing had happened.

The morbid thoughts of crucifixion never came back into my mind or returning to Lester and Mary. I was quiet about being Jesus. I stayed a couple of weeks longer and wrote a couple of autobiographies of people Robert knew in Pentecostal circles. I was told later that Lester had justified his acceptance of me because "I had lost my mind to "New Age" while in California."

The first little book was written for Johnny Barns of the Assembly of God's Royal Rangers called "Johnny the Barefoot Dreamer." It sold about 10,000 copies primarily to the kids in the Royal Rangers. The original book is still available on Amazon and perhaps other sites. My total take was the $100 advance.

The Royal Rangers are a knock-off of the Boy Scouts of America. They wear uniforms like the traditional scouts and have (all) male leaders from church congregations that act as "Scout Leaders." But even now, of course, the Royal Rangers deny membership to any little kid that is deemed a homosexual.

Robert then lined me up to ghost-write an autobiography for an ex-Hell's Angel, newly converted and quickly ordained into a Full Gospel Evangelical denomination. I first met him in Ft. Worth, as… hmm…a "youth leader" at a youth center he had supposedly founded and began to record his grossly exaggerated recounts of riding with The Angels. I finally finished the saga at his rented home in San Jose, California some weeks later. He had a story of being shot in a gang fight. Like Lester, he had found Jesus while in the hospital recovering from a near-death experience. Like me, he wanted the world to hear his come-to-Jesus story.

I sent the draft to Robert and his publisher. I never heard a word back from either. I can't really blame them. It had maybe 40 or 50-thousand words and might have made a script for a B-movie. I never received one dime in compensation.

What was I doing? I thought.

It seemed to me that I was just filling time with activity to keep from being criticized for doing nothing. It didn't matter what I tried to do. So much of my thinking and energy was going out of me. To be Jesus, I could be nothing else.

I returned home to California more broken than when I left.

Out of money, out of a job, and deeply despondent, I took Aquarius, the family dog, and went out to Crystal Springs Reservoir, just South of Daley City, to meditate. This was one of the most beautiful places on God's earth.

The fragrance of the towering eucalyptus trees filled the air. The waters of the turquoise-blue reservoir were so beautiful that you could see the stone formations on the bottom almost fifty feet deep. I took my dog and walked along the shore of the reservoir with me and found a place to sit and meditate. Aquarius quietly laid down on the ground near me. It was such a beautiful and restful place. I began to pray. The effect of the infilling of the spirit of Jesus was immediate and almost overwhelming.

Peace surrounded me as I meditated on *at-one-ment* with Jesus. Once again, the joy of Christ filled my soul. Heaven seemed to descend on me as I opened my heart and soul to the presence of Jesus Christ and entered his being. I was Jesus. I found *at-one-ment* with Him once again.

It seemed that I was far happier before I went "home" to Texas to share the joy of being Jesus with my Pentecostal parents. Of course, they were stand-offish like I sort of expected, but I was still Dave, the eldest son. *C'mon, guys, I'm still the real deal*, I had thought.

The experience in Texas seemed straight out of hell. I was constantly and unconsciously looking back over my shoulder, running for my life.

Being Jesus back in Texas was like being a wanted bank robber on the run. But destiny was taking me back. I was out of options.

I decided to take the family and move back to the place where I had met and married Dorothy Louise. There, at least, we had a place to live.

Her mother, Pearl, sensing our obvious plight, offered to help us reestablish. We decided to accept her offer. She offered us one of her empty rent houses near downtown Houston. It was the house that Dorothy Louise was living in when we married. We only had to get there and settle in.

I rented a Ryder truck, loaded it with all we owned, and, in the summer of 1975 with family, dogs, and earthly belongings, returned "home."

Back in Texas, it seemed that still, nothing I tried worked. We stayed a few weeks with Pearl, while I applied for job after job. She had a couple of gay men that were moving out of the house she was providing to us. I was still out of work when we then moved in. The old neighborhood, Montrose, had turned decidedly gay.

I tried new sales jobs, selling door-to-door encyclopedias and insurance. My heart was not in anything. I knew what I was doing was not what my life had for me. Here I was, a former successful middle manager for a giant pharmaceutical company and I could not even find a job selling encyclopedias. But I had to put up a farce, like before, doing something to fill time. I knew if I didn't want it, I would never get it. But what was it I was seeking?

Finally, I took the one job I knew I could get, rigging and iron working for my old company, Brown and Root, Inc. It was hard manual labor at an hourly rate. But I had to start at the bottom. I took it. I went back to the common, back-breaking, 12-hour work days for Brown and Root in Green's Bayou, Texas, home of my first real job.

I won't even try to describe the actual experience.

I was taunted and treated as though I had been sold into slavery. It was like going to prison. It was prison. No one remembered me for what I once was. I was now a "city boy" that somehow had bought a job. I had to get up and leave by 5:00 am and drive fifty miles to the job site to punch in. But I stuck it out. Work started at 6:00 am.

Like Icarus, I had flown to close to the sun. It melted my wings, and I fell back to earth.

Dr. David P. Summers

Chapter 16

A Silver Lining in a Dark Cloud

In England

Begin –
Again—The finished past
The price paid
The victory won.

Life is like that.
Likely a small celebration
Surge of emotion, a spark of joy
The past and marked in the leaves
Of memory.
Crossing then into newness
With all the same apparel

New hope
And pain erased
Born again, Again.
Haven't we met before?
The dismal list of unfulfilled hopes
Suddenly fulfilled—alive—vibrant
With laughter—glory and newness.

Once the bell tolled again, it's mournful message
The bewildered and sadden came to pray.
Again, darkness fell upon the Spirit, and it withered,
Falling finally exhausted of meaning.
Farewell, old cherished friend.
Fare-the-well.
For today.

(poetry of a desperate attempt to joy in my life ca.1977)

Now back in Texas, I was desperate. There were no "hippies" freeloading on the streets. I needed money and power, brothers and sisters, and I didn't have either. Mama Pearl was looking for handyman jobs for me to do in her apartment houses, and I didn't even have a pair of hard toed shoes when I started. But, after a week or two of painful anguish, I found a way to get them …legally…the hard way. I drove some 70 miles to the back side of Houston where Brown and Root was still paying slave wages for manual labor in their marine fabrication yard. It was long hours of barge-rigging and structural iron-work in 100 degrees (38 C) in burning sun on red-hot steel in their fabrication yard. And I was sent to work the top. …Any ole iron-worker-connector knows that meaning -- it means working 200 ft above the ground. It provided the needed money for work boots, gasoline, and getting away from the house with my mother-in-law. It kept me busy and gave me a little legitimacy with Pearl. Within a few weeks, I was making the kind of checks that I used to make.

It was 1978, but after about a year as a rigging specialist with Brown and Root, the company I sort of grew up in, I had learned all that I cared to re-learn. I was ready to quit, or more likely, get fired. Obviously, my experience as a top pharmaceutical executive, ministering to doctors and nurses and hospitals with goods and services were of little help when returning to 12-hour days of back-breaking manual work.

So, what's so backbreaking about rigging the eyes of four each 3.0" braided steel strands wire rope pulled from a huge wooden spool? How about having to physically pull the strands of cable through the eyes and rebraid them by hand using a big vice and steel marlin-spike. Then being lifted to a couple of wooden planks used as a walkway atop the steel fabricated oil-drilling platform to hook-up the lifting slings. What about manually pulling those four lifting slings used to move fabricated steel and platform components by the giant 300-ton crawler crane to the edge of the platform for hook-up? Or when ready to load onto the sea-going barge, the 600-ton barge crane? And how about all the smaller choker sizes that are routinely used for lifting/moving/loading/unloading all the production equipment that sits atop these giant platforms? And the rigging work in any offshore structural fabrication yard? The common denominator is that we had to pull and drag them from one crane to another, dragging four 50 ft cable slings over to a 100 ft steel tubular to be erected on a structure. Yes, friends, that was work for a 34-year-old pharmaceutical executive.

You do this all day long, walking from one end of the yard to the other…until finally it's quitting time! Structural marine ironwork means off-shore drilling/producing/pumping platforms built from both tubular and beam steel, some having a diameter or width 3 feet to 48 feet, and 300 feet when upright. They stand hundreds of feet high on the sea-going barges to be then taken out to sea to the emplacement site in the Gulf of Mexico.

Uh… what else can I do for you?

You can barely come home, eat, and fall into bed.

Luckily, my past management experience, coupled with my early marine construction experiences, was soon recognized by Brown and Root management and had me off-shore again where my old skills quickly returned with a flourish. But by now, living in my mother-in-law's rent house in Houston was too much for any of us to bear. Dorothy Louise and I decided to split up.

As luck would have it, I was recruited by a new company to manage (not labor on) an enormous offshore job complex in the Atlantic North Sea for a Chevron, Shell, and British Petroleum partnership called Ninion Complex. The project consisted of three drilling and production platforms standing in about 500 feet of water. One of the structures just happened to be one that I had originally hired out on at Brown and Root and helped build with my hands three years earlier. I happened to have just the right amount of trade and management experience. I was sent to London to live when I was not on the job in the North Sea.

Neither of us clearly wanted to separate. But, if I was to live with her in Houston and be the liberal that I was in San Francisco, well…um, that was going to be hard to do. Certainly, not living in Pearl's house and selling encyclopedias, insurance, vacuum cleaners and even with my ironworker's job driving 120 miles round-trip each day. And don't forget being a good ole, subdued Southern boy.

Not after being Jesus.

But after a few month's separation, it became clear that separation was not in Dorothy Louise's long-term game plan.

During the long months of my absence in England, she had done some deep thinking. She wrote to me informing me that she was coming to London to be with me. It was obvious that Dorothy Louise's mother was causing most of our family angst. Pearl wanted our middle daughter, Marcia, to come live with her. She did, but she soon found one of Montgomery, Texas' local good ole boys in Pearl's little red-neck retirement town and sort of fell in love. Soon this turned into Marcia spending most of her days and many of her nights with him, not with her grandmother "Moma Pearl." This was at the same time we were desperately trying to tame her long enough to get through high school. To add gas to the fire, Pearl proceeded to make matters for Marcie's maturity, manners, and self-development even worse. Without even mentioning it to us, her parents, she bought Marcia a brand new, red Buick convertible. Lotsa luck!

And Marcie to come back home to live with mom and dad? You wish! And do you think Crystal was going to stick around? No!

By then, Crystal had met a local boy called Steven Kelley, and all this was arranged all by…? Yes, Mary and Lester who had taken our beautiful, first-born daughter to live with them at Canyon Lake. Why?

"Your Mother-Daddy are not saved, honey, so better come live with us," she was told.

So, Crystal domiciled with them for about 3 months while Steve hung out around Lester and Mary's house like a lazy old hound. Then, Lester and Mary shipped her off to bible school…as in, Southwestern Assemblies of God Bible School in Waxahachie, Texas. That lasted about 6 months until one starry night an old Justice of the Peace offering matrimonial services, just up the road from the local motel in Pharr, Texas, just right on their way to Mexico married them. (They were headed to Mexico but didn't make it.) They were now living in Wimberley, a little scenic town in Central Texas and expecting a baby. (We knew that was coming.) Our little family was dissolving rapidly into pieces in Texas.

This realization finally made it beyond Pearl's rope-line reasoning with Dorothy Louise. So, she grabbed Sherry (who, by the way, also had other plans) by the scruff of the neck and put her on the same plane with herself bound for London. I met them both at Heathrow.

When they arrived, Dorothy Louise, Sherry, and I moved into a chic flat on Melbourne Place right off Edgeware Road, in West London. Sherry enrolled in The American School.

England was a life-changing experience. Although I spoke the language, (sort of) the attitudes and mores were so different that I could have been transplanted to another planet. But I loved it! So did Dorothy

Louise. We began to travel in Europe on my time off.

My job was to oversee the management of over a thousand (mostly Scottish) off-shore construction "lads" on a huge offshore oil drilling platform located smack in the middle of the North Sea, midway between the Shetland Islands and the west coast of Norway. The nearest landfall was Bergen, Norway about 125 miles due east. We were above latitude 61 degrees. At this latitude, the sun shines about 19 1/2 hours during the summer solstice and only about 5 1/2 hours at the winter solstice. During the winter period, the sun barely rises above the horizon's sky. For most of the year, the weather was one fierce gale sweeping in from the Arctic after another. Thirty to forty-foot waves were routine.

For almost two years, I rotated two weeks (a fortnight) of 12-hour days on the site and two weeks back in London. I would leave London on a Sunday and fly a commercial jet to Aberdeen, Scotland, then a smaller fixed-wing to Lerwick, Shetland Islands, landing on a short airstrip that could only accommodate small planes in those days.

Then, as the entire crew change gathered at the small airport, I and hundreds of other crews would don our bright orange survival suits, without which the chances of surviving more than four or five minutes in the almost freezing water were next to nil. Boarding giant 20-passenger Sikorsky helicopters, we were lifted off the helipad to find a tiny spec of a floating semi-submersible barge 105 miles due east of Lerwick.

Usually, the wind, fog, and rain would be blowing thirty or forty knots as we put our lives in the hands of the expert, former Royal Air Force pilots who manned the controls and headed off with only compass and radar guiding us to the big Norwegian barge.

I can't say how much I admired and respected these former RAF pilots as they pitched and weaved their way to the location. Once located, setting down a huge Sikorsky helicopter on a heaving and rolling barge in 20-foot waves was a feat forever etched into my mind.

The helicopter pilots would hover over the small helipad and begin to maneuver the control stick of the aircraft in a graceful dance with the barge eight or ten meters below. They timed the pitch and roll of the barge until suddenly they would set down on the pad at the exact moment that the barge reached its apex.

At just the right moment, the pilot would reverse the rotors while twenty or so white-knuckled passengers leaped from the craft. With the rotor blades reversed holding the helicopter "down" on the pitching pad, almost at the same time the change-out crew, waiting to return home, jumped aboard, homeward-bound after completing their fortnight on the job, they left for two weeks' time off at homes in Scotland, England, Ireland and France.

For two years I shuttled back and forth to my job in the North Sea while Dorothy Louise and I patched up our marriage (forever) and began anew. To make it worthwhile, sometimes on the free fortnight, we took holidays on the European continent to France, Scotland, and we toured England. I was making a lot of "dosh" (dollars), so skiing in the French Alps to taking a Mediterranean cruise to Athens and the Greek Isles was no big deal. It was a great project, and my management talent was beginning to produce new employment offers. I attributed my success to knowing (since I had worked my way up from the very bottom) the work. And the exhilaration of success, any success, drove depression from me… at least temporarily.

I didn't lose life or limb from a single man out of my thousand-man crew.

After returning home from London, I was put in charge of a similar job in the Gulf of Mexico. I began supervising a project that was a mirror image, though an order of magnitude smaller than my North Sea project. Given that the North Sea has perhaps the most violent weather on earth, the job was much simpler as the Gulf is much calmer. Most of the work was pre-fabricated in Texas in Brown and Root's Marine Construction yard – the same locale that I landed in when returning from California.

As I stated, I was recruited to manage the construction, fabrication, and start-up operations of the nation's first offshore supertanker port off Louisiana. Called Louisiana Offshore Oil Port or simply LOOP, it was built to allow huge supertankers to off-load their cargo of petroleum 50 miles off the coast which was then piped ashore to be partially stored in the giant salt caverns in Southern Louisiana with the rest of the oil shipped to refineries on the Gulf coast.

It was during the second Saudi-inspired OPEC oil embargo (Remember those 3 and 4 blocks long gas lines?) and President Carter had determined to free the country from the grip of another Middle eastern political move over Israel. President Carter decided to store enough oil in the giant caverns in Southern Louisiana to run the country for at least two, maybe three months. It is still called the Strategic Oil Reserves. And it is full of oil as we speak.

My job was soon to oversee the entire project from the procurement and mobilization to the final test and startup. It was a hell of a resume enhancing position, though it was another one of those jobs where I worked offshore for about two weeks and then took two weeks off. I put my spare time to good use and enrolled in Pepperdine University's Texas campus for MBA's. Dorothy Louise and I were quite comfortable by now. I had a company car again and a salary to go with it. Sherry finished high school and began to law-clerk for a local attorney. It was all idyllic until Sherry began to run with a biker-boy who loved to tantalize me by doing wheelies on my lawn at 2:00 am. Thankfully, she soon dropped him for a more sedate and hard-working boy from Florida named Gary who had recently moved to Texas from Florida. After two years I finished that job, on time, and under budget. Sherry and Gary married. Then I was fired.

My infraction was to bring a bottle of whiskey aboard the platform and celebrate our success. I guess I knew what was in store for me because I had indirectly informed one of LOOP executives that I had planned to throw a little "project completion" celebration to the successful final test and check-out. And again, and not the least, not losing a single life or major accident on the project.

It was not my success that I wanted to celebrate, it was those engineers and tradesmen that made the job a success that I invited to share a drink. None of the above mattered to the LOOP executive who fired me for a drink of ye ole *"uisge beatha"* or Gaelic for Scotch whiskey. Se la vie.

Back on shore, now jobless again, and with a little time on my hands, I was yearning to revert to my old hippie ways, but with a little more street smart. I wrote my Master's Degree thesis on the hypocrisy of marijuana prohibition. I had to have a statistical study of the local real-world pros and cons, so I carried out a sample survey in my neighborhood.

Using the chi-square sampling technique and expecting to find most of my neighbors in our toney NW Houston neighborhood antagonistic, I was astounded to find that the fe (frequency expected) did NOT come close to the fo (frequency observed) and my null hypothesis was invalidated by a solid majority! This meant that my neighbors were for legalized marijuana! And this was in 1982. Ronald Reagan was President and the "war on drugs" was in full swing. Typical of one of Reagan's "B" Cowboys and Indians movies, where sheriff Reagan orders his DEA to round up as many pot users (Indians) as could be found holding even a tiny bit of sacred weed and filling the prisons with as many, mostly

African Americans and Latinos drug users as they could find.

And the irony of it, the same year, Texas changed its incarceration laws and legalized for profit prisons. Gotta make a buck off this war on drugs, you know. Legalized pot- prisons, full of illegal pot smokers begin to fill our prisons. Irony. But as partial justification... these guys paid taxes on what they raked in on non-stop imprisonment! Such a deal!

It was getting a little hot for the guy (me) who surveyed the neighborhood on marijuana usage and the effects of prohibition for his MBA thesis. It was time to get out of Dodge.

America was still thirsty for oil and within a few weeks, I was recruited by Morrison-Knutsen Construction Company to run a state-of-the-art project in Central America. The job was to oversee the submarine piping and mooring facilities on the Trans-Panama Pipeline across the northern Isthmus of Panama. This project was almost a mirror image of the LOOP project, except the pipeline traversed the northern isthmus, and over the three-thousand-foot mountains of Panama running from a small town Charco Azul on the Atlantic to the other side of the Isthmus and to another small town called Chiriquí on the Pacific. My job was on the Pacific side where the pipeline and job ended.

Our living facilities were literally cut out of the jungle about ten miles up the mouth of the Chiriquí river. Camp Rambala, we named it. There was no road in or out other than the gravel road leading from the camp back to the mouth of the Chiriquí which had a small village also named Chiriquí'. The mouth of the river was dredged out into a port of sorts that accommodated barges bringing heavy equipment needed to cut a boat landing of gravel and rock to serve as the off-loading site for the equipment.

As soon as the road was cut from the jungle to the construction camp, we were brought in by barge with about 50 small living trailers that had just enough room for a bed and bathroom with a shower on each side and partitioned in the middle. They housed the job's supervisory personnel. The Panamanian workers were housed in several large dormitory-style buildings.

At first, the job was routine: I inventoried the supplies and essential materials, etc., the submarine hoses and fittings. The submarine pipes were twin 36 inches in diameter and ¾ inch wall thickness, steel pipes, and each joint was 30 feet in length. There wasn't much to that. They were what they were. We welded them together in dual 90-foot strings. The submarine hoses were 12 inches in diameter and 50 feet in length steel reinforced rubber. I mobilized them at the river's outlet into the lagoon.

And with a little smoke from the friendly natives, I from time to time became Jesus again. What else was there to do in the middle of a Panamanian jungle?

Although blasphemous to a religionist, I always felt that I was protected while being the being of Jesus. In other words, eliminating the separation between God and man and simply stepping into the WWJD in the here and now, present moment. This belief was especially true in Panama where I could literally feel the spiritual polarities when I toked up. There was something about the Equator and the division of the North and South Hemispheres. Spiritual energy was palatable.

One afternoon I was up on our storage tank hill while our dynamite guys were blasting out the flattened plateau on the hill. I was assessing the layout for our pipeline and pumps leading to the Chiriquí lagoon where I was to install the floating buoys that the tankers moored up to.

I was paying little attention to the dynamite gang who were at least a hundred meters away. I was being Jesus and simply surveying the work that I had to do. I didn't even hear the familiar, "fire in the hole," only a swishing sound as a large boulder about the size of a basketball came blasting by my face, hardly a foot away. I felt the wind it made as it rocketed by at the speed of sound pushing my head back in recoil.

"Thank you, God," I said. "Thank you, you're not mad at me today!" That was not the only near-death experience I had in Panama.

In the meantime, we built a small landing strip paved with gravel that enabled us to receive supplies via two ancient World-War II Douglass DC3 aircraft that flew in with food, water, and other supplies a couple times a week from the city of David, Panama the capital city in the Provence of Chiriquí. We had two smaller aircraft that came and went daily, bringing small parts, mail, and crew as needed.

Every member of my construction crew was an indigenous San Blas Indian. They came into Chiriquí every morning by crew-boat from the San Blas Islands that lie only about 12 miles offshore from Chiriquí. They were great workers, quite different from the Hispanic Panamanians who were hired in Panama City or David and flown in to work for the duration of the job. Admittedly, sometimes I was a little arrogant of my special relationship with God when being Jesus. I sort of took the role of chief. Like almost all indigenous natives, the San Blas had a Chief that negotiated the terms and considerations for the entire tribe. We worked well together. Most of the considerations he asked for had to do with work breaks, overtime, and safety. I was able to take care of all of these, but there was more to come.

The pipe laying crew started on the Pacific side of the Isthmus and were working their way over the mountains to the Atlantic. Everything went well until the pipe-laying crew of Americans reached our camp. The crew's "boss man" was an older experienced man named Benny Hill. (*fictitious*) Hill and his crew worked for another company but were subcontracted to do the pipeline. Benny's crew were all from Mississippi and Alabama, and all were white Anglo.

There were only about two dozen of them, and this was their second foreign job. Rowdy did not really describe them. They were "good ole Southern boys," (as they say) who, as soon as the work-day was completed, began boozing and hustling the native girls for sex. They had just completed a big job in Somalia before coming to Panama. There they had no prohibitions on relationships among the work crews and the native workers.

The Somalian laborers worked for a few dollars a day and had no job protection, few safety regulations and no respect from the white men on the crew that oversaw them. Benny's crew were a cocky and arrogant bunch of redneck immaturity that had absolutely no respect for their Panamanian co-workers. As the mistreatment grew, I knew that we were headed for trouble.

The Panamanians were highly educated and respectful of us, and what tipped the scale in favor of the Panamanians was the worker's union that protected certain rights like the level of pay, the hours worked, and had certain safety regulations that the pipeline guys mainly ignored, like sexually molesting the local females that worked in the camp.

"Benny," I said one evening as shift ended, "you've got to tell your crew to lay off the booze and local women, or we are going to have problems." He spat a wad of tobacco spit onto the ground near my boots.

"Screw you Summers," he replied. "Mind your own fucking business, and we'll get along!"

"Benny, you're pissing off the Panamanian shop stewards. And we don't need labor problems. We're almost done." My position as Project Manager of the Submarine and Offshore facilities gave me certain authority over Benny, but all I could really do was complain to Morrison Knutsen project executives. My authority started where Benny's ended. At the water's edge.

But he ignored me, got into his pickup and drove away.

"I need to talk to you Benny," I yelled. I got into my pickup and followed him to his crew shop, a small trailer with a desk and shortwave radio facility. We both pulled up at the same time. He walked into the trailer, and I followed.

Benny turned to me.

"Have you ever had your ass whupped?" he snarled. He now had backup. A couple of his side-kicks had walked up and stood on each side of me. One took out a large Bowie knife and began cleaning his fingernails with it. Typical macho-man stuff, I thought.

"Yes, Bernard. (I called him by his given name) I have had my ass whipped…more than once." I replied. He wasn't quite prepared for my honesty.

He paused and stared at me, "well, you're about to get it whipped again."

"Maybe so, Bernard, but what I told you is true. God is my witness, I'm right," I said.

He gave me a strange long stare and said nothing more. I stared back. I knew I had penetrated his hard heart. I stared right back into his soul.

"Get out of here and go back to your business," he mumbled.

"No," I said, "you've got to stop messing with my crew. They've already assembled 90% of the hose-sections and will have the underwater pipelines ready to pull by Sunday. Keep your boys away from my men and let them finish," I directed.

He looked away, and I turned and got back into my vehicle and returned to the construction base. When I got back to my little trailer, the Chief and I had a talk about what to do about Benny and his crew. The Chief mentioned that Benny's boys were making life hard on the Indians as well as the Panamanians. The San Blas had certain customs that they place a high value on. Benny and his boys totally ignored and abused them. I asked the Chief if he could join me in a little smoke. He knew what I meant. A pow-wow with God. The next evening, we lit up the sacred buds and talked about what God was to us. Simple personal stories. His from the ancient Guna religion. Mine was about Jesus. We both agreed that we were in "one accord." That was all.

I waited to see what would happen. The tension in the camp was palatable.

The next day the Panamanians called a surprise labor strike. At the same time, they put an armed worker at the entrance gate to our compound. They moved several of the big earth moving dozers and graders out onto the landing strip that prevented any aircraft from coming or going. It was more than a labor shutdown. We were being held under armed guards inside the camp. It was more like a revolt than a labor strike.

This did not go well with Benny's crew. They felt unique and were used to driving Camp Rambala down the little gravel road eight miles to the small village of Chiriquí, drinking beer until eleven or twelve o'clock at night. Buying sex and disregarding and disrespecting the local indigenous people till the wee hours of the night. Then, they all left together, driving back at high speed up the gravel road in a convoy of company pickups back to the camp. There, they fell into their bunks to catch a few hours of sleep before starting a new day was redneck routine.

The lockup continued through day-three when three of Benny's pipeline crew decided that they would break through the guarded perimeter, go to Chiriquí, get a boat and take it across the lagoon to the small town of Boca del Toro. Boca had a few retired American and British ex-pats living in the picturesque little banana port on the West Coast of Panama. They didn't think the Panamanians would follow them there.

It didn't quite work out that way.

They decided to avoid the guarded gate on the primary road out of the camp, and drive across the landing strip and pick up the road on the back side of the strip – which led straight to Chiriquí village. Three of them piled into one of the pickups and took off at high speed heading across the landing strip.

As they rounded the compound, driving at breakneck speed, one of the young Panamanians jumped out in front of the speeding vehicle, waving an AK 47 automatic rifle and ordered them to stop. Rather than stop, the good old boys floor-boarded the truck and…ran over and killed him. On the spot!

That didn't stop them either. They continued wildly driving down the gravel road toward the Chiriquí boat slip hoping to find one of the crew boats that took Indian crews to and from a series of small offshore islands. These were the same islands that supplied my crew.

The Panamanians had radio contact with others who had vehicles, and three or four of them were in close pursuit down the ten miles to the town. Arriving in town, they found one of the crew boats tied to the dock and jumped aboard. Hot wiring the ignition, they got it started and took off toward Bocas del Toras, a small town directly across the lagoon on the Pacific. It was a quaint little town which at one time was a company town for United Fruit Company. There were a small group of American expatriates that had retired in Bocas del Toro. The good old boys hoped to find refuge there until they could flee the country.

Only, they didn't make it. The Panamanians had already grabbed another bigger and faster boat. In close pursuit, they rammed the fleeing pipeliners. The boat took on water and began to sink. The motor stalled, enabling the Panamanians to quickly board and capture all three of Benny's crew.

The rest is history. They beat the pipeliners mercilessly on the way back to deliver them to Chiriquí's Guardia National – consisting of a couple of armed locals given a uniform, a bit of authority, and work for the government police force. Once back ashore, the good old boys from Mississippi and Alabama were thrown into the small one-room cell.

And left there.

But this was only the beginning of things to come.

El Presidente of Panama, Manuel Noriega, was finally persuaded by both the company and the union to get involved. After all, the dispute was between one of the largest construction companies in the United States and the national union of Panama. He flew in on the Presidential helicopter from Panama City, Panama thus avoiding the obstacles on the runway. There were a lot of politics at stake. The Panamanian unions, the Company, the death of a Panamanian worker – it all took a grueling week of negotiations. Finally, President Noriega made his decision and we were freed.

The only casualties were the Panamanian laborer and the three "good ole boys" who were transferred to a larger jail in the city of David. With the Noriega decision, Benny's boys were quickly put on a plane and flown out of the country.

After completing the final testing and checkout and certifying my portion of the project completed, I packed my bags and returned home to Houston. But there was still a little left to do. I ran into my San Blas Chief on the way out.

"I am now a Jesus friend," he said. "He has come to our tribe!" We grinned and shook hands goodbye. I knew what he meant.

When a tanker arrived in port, the ship was to slowly move in and moor itself to one of two large floating buoys. Then using the gaff booms, the ship's crew picked up the floating portion of the hoses and lifted each hose onto the ship. Then the crew connected the hoses to the ship's discharge nozzles on deck, and when hooked up, the ship's massive pumps began pumping the cargo of oil out of the ship's massive holds into my hoses and underwater pipeline to shore. Thus, the oil tanker never needed to be tied up to a dock. The entire procedure was run exclusively by the ship's crew, and the entire discharge procedure took only about six hours. Once the cargo was pumped out, the ship could be on its way back to Alaska for another round trip. Smart engineering!

As soon as I got home, the phone in my small office was ringing. It was news from Panama.

The second or third ship to come into the lagoon to unload had accidentally hit the mooring buoy and damaged it, making the system inoperable. The entire system was shut down from the Pacific to the Atlantic. Losing millions of dollars per day, the new owner of the pipeline quickly took my bid to repair the buoy and put the system back in operation. This time I was joined by Dorothy Louise.

She returned with me to Rambala as an assistant contractor manager, hired to repair the damage done by an oil tanker to one of the offshore loading buoys. The Central American jungles of Panama was a place that she had never been. It was exciting to both of us. It only took about six weeks to repair the system, and I returned home, this time a proud contractor instead of a project manager. But before we left, we both experienced a few miracles.

We had a small work barge that held our welding machines and other needed equipment. The work was finished except one brace that had not been welded. We needed the rain to stop – just for few minutes to provide me just enough time to finish the weld on one beam.

Dorothy Louise stood in the rain.

"Oh Lord, this is my prayer of faith. Please make the rain go away," she prayed. As she did, the clouds above instantly parted as we both watched, eerily resembling (I guess) the parting of the red sea. I quickly completed the welding just as the next tanker came into the lagoon.

Mundane? Yes, but something moved overhead. It was her special answer. As we moved our work-barge away the huge tanker tied up to the buoy. She was thrilled to see her prayers answered in such dramatic fashion. It was a first-time experience!

Another funny thing happened on that trip back to Panama. I ran into Benny Hill. He was at the offices of the Panamanian contractors – all dressed up, new shoes and a new shirt and tie. He was glad to see me.

"I want to tell you something, Summers," he said.

"Well okay, Benny, tell me."

"I found the Lord Jesus."

I grinned and said, "Congratulations."

In 1985, I changed jobs…again. It was for one of the country's largest pipeline companies located in Boise, Idaho. It was a subsidiary of Morrison Knutsen and appropriately called MK Pipeline Company.

This time Dorothy Louise was with me from the beginning. We flew to Aberdeen, Scotland where the new job was already in progress. Here my team completed the design and engineering of the project. Once the engineering was completed, we flew over to Copenhagen, Denmark to survey and lay out the landing area where the pipelines were to come ashore in Denmark. Copenhagen was enjoyable but short-lived. But the two or three days there allowed us to walk around the uniquely Danish waterfront and tour Tivoli Gardens, one of the most beautiful public parks on earth.

Then we took the "fast boat" across the Baltic Straights over to Malmo, Sweden where we stayed until I finalized the long strings of floating sections of pipe that were floated out to points in the Straights. Once floated out into the middle of the Baltic Straights, they were welded together, and then temporarily dropped to the bottom of the sea to await the next section of pipe to be floated out from the Swedish side of the Baltic Sea.

The submarine pipeline system traversed the entire Baltic Straights supplying Sweden with natural gas from Scotland (some of the gas coming from my old Ninion Project) and the North Sea. The job was a huge success and quite a big deal all over Scandinavia. At last, Sweden, Denmark, and Finland would have plenty of fuel for heat and transportation.

It was sort of like the topping on my occupational cake. I started with the Ninion Project in the North Sea, building the drilling and production platforms in the late 1970s and completed the Trans-Baltic pipe project seven years later with natural gas flowing to Europe and Scandinavia. A lot had transpired between those two projects, but again, we never lost a member of my construction group in an accidental death during the seven years that I was back in my old trade.

When we returned to the states in the fall of 1985, I was told that Mary had been diagnosed with ovarian cancer. Cancer had killed her mother back when I was in my early twenties, and it was the one disease she always dreaded. Hearing the awful diagnosis from Robert, Dorothy Louise and I decided to drive to Dallas to visit before her scheduled surgery.

Never wanting to spend more than a few hours with them and never to spend the night, this time we did things a little differently. We arrived in the evening and settled in to make the exception and to spend the night at Lester and Mary's home. They were gracious, and Mary prepared an excellent meal, but no one had much of an appetite.

As usual, Lester was up at five in the morning, television blaring and reading the Dallas Morning News. This was deja vu all over, and I was momentarily taken back to my boyhood. Soon Mary and Dorothy Louise joined us with the two separating from the men (Pentecostal custom) and prepared a quick breakfast of scrambled eggs and bacon. We ate in relative silence, and after the meal, all of us gathered in the living room. My brother Robert showed up and joined the group, and we chatted quietly. I knew Mary wanted us to pray over her. She was due to be operated on the next week.

The prayer started with the customary "laying on of hands." This time, instead of Lester or Robert, I led the prayer.

"Oh God," I prayed, "we take this affliction from our dear sister, Mary. We take her affliction upon ourselves, Oh God, and we commit it to the "sea of forgetfulness" of the Holy Spirit according to thy word."

I knew they had never heard a prayer that asked God to give the affliction to one of the prayers. I learned that some religions do ask for the afflictions of the sick to a Chief such as the Guna, (God of the San Blas) or the Eckist, (Eckankar Cult, the Majanta takes the karma from the patient and commits it to the Sugmad/God) or the Iroquois (Native Pantheon of Great Spiritual Icons) do the same.

Disease is an attraction of negative energy, believe it or not. If you can break the negative attraction/bond, the dis-ease has no energy to hold on to the body. I knew that if we could get Mary to release this negative energy manifesting in her mind and spirit as cancer to us, or at least to Dorothy Louise and me, we ourselves, who had no place for the negative attraction, could heal Mary.

"Yes, yes, Lord," repeated Robert. Lester began speaking in his same unknown tongue I had heard so often. I knew his opening phase by rote and so do all my siblings. It starts with, "shaun da la ma hala…"

It was soon over, and Dorothy Louise and I left Mary weeping. Saying our good-byes, we quickly left to return to Houston. We accepted her healing, but the vibrations at Lester and Mary's house were just too rough to be comfortable.

And yes, we stopped on our way to Dallas and bought a bottle of Jack Daniels whiskey and some cokes to celebrate Mary's healing. It was sort of like the Voodoo in Panama we had witnessed, only we didn't spew out the alcohol on the ground. The effect was the same.

The next week I got a call from Lester.

"David, would you come back up here and be here for mother's surgery tomorrow?" he asked.

"Dad, she is healed," I said. "There is no need for surgery."

"But the doctor x-rayed her a few days ago, David. She has a cancer that should be removed, the doctor wants to operate."

"She's healed, Dad." I had total conviction that Mary had been healed. "Her cancer is gone from her."

"Please son, mother wants you to be here when she gets operated on."

"I'm not coming back up, Dad., she's healed. We took her affliction from her when we prayed for her the other day."

"Please come, David," he begged. He had never begged me to do anything before.

"No Dad, I'm not. There's no need," I said and hung up the phone.

The morning of the scheduled surgery I received a call from Robert.

"David," he said, excitedly, "Mother's not having surgery today." I didn't respond. I knew she had been healed.

"So, what changed your mind on surgery," I asked

"Well, she was admitted for surgery, but the doctor wanted to do one last x-ray," he said. "The tumor turned out to be a cyst. And it burst this morning… it's just a cyst, Dave. She doesn't have cancer."

Lester never again mentioned the incident. Neither did I. Neither did Robert.

Chapter 17
Haven't We Met Before?

Memories Still

Funny how
He never thought of it before
Yet one night it struck him

What would they all say
When he presented his petition
To the elders?
A little epistle of regret
A few sighs, Some tears?

He should have
Stayed a while
Just to see
What they said.

But he could not wait,
You might say.
He just turned in his badge
And walked away.
An epitaph?
Come now!

An old-grey banjo player strums
An even older tune
In double-time
And makes you happy
For a while.

"Carry my troubles away"
Away, away So far away.
(To my deceased friend, Austin Basset, 2017)

Upon returning from the Panama job, I struck out to develop my own business. I founded a small biotech company called American Biomed, Inc (ABI) and took it public in 1992, raising about $4.5 million in an initial public offering (IPO). Not much in today's currency, but once again, I felt like a born-again man.

Since the US Postal Service and Ma Bell were our sole means of business communication, one could easily lose the chance to take a call from a friendly solicitor for services of (and it happened) to take a call from Pfizer or Johnson and Johnson. So, Dorothy Louise and I opened the office every day precisely at 9:00 am. I really wasn't adept at public offerings (IPOs), commonly called "Initial Public Offerings." I hired an ex-banker for my CEO— Don Sedder—to head up our business organization. He brought with him two young accountants from the recent Arthur-Anderson failure.

I traveled a lot. And I mean really a lot. I went anywhere I sensed an opportunity to help ABI grow into the company that I proposed it to be to the many investors who bought into our stock offering, which, was just that…a promotion, not reality.

As usual, the Republicans under Reagan sought to cut the cost for decent benevolence (helping the poor, unemployed, sick and liberals, meaning libraries, environment, women, anti-war activists, etc.) from government budgets wherever they could. (A sort of Republican modus operandi, I suppose). They were also law and order junkies; most had never even gone out for junior high school sports but were now eager to show how "tough on crime" they could be. The subliminal national psyche was "I really want to show big daddy how tough, efficient, different from liberal hippies, pro-war, and how America-first I can be."

I continued to smoke pot whenever I could and be Jesus whenever I could while devoting my time and energies to growing my company – whenever I could, and keep it secret (sort of), whenever I could. It was a strange psychodynamic. My logical, left-brain, straight-business-man rational state and my right brain, hippie, pot-smoking, spiritualistic Jesus state began to lose sight of each other. Jesus seemed further and further away while I tried to be all business. It seemed that I was only close to him or entered that *at-one-ment* with him, when in my right-brain, that conceptual, holistic state that I could only induce with a few free moments and a puff or two of weed. And that opportunity became more and more rare.

This only happened when I managed to find a few minutes peace (usually while alone driving) trying to mind my own business...in Houston traffic...and hoping some jerk doesn't cut me off shoving the real world back in my face.

In my old pharmaceutical job, (ca.1975) I had worked with Houston's renowned heart surgeon, Dr. Michael DeBakey. (*deceased*). Even after I left the company, I kept the contact warm knowing that he wanted to develop and clinically implant a small self-contained artificial heart for patients who otherwise could live another 40 or 50 years if not for heart disease or trauma.

After starting American Biomed, I applied for a National Institutes of Health (NIH) grant and received $500,000 grant shared with Baylor College of Medicine. I began to mentally noodle on a small pump design with Professor Ned Hwang at the University of Houston. The concept was based on the "Moineau Pump" principle that I had filed for a patent for a couple of years prior during the first Arab Oil Embargo on pipeline pumps for coal slurry. A Moineau pump is a progressive cavity pump that also can act as a motor. Unlike other heart pump designs at that time that had reciprocating piston type or balloons open and squeeze the blood through the body, the Moineau can run without any of the operating parts ever touching each other. The idea arose from my experience in my oilfield days, where they were used for mud motors...as in drilling mud. I took the concept to Dr. DeBakey, and we went to work on his lifelong dream, the implantable "DeBakey Heart Pump" as it was reported in the national news.

During this period, Dr. DeBakey hosted a group of Russian surgeons and cardiologists to come over to work with him in his clinic and see firsthand what freedom and democracy could do for medicine. It was during this same time the Soviet Union was coming apart at the seams. Mikhail Gorbachev was Secretary of the Communist Party (head guy) and had initiated a program called Glasnost which was designed to open Russia to the West and install full democracy in Russia. At the same time, Gorbachev hinted that his country would be open to free trade with the West.

Dr. DeBakey was willing to help by training Russian doctors in his state-of-the-art surgical techniques. They were eager to learn from the "master," (DeBakey had flown over to Moscow a year earlier to treat Gorbachev's wife Raisa who was suffering from heart disease) but also wanted to promote their own manufactured surgical instruments into the American market. I made an appointment with Dr. DeBakey to discuss how this might work out for ABI and he informed me that a famous Moscow physician named Prof. Eugene Chazov, (*deceased*) Minister of Health for the Communist Party, was coming to Dallas, Texas to present some unique Russian breakthroughs in coronary disease to the American Heart Association's annual meeting. The Cold War was thawing, and I saw an opportunity in the making.

With my new company president, Dan Stacy, we drove the 250 miles from Houston to Dallas on the day that Prof. Chazov was to speak. I hoped to somehow finagle an invitation to visit Russia from him and to be the first to capitalize (as in Capitalism) on the yet unknown opportunities of the old Soviet Union. Dan and I arrived at the Dallas Convention Center in plenty time for us to register and get into the meetings that were presenting break-through technologies. Prof. Chazov made his presentation and received standing applause from the mostly American doctors in the meeting hall. We positioned ourselves just outside the big entrance door of the convention knowing that Chazov would have to walk through. Dan had hired a couple of Dallas photo and video hogs who were to record the event. Just as planned, Chazov walked out the doors, and Dan and I stepped up to introduce ourselves and congratulate him on his presentation. I will cut to the chase.

Dorothy Louise and I flew to Moscow and met with Eugenia Chazov (*now deceased*) and his physician-disciples for several days. We were introduced to a manufacturing representative from Kazakhstan whose plant made surgical instruments for the Soviet Military and who was a medical specialist in the country. We were put up in the best hotel in Moscow, built by the American oil magnate, Armand Hammer, before taking a train all day and night to Astana, Kazakhstan to visit their plant. The Russians graciously put us up in one of their dachas (holiday lodges) which was reserved exclusively for the upper members of the Communist Party. It was about a 30-minute drive outside the city.

It was a beautiful setting set on the Volga River, and it was summer in Russia, and everything was green. To show their acceptance of me as one of them, the Russian doctors suggested that I become honorarily initiated into the All-Soviet Medical Society. They told me that to become an initiate, I had to undress in the "banja" (sauna) situated in every dacha of any preeminence.

The sweat-lodges called banja were low-lying wooden structures dependent on a fire lit inside to provide heat. I was soon joined by a half-dozen other doctors and female companions who were assigned to make sure that Dorothy Louise and I enjoyed Russian hospitality. After I had been thoroughly steamed and "sweated," we all anointed our naked bodies with tallow from a Russian tree.

As I lay resting on the wooden benches, my host appeared and told me to "put your hand over your genitals." For a minute, I froze as old sexual memories flooded in. But then, as he took a bunch of young birch reeds and literally thrashed my body red (to stimulate the effects of the heat, tallow, and steam), I knew that it was real. There was no modestly covering of my privates, no prim or proper form to it. He just beat me silly with soft birch.

Then, with a wink and smile, I was particularly assured of its health benefits. Once initiated, I was considered a good Russian and a member of the society. "Now we can drink vodka," my host said. I took that to mean now we could get drunk together. I was correct.

We spent a week in Kazakhstan before returning to Moscow. It was not only great fun, but it turned out to be quite productive. Dorothy Louise, already a kitchen master herself, integrated into the cooking at the lodge (which went from 4:00 am to midnight) and though none of the female cooks spoke a word of English, and though Dorothy Louise spoke only a word or two of Russian, all became fast friends sharing American and Russian cooking secrets. She loved it. And they loved it. Every aspect of the preparation of meals had to be demonstrated both ways. She took over the potatoes (boiled) and the steaks. Her counter-part prepared the bread baked from scratch and desserts.

The meals were indescribably delicious.

We were part of a group of about a dozen or so "guests" of the Communist Party. Only one or two of the doctors spoke English. It didn't matter, as we all got along famously. After a huge breakfast in the morning, we visited the plant, and, in the afternoon, we napped, swam in the Volga river and picnicked on its banks…and drank a lot of vodka. I never drank so much vodka in my life! But, Dorothy Louise and I returned to the U.S. with an exclusive agreement with the Russians. They agreed to license our little company to sell their surgical instruments into the entire U.S. market.

We returned home with great expectations as the surgical products manufactured by the Russians were of the highest quality, made of stainless steel and titanium. With Dr. DeBakey behind me, what could go wrong?

Yeah, what could go wrong?

Unfortunately, President Reagan had appointed a guy named Dr. David Kessler who was an outspoken and conservative physician who felt that too many drugs and devices were being approved for the American market to head the Food and Drug Agency (FDA).

My new biotech inventions and the Russian instruments were completely blocked by his Agency who that year only approved eight medical applications. And those were drugs from Big Pharma.

It was maddening. I had done my good American thing and helped Dr. DeBakey, and thus, the Russians achieve part of what the entire world wanted, peace and coexistence with our former arch-enemy. What was to be a simple 510K (a submission that shows that the product is substantially equivalent to another, already approved product) notification to the FDA languished somewhere in the bureaucracy of bureaucratic red tape and was never approved for the U.S. market. No amount of resubmission, revisions, or outright pleading with the Agency turned into the approval of Russian surgical instruments.

Someone somewhere had tagged our applications with perpetual inaction. I had hired representatives all over the country who were ready to compete and sell these instruments. And we were continually blocked. It wasn't just me. No one was getting approved. I even took a phone call from a reporter from the New York Times who asked me questions for over an hour. My legitimate complaint was printed in the New York Times but to no avail. Kessler was impossible. He just would not budge.

After over some 20 months of delay, of what was a usual 3-month review for this type of application, we should have had our official approval to market in the U.S. -- and by law! The Agency simply ignored its own rules. The law says an application is reviewed and approved within a period of no more than 3 months unless the FDA finds that you are a drug, or you are running a criminal enterprise, these things always go according to the rules and regulations put out by the FDA and are open to the public.

I was unbelievably frustrated. The company had hired several sales reps to sell the Russian instruments and a dozen or so new employees to work on my own invention to follow. It was an endovascular medical instrument to be used by Dr. Debakey to minimally surgically remove the buildup of plaque in patients' arteries without cutting them from sternum to gut. We called the new device the OmniCath™. It was simply a "plaque scrapper," attached to the end of a long endovascular catheter, but it worked. It gently removed the vascular obstruction without traumatizing the blood vessel. I was running out of time and money.

The company was soon broke. It was time to fire all those good and loyal employees that I hired to fulfill my promise to my investors to enter a highly profitable market with a patented and therefore exclusive product required to avoid open chest surgery.

But I was blocked somewhere along the line by a powerful conservative influence from a government agency. No Russian surgical instruments— even if endorsed by a world-famous legend such as Michael DeBakey, M.D.—were to be allowed on the American market.

I thought Reagan went to Reykjavík, Iceland to remove these types of obstacles!

Yeah, right.

In my desperation, I hired a so-called "turn-around manager" who came recommended by one of my old Bard managers from back in the 1960s. The Board made him President, and he moved his family from Providence, Rhode Island to an exclusive home in The Woodlands where ABI was located, put his kid into private school, joined the exclusive Country Club. All the while he assured me that he could turn the situation around. But then…promptly began to sell off the assets. Within a few months, he put the company into bankruptcy before I knew what he was doing. He then called a meeting of the board and fired me.

He had killed my dream, American BioMed, Inc. Chapter 7 (liquidation) bankruptcy was its final breath.

WWJD now?

Not to be completely deterred, I received my MBA from Pepperdine University after two years of weekend work during the interim, and… started another new company called Endovasc, Inc. It was incorporated on June 5, 1996.

Dr. David P. Summers

Chapter 18

Bye-the-way, How does the Cotton Grow?

Soul Mate

So, it is with Woman I find friendship.
And with it, the keys to eternity.

The rose, her essence of beauty
Is the fragrance of all life.

To all who have hated Woman,
She shall own you as she owned her children.

Woman, my mate
My soul

(poetry in seeing the travail of woman ca.1990)

    In the fifteen years that followed before Lester's death, we both found something in each other that neither of us had ever known. We were really friends for the first time in my life, but it was never the lost "father-son" relationship that I had yearned to experience. Neither of us wanted nor now needed to resurrect that lost experience. About three or four years before he died (losing his battle with Alzheimer's), I came to visit him to say goodbye while he still knew me. I talked about jobs and business deals.
    Cheerfully, he lapsed into another old discussion about churches and religion He kept saying "I'm getting ready to run up to Wellington and see that guy."
"What guy, Dad?"
"Oh, you know, that guy out West."
Hmm, out West? I pondered the significance of "out West." I couldn't

figure out what he was saying until I realized that he was having a reoccurring memory of his first church – a tiny church in the tiny West Texas town of Wellington. That's when you know you are dealing with big Al (Alzheimer's disease). I did say goodbye, but I don't think he got it.

I did the same with Mary, a few years later, visiting her in her nursing home, telling her that I wanted to say goodbye while we were both lucid and could answer and discuss any lingering questions either of us might have. There were none. She gave me her love, and I her.

Mary died in the winter of 2004. Lester died in the fall of that same year. My sibling Robert conducted both burials

---

I guess my resurrected Jesus didn't need that father/son relationship either. You know what I mean, God-the-father/Jesus-the-son, abandoned at the cross. The child of God who was left to die, I could go on and on. It was sort of like we were business associates. I guess my relationship with Lester in the final phase of his life was: "I'm ok, you're ok." Nothing ever changed. His emotions remained the same. His memes reinforced the responses. "Operant conditioning," sayeth B.F. Skinner.

After that, we never talked about personal religion again. The effect of my freedom from his perpetual religious state of being was ecstatic and transcendent.

And temporal.

My Jesus trust (that dreamy promise that all things work together for good for those who love him) was betrayed in the real world once again. Oh well, this was the Jesus drama as anyone who ever played a leading role in WWJD has experienced. I was testing Jesus as he was testing me. Life goes on.

So, with the "just business" as a life model, I filed two lawsuits, one in state court and one in federal court and promptly won an $820,000 judgment in federal court. I also won back what was left of my old company in state court, mostly consisting of the intellectual property (IP) I had previously conveyed to it. The judge determined that the acts of Board of Directors were so deceptive and criminal that she applied sanctions against all who were involved. She also determined that my removal was so inappropriate that she reinstated me for the period that I had been removed. She ruled that I effectively had remained the sole officer and director of the company, which she handed back to me from the hands of BoD's fraudulent actions.

A small victory for ten years of work on that one!

By then, they had filed Chapter 7 Bankruptcy.

There was so little left to work with. The company was broke and in Chapter 7 bankruptcy. The company that I had worked so hard for and had given so much technology to had declared bankruptcy before I could return and restart it. Kicked to the curb once more. When do I get this? I kept thinking.

WWJD?

Two years later, Dorothy Louise and I were finally able to buy the assets of my old company from the Bankruptcy Trustee. We planned to use it as a "shell company," a new investment and to establish a new business based on what we bought back from the Trustee of the Court.

So, I took over. But the lawsuit to recover the lost royalties on one of my patents that the company had depended upon for a revenue stream remained unsettled. This was where the $20 million came in. We sued the licensee that had defaulted on royalty payments connected to one of my patents and the patented product that was protected by it.

I filed a $20 million lawsuit against a big Utah company that had taken the product to market but had defaulted on paying its royalties. The meme that compelled my dramatic action was…um, David slaying Goliath. It was first imprinted when I was about four-years-old, I think.

I may be repeating this, but I had to do it. There is no life without experience. Experience is the "cost of doing the business" of life. Someone once said, "life without experience is simply life as a philosophy" and further, "philosophy without experience is simply ignorance."

Life is obtained at a price – let there be no misunderstanding. During this experience, in the summer of 2010, my sister Mary Helen decided to hold a family reunion at her and husband Paul's beautiful lake-side home on Flathead Lake in Kalispell, Montana.

Expecting to be met as the usual "lost" member of the tribal family, I put off accepting the invitation until the spring of that year. Upon finally accepting I got a group letter from my loving, ever-so-authoritative sibling, Mary Helen, instructing all "senior" family members, meaning all of us bros (Donald, Robert, and me) to write a short memoir of our life to date.

She thought "it would be fun" to read "a page or two" aloud to the entire gathering. Why I accepted this additional karma, I can only attribute to the idea that I'd already for two years prior thought of writing my own life's story, if for nothing else, to commit to paper a memory of the past. This would be my motivation.

I had begun working on a draft a few weeks before, but only a couple of weeks before we were to leave did I feverishly come up with anything like a semi-coherent memoir. That decision, dear reader, is the reason you are reading what you are reading today.

I decided to tell it like it was and is without the exaggerated sugar coating that I always heard tell as a church lad when Lester (or any other preacher) would tell a story of an experience he had, invariably telling it to picture himself as blessed in the very best of light. That memory had been my meme for self-promotion as a blessed creature.

The little 68-page story kick-started my memoir. It's more than that now. I wrote it partially as justification for leaving Pentecostalism and the family religion. I called my story "Escaping Pentecostalism". Unfortunately, leaving my religion was the same as leaving family. You see, the story just kept unraveling, going and going, one painful revelation after another. We all gathered in Kalispell at Paul and Mary Helen's beautiful lakehome on Flat Head Lake. There's more to this little gathering a couple of chapters ahead.

So now, for the trial.

Picking up four years later in August 2015, I had just returned from Salt Lake City where my first lawsuit was filed in August 2005. Since I had been in the court and had worked ten years, I expected to get justice. (Just as you might expect Jesus would do had he petitioned Pilot's Court after the resurrection.)

The lawsuit was an attempt to collect unpaid royalties on a patented dietary supplement that I invented and licensed to the big company in Salt Lake City. We were asking for $20 million.

There is not too much to say about the trial other than we seemed to be fortunate to have a good Mormon judge. What I didn't know at the time was all the Board of Directors of the big pharmaceutical firm that I sued were all "Mormon elders," and well…enough said.

Of course, I did not know how the trial would result, but we laid out conclusive evidence to the court that my company was owed at least $6 million dollars out of an original complaint for $20 million. Throughout the trial, my original exclusive license agreement was put before the Court.

We pounded away with our argument that the three amendments purposed by the Defendants which my company willingly reviewed and discussed but never accepted should have been sterling evidence of continuing warranting of the original covenants. The defendants had but one witness, and he was the founder, Chairman, and CEO of the company. The royalty agreement had never changed and was never rejected as evidence of the "plain reading" of the royalty agreement.

My patent attorney was brought in and testified as to writing the original draft that was hardly changed from its earliest form. Then, another attorney of ours testified to the difficulty in trying to deal with the defendants who never returned phone calls, who would not see our erstwhile President of my company and the company attorney.

We showed the Court how the opposition CEO of the Defendant company failed to pay my company royalties and would not take telephone calls regarding payment. Even after finally setting an appointment with my company's President and attorney and making the long trip from Houston to Salt Lake City, upon arriving, we were told the CEO was "too busy to see you.". They had no choice other than to turn around and return to Houston.

We even showed the Court that the opposing party had filed an almost duplicate USPTO patent application on a "knock-off" product to the licensed product and in doing so, glaringly demonstrated the malicious intent to commit a fraudulent act. All of this was brought out in the three days of testimony.

On the other side, the only evidence laid before the Court was the testimony of the old Chairman of the Board and CEO who took the stand to testify that he "never considered the contract to be exclusive." He testified that he told the president of my company that he was not going to abide by the contract that he signed. But he never formally (in writing) notified my company that either (1) the contract was terminated, or (2) that he was not going to pay the minimum royalties provided for in the contract. This illegitimate action did not terminate an on-going contract, especially since he was surrounded by his own attorneys.

The trial was enormously taxing for me emotionally. Yet, dragging myself back to Texas on a late flight in the middle of the night, I somehow felt that an enormous emotional and personal victory had been won. After a few days' rest, the inner feeling continued to grow more positive each day. What a feeling! The clouds of depression were swept away, anxiety over the next step in my life was nowhere to be found. What…a…relief! I just knew that I had won my case.

Until I lost.

Buzz! (wrong)

Story-book faith in action.

The judge sent the case back to the "cartographer," meaning that the case was to be re-litigated from the initial development of the royalty agreement forward. I had already spent about $300,000 on attorneys over seven years of litigation and was nearly broke. The lawyers demanded another $50,000 to file the inevitable appeal.

I settled our lawsuit with a simple return of my intellectual property and the patent for (US Patent Number 7,074,812) the online sports and exercise dietary supplement that had grossed over $10,000,000 its first two years on the market; no money, and no more attorney fees.

Here I was, having worked for 14 years in a WWJD dream-state and still thinking about all the good things I wanted to do when I grew up (thinking into the future) just like I did as a child. I just couldn't help myself.

What is this thing called "tomorrow?" I asked.

The answer quickly came back - "it is an illusion, always somewhere out there beyond today."

And then, "keep the faith, brother!" I learned an invaluable lesson.

Chapter 19

Keeping the Faith

Souls and Karma

There is in every man's soul to give
From the depository of dreams of those
Who came before and sought this solace from within
To use, to live and ultimately forgive
Over and over.

"Oh, I've done you wrong?" Nah.
Just following my destiny's script.

Then let us re-write it together.
Playing the cards dealt
Let us begin with a new contract

That love shall rule our karmic actions
There are no rights or wrongs
Our tribes can meet
And be friends.

And If you want
And we can form a pact.
To follow Soul In peace.

(poem on beginning once again, life ca. 2010)

Let me say a word about faith. Of course, I still have faith…faith in the goodness of others…faith in myself and most of all, faith that whatever I do in the "now" (the present) is in the "will of God." I don't worry that Jesus may return in the night and I may have forgotten to repent of my daily sins. I live life as I encounter it. Without trepidation or regret.

Religion is built on a different kind of faith. It is the taught belief that we must live according to teachings of ancient, Middle Eastern Jewish tribesmen/fishermen/priests that controlled tribal social activities with ceremonious rules and regulations that benefited (mostly) the ruling class of Jews who constituted the priestly families. It meted out terrible punishment for disobedience – like killing an entire tribe of people for the sins of one of the members. It motivated a lot of simple, gut fear. Hence, religions motivate fear. It's not that fear that my faith delivers me from. It is the faith based on an illusion that the myth (or biblical story) is their highest truth. Believe the story, and you have faith. It requires a belief in symbols. The symbolic miracles demonstrated to the believer that his faith is "true." Unfortunately, it is not the faith that God has produced the power of the story in you.

It is that the story has produced something to believe and that belief becomes the foundation of your faith. In other words, it is coming from the outside in…not from the inside out.

And, oh yes, God spoke to them in an audible voice…out of a burning bush to Abraham or from Mount Sinai to Moses and responded to his voice by parting the Red Sea as they exited out of Egypt. Almost all these stories are either told in earlier civilizations such as the Sumerians, Persians, Greeks, or other versions in historical chronicles in man's mythologies.

The Old Testament is full of audible words from God spoken to people who believed that they were conversing directly with Him. But, so were all the other cultures and civilizations who had Gods who "spoke." God "talked" to them all. Not just God, but their idols spoke as well.

I cannot accept words that are spoken out of what we know were hallucination states interpreted as God speaking any more than I can accept the glossolalia or speaking in tongues as divine communications. It may feel divine to the individual who is speaking, but it no more divine than a preacher who convinces himself that he is replacing Jesus as the oracle of Christ. If one looks at tea leaves long enough, one will find some divine message.

But bear with me on this topic a little while longer. This doesn't mean that the stories of the words heard were not true, it simply means that acting upon one's instincts is sometimes mistaken for "God told me…" but if you can't bring God along as your witness, even better, as Jesus said, bring "two or more believers" that also hear God's words, then it is a hallucination.

Those that say, "God told me to tell you this…" are just hallucinating within the chambers of their mind. BTW, if God wanted me to know what he told you to tell me, then why didn't he just tell me? I plan to write about that at another time. In the meantime, if one wishes to delve into the thoughts of these primitive men now, one might read Julian Jaynes book *The Origin of Consciousness – In the Breakdown of the Bicameral Mind* (Houghton Mifflin Company, New York, ISBN 0-618-05707-2).

Jaynes graphically details how the ancient Sumerians, Persians, Greeks, Egyptians, and even tribal Semites (who came a little later, originally called the Khabirus) all heard voices which we now know from ancient hieroglyphics, Sumerian cuneiform, and other proto-literate writings and symbols both originated and terminated within their minds.

According to Jaynes, the Old Testament also indicated that one of the types of idol referred to as the Terap could speak (Ezekiel 21:21) and describes the King of Babylon as consulting with several of them. Further direct evidence comes from America. The conquered Aztecs told the Spanish invaders how their history began when a statue from a ruined temple belonging to a previous culture spoke to the leaders. It commanded them to cross the lake from where they were, and to carry its statue with them wherever they went, directing them hither and thither, even as the yet unembodied bicameral voices led Moses zigzagging across the Sinai desert.

There was no "voice" coming from the outside that was ever verified by a co-witness who was not himself part of the hallucination. There was evocation, but no counter-argument to the cultural conclusion. Primitive man only spoke in symbolized speech and spoke in left-brain, linear thought processing. His speech came from left-brain memes, originalized in meme symbols formed from neural arrays of memory. The memes formed left-brain dominant/linear/logical-thinking neural nexi that controlled his outer reality. Early man was symbolically rational. He sequenced one meme after another.

But these were not sequences of words.

It might be more accurate to say they were sequences of memories. Men and women were not conscious as we are and were not responsible for their actions; therefore, they cannot be given the credit nor blame for anything that was done over the vast millennia of time.

Instead, Jaynes tells us, each person had a part of his nervous system which was "divine," by which he was ordered about like any slave, a voice or voices which indeed were what we call volition and empowered what they commanded and were related to the hallucinated voices of others in a carefully established hierarchy.

To use these examples today as models for behavior and to conceptualize a divinity to seek and obey in today's world is like early explorers setting out on the vast stretches of ocean with no more than simple compass and sundials seeking discoveries of the new worlds (new truths).

The opposite hemisphere (right brain) of the mind simply conceptualized reality into groups of emotions of the thinker. His mind did not begin to rationalize thoughts within the dominant, thinking hemisphere until a millennium or two later. When it did, the dawn of self-realization and consciousness began. The neocortex of the brain began to communicate in a new way – crossing the corpus callosum -- a holistic and contextual process that heralded the origin of self-consciousness and the ability to see oneself as others see you, self-realization.

According to Jaynes, the primitive proto-conscious man only spoke in symbolized meanings which conveyed language in linear stream-of-consciousness based on the memes of five emotional senses, and no more. All his thoughts were sequential. For example, he notices a particular rock which brings forth a memory, and then a meme-image of an ax, which brings forth the meme-image of a piece of wood or the head of a fish, which then brings forth a feeling of hunger, etc. The words for such memes were exclusively captured by the senses of sound and hearing, not mental rationalization as we know it. They were mono syllogisms and guttural expressions that coincided with the meme that was prominent in the consciousness.

In his captivating book, Jaynes details graphically how the ancient Sumerians, Persians, Greeks, Egyptians, and, of course, the ancient tribal Semites who became Hebrews heard voices which we now know both originated and terminated within their minds. Some saw outside their heads like Moses and the burning bush.

Jaynes details how these ancient cultures captured the sounds of thunder, screaming wind, the burst of lighting, the groan of trees of the forest, the startled surprise of a wild animal, an eclipse of the sun and moon, into a sort of narrativization. Narrativization is a single word for an extremely complex set of patterning abilities (memes) which have multiple ancestries arising as a codification of which later evolved into proto-speech which had no conceptual meaning in the present tense, only in the past tense.

Why no ability to converse in the present tense? Because his right brain hemisphere had not learned to cross the corpus callosum bridge in his brain, thus, bringing to his left brain the conceptual memes and memories needed for a holistic realization of the event in real time. In fact, ancient man had no subjective consciousness until the barriers of the bi-cameral mind began to break down.

As the paleontology of consciousness slowly developed onto crude markings and cuneiform symbols, then upon early parchment that conveyed the awakening of self-consciousness (self-realization) that Sumerians, Persians, Greeks and even Hebrews experienced early as voices of the gods heard as sort of a "mindfulness" which we now know was a sort of ongoing hallucination.

I join with Jaynes in believing there was no voice of God coming from outside the mind. There was evocation, but never counter-argument to the cultural conclusions. The primitive man only thought from out of his rationalization-forming, logical left brain, the opposite hemisphere of which simply conceptualized sensory recollections into a repertoire of emotions of the thinker. It did not rationalize with the dominant, logical thinking hemisphere. This side of mind was quiet when the subject spoke.

As Jaynes writes, these expressions, around four to five thousand years ago, were of early myths, dictated by so-called gods, the gods themselves taking the place of consciousness.

Jaynes writes, "If we erase all our preconceptions…except for its later accretion, the epic (speaking of the Iliad but just as likely the early biblical books) itself was consciously composed, not consciously remembered but was successively and creatively changed with no more awareness than a pianist has of his improvisation."

"Who then were these gods that pushed men about like robots and sang epics through their lips? They were voices, whose speech and directions could be as distinctly heard by the Iliadic [and biblical] heroes as voices are heard by epileptic and schizophrenic patients, or just as Joan of Arc heard her voices. The gods were an organization of the central nervous system and can be regarded as personae in the sense of poignant consistencies through time amalgam of parental or admonitory images [and voices.]

The god is a part of man, and quite consistent with this conception *is the fact that the gods never step outside of natural laws."* (Emphasis mine)

As the bicameral mind (left-brain/right-brain) broke down and the two hemispheres of the frontal lobes of the brain began to communicate with each other across the corpus callosum in synchronistic congruency and harmony, precipitating the rise of human self-consciousness, time, as we see it, commenced.

To have consciousness, one must first develop self-awareness. One can only have this "gift" when both hemispheres of one's brain commence to communicate with its opposite hemisphere. In other words, the two hemispheres of the mind must first get acquainted with each other. Then self-realization begins.

Immanent means all-pervasive and inherent in, and spread throughout something else — it's innate, intrinsic, inborn, and eternal. Immanence is truth. It describes God if you need such a description. This is not the god of sight and sound, only speaking and controlling through the five senses. Immanence is beyond that.

The immanent God does not speak to man in pithy metaphors or amalgams instructing one tribe to go kill all the men, women, children, cattle and burn the homes and fields. These biblical passages cannot be read in any other context than tribal stories embodying popular ideas on natural or supernatural and social phenomenon.

Can anyone find a single instance where Jesus said that God (the Father) told him to say or do anything? No! Jesus simply acted out his life on the stage of moral judgment and understanding of human nature. He knew that he was divine just as anyone who puts faith in the immanent nature of God. But I'm being preachy now.

Let us go further with Jaynes. "Consciousness" is a much smaller portion of our mental life than we are conscious of because we cannot be conscious of what we are NOT conscious of.

How simple, that is to say, how difficult it is to appreciate. It is like asking a flashlight in a dark room to search around for something that does not have any light shining upon it. The flashlight, since there is light in whatever direction it turns, would have to conclude that there is light everywhere. And so, consciousness can seem to pervade all mentality, when it does not."

How embarrassingly profound!

The immanent and eternally present have been with us always as omnipresence. The dynamics of the present here and now is the universal force that co-creates omnipotence and synergizes the positive actions of man. This is called co-creation. The true immanence simply observes, just as nature observes the negative actions (perturbations) but adds no synergy to it. Like a stone thrown into a pond, the waves only represent the perturbation of the water. Since there is no right or wrong action, the waves soon settle back to homeostasis. (Of course, there's always that lesson to be learned in expending unnecessary negative energy.) For example, the man fishing in the pond below the stone. His fishing may be ruined for the day!

This concept of God is denied by most religions.

Religion, especially those that lean toward fundamentalism and literalism, have an inherent need to be emotionally attached to a personal god, a god whom you can call by name, a god whom one can ask favors, seek advice, do good deeds for, or generally worship as a sort of super parent. On the other hand, the immanent God is not a person but an omnipresent intelligence and omnipotent energy.

Like the voice that is produced by a radio frequency, in all dimensions, it is an electromagnetic transmission of the truth of all that is and all that will be contained within the vibrations of electronic particles and atoms of the universe. And yet, it is more than that. Who knows what other dimensions of space, time, and energy God may present Itself? But one thing is certain: God is beyond the limits of religion.

Even "mainline" religions see God as a personal being or He-who-is

Elohim, Yahweh Jehovah, Jesus, or Allah. (I did not include the Gods of Asia which would add about six or seven more to the list of mythical gods.) All of these Gods exist within a story or myth with an evidential paper product (Christian New Testament, Torah, Koran) providing proof-of concept by the literal reading of repetitive, humanized stories of (mostly) male genderization and divine patriarchy.

Jaynes continues, "'He-who-is'" [Elohim, Yahweh, etc.] is a visual physical presence, the duplication of his creation. He walks in his garden at the cool of the day, talking to his recent creation, Adam. He is present and visible at the sacrifice of Cane and Abel, shuts the door of Noah's Ark with his own hand, speaks with Abraham at Shechem, Bethel, and Hebron, and scuffles all night with Jacob like a hoodlum."

There is no subjective self to narratives into a relationship with these descriptions of God. There is only obedience.

Jaynes writes of Moses, saying that only in a single instance does he (Moses) only speak of God (Elohim) "face-to-face, "as a man speaketh to his friend." (Exodus 33:11 KJV) And another time, there is a group hallucination when Moses and the seventy elders all see He-who-is (Elohim) at a distance standing on sapphire pavement (Exodus 24:9-10). But that ended the intimacy with God. Subsequently, in all the other instances, the hallucinated meeting is less intimate. Visually, He-who-is is a burning bush, or a cloud, or a huge pillar of fire. And as visually, the bicameral experience recedes into the thick darkness, where thunders, and flashes of lightning and driving clouds of dense blackness crowd in on the inaccessible heights of Sinai. Here I must pause.

We approach the greatest teaching of the entire Old Testament, that, as the last of the Elohim loses his hallucinatory properties and is no longer an accessible voice in the nervous system of a few semi-bicameral men and becomes something written upon tablets, he becomes law, something unchanging, approachable by all, something relating to all men equally, king and shepherd, universal and transcendent."

This is God for whom most of the world still yearns, yearning for that illusionary experience of Moses, Noah, and Jacob that is gone forever. But yearning is the limit of this existence. And until man finds himself, he will never find God. Like the flashlight example shining around a dark room, the only mental conclusion is that there is light everywhere. There is not.

On the other hand, the Immanent God that is, "IS" the entirety of all, without a hierarchy, without hordes of worshiping invisible beings called angels, or sacrificial sons, or slaves or a competitor called the devil, or even having the need for a time of past or future. Believing in this God, there is no yearning for divine perfection or a sinless existence because the immanent God is…what you are or (fill in any blank).

To put this simply…God IS. How can one write of the totality of the immanent God? And get this…the immanent God is completely verifiable and provable at any given moment since, like quantum time, which does not exist until observed, neither does the immanent God in man until one observes the moment! But IT's there! The physical reality of the immanent God in the observable moment. It is, then, the cooperation of life in the here and now.

This puts the emphasis on the synthesis of omnipotent intellectual comprehension. The immanent God doesn't need a religion to give to mankind an illusionary burning bush, a talking snake, or a cloud of fire, immanence provides reality in any given moment in that it is inherent to be. The Immanent God encompasses the love of Christ of the past and future. Just like the present moment, immanence has the same quality and cannot exist or be imagined without the here and now. Is the present moment real? Yes. Is the past moment real? No. Is the future moment beyond the present moment real? No. Reality exists in only the moment here and now, the present moment. So, look no further.

Religion's contemporary Gods are the telling/preaching/teaching of ancient moralistic stories with crass quid pro quo of the recipient's behavior. "Salvation" is based on how well one can promote his act of becoming "saved" on the stage of life that best reflects these ancient truths. This is a God that lives in its beginnings (the creationist God) but needs a past and future (or time) to exist.

This type of religious "faith" is life in the futuristic lane and regret in the past. It's like a contract business deal where you are working for an "outcome." In Fundamentalist Christianity, you arrive at the altar of salvation a worthless, pitiful sinner, (already born in sin, thus, just being born is a "breaker" of God's laws) until you are saved(!) from this worthless condition. Then, you must commit to a lifelong contract to pay for your salvation by acting a certain way, and you are paid (rewarded) by God for your daily work. A version of this contract is called the true believer's faith. A true believer sees God as doing everything for him or her, continually sending tests, temptations, disease, pain, suffering, but also, answering his/her prayers. If not here on earth, then (pardon me, OMG) in Heaven, behind large pearly gates that keep the Devil out!

That's fine and good for the immature intellect of parent/child dynamic, (divine father God/human child of God) but living entirely by the hope and faith in tomorrow's future (God's goodwill or grace) which leaves one (the human being) as a child of God in perpetual child-like dependency. Not to say that one may, over time, adjust to begging the parental God for sustenance (think Mother Teresa or the Little Sisters of the Poor) but it's not what Jesus demonstrated in his life. There is no "grown-up, Adult God" in this room (read: state of consciousness) where…

…there is no room for an adult.

Living in the present now is different. When filled with the sense of the immanent Christ, one encounters love that doesn't leave you when you walk out of the church doors; you need no book of dos and don'ts. This is unconditional love. This divine, unconditional love lingers and lives in you, and your life results in right living -- naturally. It is not a love of superiority over those religion considers "lost" i.e. "the world" or even those who one knows are truly seeking the love of Christ. It is love that simply encompasses everything else. This love conflates with the divine immanence of eternity. There is no death in this love.

Living in this truthful reality inevitably puts one on a different plane of experience than those around them. There are times and places when even the perception of truth differs markedly between one's self and those around you. This experience is exemplified as the time when Jesus and the disciples were out on the sea fishing and a storm arose unexpectedly. The disciples saw big waves and feared for their lives. Jesus saw a calm and peaceful sea and then demonstrated faith in what he saw by walking out on the sea. Jesus rebuked his disciples and asked in Mathew 8 "Why are you fearful, oh you of little faith?"

Jesus was not attempting to belittle his disciples by remarking on their lack of faith. One sees the bigger picture since Jesus was co-creating the entire dramatic event in cooperation with the immanent God. He was attempting to lure, attract, or otherwise induce his followers to the calm and peaceful state of perfect faith that he, Jesus, was experiencing.

How does this same spirit of Christ affect us now, some 21 centuries after his death? By understanding that love is something that is made. It does not exist until the idea or the desire to "love" has been developed through desire, will, intention and self-sacrifice. It comes from the will of man.

Simply put, you can't love someone or something without some sacrifice of yourself to that loved one or loved thing. The eternal mystery is how Jesus, a lowly Semite, who was not even of the priestly order, came to fulfill his mission of demonstrating a love so high in the realm of consciousness that it hasn't been yet over-reached by anyone else in history. Many of the early saints acted out this historical drama, but few even know the names of the thousands of martyrs who also en defacto gave their lives. Then, why Jesus? He desired, willed, and intended to sacrifice himself in order to demonstrate love to the world. It was the only way the merit-believing Jews could understand the process and subsequently, mankind coming later could understand. If one of us tried to do the same, we would be picked up and put into a mental health hospital and put on suicide watch. As the saying goes, you will know it when you see it. Love is the magical key to all our needs, wants, and being.

Love is the quantum field of all potentiality.

Co-creating with the immanent God of the here and now produces life based on what is commonly called the real world. It is what happens in the present moment to make life fit your needs. Needs are always fulfilled. No one has any needs in the present moment. But one may certainly have wants.

Wants are different from needs. Wants are desires of the imagination. The place for wants is in the quantum potential (spirit) and should be left there to be fulfilled in due course. There ought not to be a continuous attachment (binding/longing) to one's wants. Living in a state of wants is simply living a vain, glorious life. If you are religious, pray for them and leave them there with God. Or, if you don't believe much in prayer, put your wants into the quantum field of all potential and leave them there. It is the same thing. In Christianity, your needs are known before you ask. (Mathew 6:8 KJV)

As I said, needs are different. They are already fulfilled by the immanent God. So, if you live "as if" it is already here in the present here and now, your needs are always met; you become self-realized with what you idealized; you are then a co-creator with God Now, let's return to the story.

The Court's decision was not in my favor, but it was not in their favor either, as you may have thought. The following is rather hard to read, so if you would rather skip over dull Court proceedings and its relationship to my life…feel free to pass go and go directly to the next chapter.

To sum up, the judge was unable to decide on who was right and who was wrong, so he sent the case back to the beginning and instructed the writer of the original document (my patent attorney) to re-write the agreement. Then, the judge said, we could resubmit our claim and start the litigation all over again (after already having spent eleven years in litigation). I kid you not!

I guess, had I won, I would not have written this tell-all story of my life…hmm, I could think of better things to do perhaps, like sitting on a beach somewhere down in the Caribbean with a cool drink in my hand.

Wouldn't you? Yet in reality, the decision was in my favor as a needed life lesson. But certainly not in my favor as what I wanted. My want was an illusion. I hardly needed "all that money." So, why did I want "all that money?" I don't know, but I certainly learned a brutally honest lesson – I was chasing the future which was an illusion. I had gotten out of my treasured here and now present. (And I secretly knew it in my subconscious mind.) I hope that will be my last lesson on chasing wants. The Court had given me my patent and other intellectual property back; so, for my part, the case was closed. I was back to where I had started.

So, it was, back to the same day-by-day living that I had been living the past 13 years. But, guess what? I won anyway. I won a hard lesson in the here and now but failed a hard lesson in the value of illusion of the future. Is that sort of like trying to get to heaven by doing all the right things?

It feels like many years have passed since I last entered statements into this chronicle of life-as-I-lived-it. But it's only been a few days, weeks, and months since I abruptly learned that lesson; in fact, it was in the same moment of thought, when I began again to apply the life-lessons that I have learned.

First, there have been no pass/fail experiences in my life. There have only been lessons. This is the world of duality; cause and effect are of the same dynamic and only exist in a world of the five senses. As a co-creator with the immanent God there are simply experiences that we are destined to have; all have been steps out of this world of cause and effect, heaven or hell, the place of bliss or eternal torment, in finding the abode of God, still just a day away from today's here and now experience.

If you can get this one thing in your head: live above cause and effect. Nothing you can do in this Newtonian world can escape this duality of life forces, of life in the cause and effect. But you make the decision to participate in the action. Yes, you can at least decide where in life you want to live. You can simply detach, or if the action is habitual, then break the chains of enslavement. As one breaks the bonds of attachment, then one begins to live on the mental plane which sees the real world of rational reality. Yes, you can get above the five senses, above the emotional memes, the world of stimulus/effect (the B.F. Skinner world of operant conditionalism (see Operant Conditioning, J.E.R. Staddon and D.T. Cerutti, Annu Rev Psychol 2003, 54; 115-144) or simply just Google it. (I'll talk about this in just a minute).

Then, when you become cognizant of this habitual behavior, break it!

Apply reverse behavior to your habit until you become free. Give it a try.

Give my theory a chance and live in my conclusions; experience that bliss that is found in this moment and not dependent on some future moment of arrival of a paid-up (through good works and prayer) ticket to paradise, a mindset some even believe is bought by martyrdom, others by purchased streets of gold by righteous living.

Yes, being Jesus in the future, culminating in "losing" a $20 million case I fought so long and hard to win…even lived, in those last few weeks in a sort of a contrived state of here and now ecstasy, was exactly the wrong way to live in the present and was itself, a "come to Jesus" moment. I surmise that the moment was the equivalent "feeling of living" with $20 million dollars that I had wanted and even expected to soon be in the bank, was…well, like living in the moment of fabulous wealth. What else could I possibly desire? Was I high or dreaming?

No.

I was betting a win-lose crap game that told me that Jesus wanted me to be rich. I thought that I had been an impoverished follower of the biblical version of believer long enough, yes, sort of the "last shall be first and the first shall be last" thing. I imagined Jesus sitting right next to me at that crap table! I never really considered whether the Jesus part of me did or did not need all that money to be complete and fulfilled. And of course, to be what I imagined rich was, was not the lesson that I needed to learn.

What's the difference between the reality of $2 dollars, $2 million dollars or $20 million, and the here and now bliss of experiencing the same emotional feeling of, well, abundance? Does Jesus really need $20 million to be what he is?

I can tell you, my friends, there is no difference when you are living life…as if. Jesus didn't need any of that money he scattered on the floor of the temple, did he? The bible doesn't say that he stopped to pick any of it up, does it?

To say that I lost the case is a misnomer or inaccurate description because I never had the real world $20 million to lose. You see, I had never had those millions of dollars that I sued for. I sued for the potential value that I perceived I had lost. I went after the proverbial "pie in the sky."

So, take a deep breath and let's continue if you understand what I've been saying. If you don't, go back and read this chapter again because this is where most "Christians" fall flat.

Life goes on and the disappointment I experienced is now an ever dulling lesson when I choose to bring it back to my awareness. But the need for $20 million doesn't exist. I will continue to act out each day whether it be posting my succinct little comments on Facebook or getting into pithy little arguments over "first cause, the observer, and/or evolution v. creationism" as I am sometimes prone to do. Maybe I still occasionally need those mental exercises of futility. As B.F. Skinner said, "my actions were a response to mentally operant conditioning." To say it another way, I acted to satisfy the disappointment meme in my behavior that I subliminally expected to receive. And this invariably became the operant outcome. My old religion helped me out a lot on that one.

The quantum physicist in me says that if you are serious about using this dimension of power in life, you must mentally project (visualize) a manifestation of your need into the quantum field of all potentiality, i.e., such as a thought that would fulfill that need, and feel the emotional manifestation of that fulfillment coming back to you as acknowledgment of your action. It's called the Helsingborg Principal (without that emotional feeling part). When you confirm the thought by feeling it emotionally, you have instantly collapsed the universal wave of electrons and protons that make up the field of all potentiality, and you now have manifested it (at least conceptually) into a real manifestation of materiality.

Yes, collapsing the wave of all potentiality of the universe, in that moment, creates a real manifestation. The more one does that, the more the visualization of what they want becomes real. To me, a person who uses quantum mechanics for personal fulfillment is doing something almost totally identical to praying to God for something that one does not yet have. The visualization is the act of exercising one's faith and believing that you will receive evokes the manifestation of feeling.

"Ask and it shall be given unto you, Seek and ye shall find." Of course, that was what Jesus said some 21 centuries before his time. You have used the power of your divine volition in the quantum field.

And the effect is the same. If you need it, well, it's already here. You only need to use your volition to receive it.

If you want it, well, perhaps you'll have to wait until the Spirit (quantum field) has it ready for you.

But to the purest, using the quantum field of all potentiality as the source for all manifestation is quite different than praying to God and asking for something. Just asking God can then turn into a motive for good behavior, correct? ("God, I'll change my ways, but I need a really good bank account and a new car.")

But, if you believe in God as immanent, being good doesn't do much to buy God's favor. Whatever you are trying to buy from God has already been given to you. The manifestation comes when you surrender yourself, unconditionally, to the immanence of the living presence of God. The unity of science and religion and the mental similarities are almost identical and are almost too good to be true! The quantum field of all potentiality is that field of uncertainty that will manifest just the same as the "Holy Spirit" does (or God/Jesus does) when one prays continuously, "believing, they shall receive."

The difference is that one who is co-creating with the immanent God has already created his/her need/fulfillment.

According to all the popular religious and spiritual gurus, all I needed do during those 13 years of legal process was to project the "abundance of $20 million" into the here and now of my meditations and contemplations. "God wants to pour out his riches on you…," I heard the televangelists all say. But, I really didn't need $20 million. I wanted $20 million, but again, I didn't need $20 million. So, I acted like I needed it. It didn't work. It was a lie, a staged drama on the stage of life. It was the same play that runs over and over in most people's lives, acting like you need something when you really don't need it.

Abundance is simply freedom and fulfillment, is it not? And freedom and fulfillment is joy.

If I was fulfilled by the pursuit, then I was fulfilled, right? How does one who has never had (nor needed) such riches know to project such a desire for riches? Will having a fat bank account provide a continuous plethora of positive feelings? No, one simply projects abundance now, in the here and now of this moment, and leaves it there. If it is a real need, you already have it, you just need to receive it. If it is a want, well, get ready to wait until you are truly ready for it.

Meanwhile, back to being Jesus in my own skin brings me to the little book by Jim Palmer, "Being Jesus in Nashville," (iUniverse.com, Bloomington paperback edition) which I just read, (and he wrote in 2012). I wish I could have read something like that when I was cruising around the early 70's saying the same thing and trying to avoid the slammer.

Really! I thought being Jesus was the loneliest job in the universe. And I also thought that anyone who claimed to be God was a dead man walking. But Palmer says on page 52 of his book, "I felt that God and I had become one. I didn't find that Jesus line and cross it; there was no Jesus line to cross. The moment I opened my heart to the love that is God, the line merely disintegrated. There was no longer separation between God and me—it was no longer "I" who lived, but Christ—the very nature and essence of God—living in me and as me."

Nowhere in his book did I find that Jim also had the fear of "the Father" that I had back in the 70s by claiming that I was God. I truly felt that I would die for being Jesus.

But I did find a fellow-Jesus traveler in Jim Palmer. On page 126 of his book he goes back to the 1st century when he says, "Although his disciples would grieve his death, Jesus spoke of resurrection and how his spirit would continue in and through any who had the faith to believe—to believe that Jesus' spirit was inside them to believe that Jesus *was* them."

(Emphasis mine)

Then Jim says: "I am Jesus."

Oh, it's so good to hear you say that, Jim. I thought I was the only person in the world going around making that statement!

I think I differ slightly with Jim on his statement on the next page, saying "Being Jesus means…letting go of Jesus."

Yes, you can "let go of Jesus," but the changes made in your life by being Jesus remain. By whatever title you use, that vessel of clay remains energized, inspired, and (to use an old fundamentalist word) sanctified as Jesus. To me then, the greatest gift that remains is the choice of when to be Jesus.

Being Jesus, I COULD NOT LIE! Smoking a marijuana cigarette during the Reagan era and hearing Secretary of education William (Bill) Bennett) casually say on NBC's *Meet the Press* one Sunday that "maybe we should have a few hangings on public squares to show these hippie drug users we mean business" in the war on drugs, was certainly anxiety inducing. Furthermore, being Jesus and witnessing young black males (and a few white males) being shot for not quite responding politely to a white police officer or having one joint in possession and being beaten and thrown in jail was not conducive to a calm state of being.

I was insanely open about my marijuana use. After all, I was Jesus. In fact, while living in San Francisco in the early 70's, I smoked openly on the streets. When I migrated back to Texas, this was almost a suicidal proposition. I was just as insanely open about being Jesus, and that provoked a similar reaction. I don't smoke pot openly anymore; in fact, I hardly smoke at all. I think the last time I passed a joint was with my two grandsons on Christmas in 2016.

And I am not Jesus openly much anymore; it's too much drama, and it's now vanity. What's more, I don't have to. Like Jim said in his experience, the Jesus that I once was is the same Jesus that I am today. That mission is over. I've been to the cross. Jesus is in the here and now… anytime you are *at-one-ment* with the Immanent Christ.

So, life goes on.

While it's on my mind, I must elaborate on the state of truth that is the overpowering instinct of being Jesus. In Christ, there is no false state of being. You simply MUST be truthful in all your dealings just as Jesus was. That is the first step of commitment: Speak truth in every word that comes forth from your mouth. That means if you are a drug addict, you admit to it. If you just enjoy getting high (like I do), don't hide it. If you are gay, then admit it. If you are a sex addict, then shout it out. If you have murdered someone, confess it. Get it out of your life! This is simply the first step of the 12-step process of Alcoholics Anonymous. Life must be built on truth.

If you want to be God, start by being what God is…truth! The truth will set you free.

Oh, the memories of blurting out the truth in polite circles (such as in a church group) and seeing everyone, wife included (at the time), want to hide under the chairs.

I would like to close this part of my story on a positive note. Something that provides a "feel good." But that's just a waste of time. By now, you have gotten to know me well enough to know that "feeling good" is simply an "equal and opposite" reaction to feeling bummed. It's a choice.

So, today is simply another day in the life of… (insert name)

With that sentence (above) we are to let out a long sigh of relief. It's over now. The end. I said it. Death, just like the first time I surrendered to death. Only now, it is as false as it was on a September day in 1973 when I showed up at the receptionist desk at St. Joseph's Hospital in Spokane, Washington and asked the pleasant little nun to check me in because "I was dying."

"Oh really? C'mon, you're joking."

Well, that completed her quota for the day for walk-in crazies, didn't it?!

Not quite.

Chapter 20

God Realization

Spiritual Comfort

Solitude carries me away
As my bones bend easily,
And my heart fills with euphoria

I am just a brief eternity
In another world.

Transparent realities appear
As a face reveals a thousand
years of knowledge.

I met stranger
And was brought
To the realization:
I AM!

Like it or not,
We are all desert flowers
We spring up
In brilliant glory
After summer showers

Yet,
We merely wither
With the morrow's consuming sun
Awaken, my friends to now
And manifest realization

(poem on reflection of here and now ca. 2008)

We shall now enter the house of mirrors at the carnival of past ideas, inspirations, and efforts, each having its own mirror and labeled, failed (but truthful) realizations. Let's call this state, the illusional state of God Realization since you have said "yes" to life and "yes" to exist in this illusion and "yes" to God realization, then, therefore, you never fail on any endeavor. But, as you enter this state, you are in the house of mirrors. Everything is you. Everywhere you step, you discover yourself. You may experience the "unexpected," (you know, the fat you, the skinny you, the up-side-down you), but that is not failure. The "you" is still the illusion in the mirror.

Let me prepare you for one of my greatest expectations and one of my greatest failures.

I thought being Jesus was being enlightened! I had heard endless talk about "God-Realization" and how one finds that perfect equilibrium, the self-realization of cause and effect of the dual worlds that lead to the God realization was where one should be.

"My God," I thought, "how much more can one be, than to be Jesus, here and now?"

Pause and think about this. You are now in the house of mirrors.

Now try it.

At first, taking on the identity of Christ, trying to be true to the "truth," and publicly calling attention to myself as god, (the illusionary reflection from the mirror). Example: when someone asked me how I knew something, I would have to say… "because I am Jesus!" I got everything from instant love and worship to being cast out from any relationship in any form (including family). More about that when I discuss family reaction to being Jesus at a family reunion.

I even became the mirror-image of what the Eckankar cult calls, "the Mahanta, the living Eck master, his holiness, Sri Darwin Gross." Remember, this was toward the end of the 60s and just the beginning of the tsunami of spirituality that swept over the nation after the Nixon Vietnam years. Their descriptions of that state of being were all so, so surrealistic, and if you wanted them to be, they could be self-confirming. ("Week of love"). Of course, being with a few friends and indulging in a mind-altering substance was thought helpful.

Like living a dream within a dream, each illusion took on its different characters and scenarios. Just like god does, I suppose. (No disrespect to the big "G," but the little "g" in god signifies the storybook god.) And for a while, it seemed that I could only make the transition from my tortuous "real" self, that load of pain and suffering that I call me, by altering my consciousness with various substances like marijuana, psilocybin, booze, tobacco, LSD, hydrocodone, or whatever else.

But marijuana was not infallible. Sometimes, pot gave me the temporary escape from my enslavement to my left-brain's super-dominate, linear, ego logical state, with its relentless state of rules, that I was so desperate to escape. Little did I realize that I was living in the quantum super-positional state. As hard as it was, I was creating it… hard! I was oscillating from creating reality to having reality create me. It can make you dizzy, bro.

When you become "God realized," you find God in every image that you see. There is no good and no bad. There is no up or down. Everything is God. Everything is a quantum particle of energy. Ah, quantum physics.

Dr. David P. Summers

Chapter 21

Flathead Lake (Again)

Untitled

Sometimes,
you just run out
of words
to describe
irony

Let me take us back to the experiences of the family 2010 reunion at Flathead Lake. Everyone wanted to tell us what had happened to them… up to that date. Karmic outpouring. Most were little tidbits of a few days. Or weeks or months. Want to know me better? Well, can I tell you what was going on in the past? Like the past 30 years squeezed into 3 minutes? Well, it turned out to be the same ole, same old, living in the past! All my religious relatives were habitually hooked (far worse than I) on getting up every morning and carrying out the same rituals.

But I was the bad guy!

All that I could tell them was that I had been doing the "Jesus" bit since about 1972 which was the first and last time I got out of my body and soul traveled. No one believed or cared, but I carried on during the entire visit.

Let me stop for a moment and describe the event.

It was a dramatic experience. I recall that I was in San Francisco just starting (once again) to live the "straight" life…forsaking all artificial means of experiencing spirituality, now using only the "tried and true" Eckankar method of mental concentration upon the "third eye," meaning the spot between the eyebrows somewhere a few centimeters in front of the pineal gland in the brain…supposedly the "seat of the soul."

It was about six o'clock in the morning and I had been roused by the maids outside my front door. I had asked the boss' secretary the afternoon before if she could direct me to some reefer madness. This was at the end of my trip to truth that I described back in a previous chapter where I vowed to speak and to live absolute truth. Even if I incriminated myself like I did at the Arizona veggie check-point.

Anyway, the boss's secretary, a pleasant, overweight, single lady directed me to the boss' son who happened to live in Marin, just over the Golden Gate Bridge from San Francisco, which was where I (just happened-are there no accidents?) to be going. I had arrived in San Francisco the afternoon before, fresh out of smoke, so I'd spent the night trashing and turning in bed. Having been aroused long before my usual get-up, I decided to try to meditate.

I began focusing on my third eye. I held my attention until I began to hear a low, rhythmic rumbling. It was sort of like someone playing the lowest note of a bass violin, over and over, zumn…zumn…zumn, the same note as I was fixated by concentration. Suddenly, I heard a higher sound, like the cork being pulled from a champagne bottle. A clear, distinct "pop." And there I was, rising out of my body, looking down and seeing my body from ceiling level. I was transfixed for a few moments in that state, staring at the body in the bed that I had rented the night before when the "soul travel" memory sprang into my conscious awareness.

"Soul travel!" I thought, "it's time to soul travel!" The one thing that I had sought for so many years was now at hand.

Hmm, let's see, what do I do now? Then the thought that I could use my mind to soul travel hit me like a bag of bricks. "It's all in the mind, stupid," I thought. I was still glued to the ceiling and still looking down onto my sleeping(?) body. How long was I out of my body? I could say, well, a lifetime. Or, I could say, only a few moments. Which would be correct? There is no time in that state of spiritual consciousness, of course.

And no one in my family wanted to hear such gobbledygook.

I have never really cared to talk about this, but it was an experience that I lived. It was an illusion so real that I called it a spiritual experience just as everyone else did. I would describe the experience as sort of the opposite of a near-death experience (NDE). And it was so real that when I soared through oceans of water, I did not need air. Perhaps reliving and curing my near-death drowning as a child, I simply breathed the water. And the weird thing was, I wanted Dorothy Louise to experience the soul journey with me, and she was immediately there.

I recall we held hands and laughed while gleefully soaring into worlds unknown to both. I have no idea where we went…to heaven? Who knows? But, we were there, joined in spirit, holding hands as lovers do, and communicating by simple thought. It was, to say the least, the ultimate trip of trips.

But, nothing lasts forever, as they say. And let's face it, when I opened my eyes to the reality of the day, it was now and that was then, just a memory, though a memory-meme that I shall never forget. My real-world work began at 8:00 am. As usual.

Ah, there is no life without experience, and experience is just the "cost of doing the business" of life. All life is obtained at a price – let there be no misunderstanding. Trying to isolate one's self from the "world" in hopes of avoiding the need to make compelling decisions of "good and evil" is an empty shell of a life and cannot rise to the expectations of God. If the contrary was so, Christ would have never made the decision to "come to this earth" to endure his hideous crucifixion.

Chalk this entire memorandum up as a recap of the summer of 2010. My sister, Mary Helen decided to call a family reunion at her and Paul's beautiful lake-side home on Flathead Lake. I recall Helen sitting beside me on their wrap-around, 2nd floor double (it had a screened-in portion and an outdoor) and asking (no, pleading) as to why I did not love my family. It was puzzling to be asked that question. To me, this was akin to asking me why the wind blew a certain way yesterday.

Now, I know the exasperation they felt trying to understand my goodbyes to each of them…30 years earlier.

We were in Kalispell, Montana then too, were we not?

And this was the story I told. We need not repeat that saga.

Dr. David P. Summers

Chapter 22

Games Religions Play

Come Unto Me

Come, my little children,
Let us play (pray)
You see
There's something called time
That man has made

Let us write a script(ure)
Of our goodness, and
Acknowledge our creation.

Say it with me:
God
Got it?

When do we grow up?
Become co-creators with God?

Let's all hide
From secret knowledge
And seek Truth.

(my poem written about the games religious people play ca. 2012)

Now, this chapter may be a tough read. I would suggest that you skip it and simply go to my last chapter if you are reading this book for amusement only. If you are looking for spiritual growth as I have all my life, then let's slowly walk together through this chapter.

History is filled with stories of totally religious cultures. I discussed this earlier. At one time before the enlightenment, whole cultures (might I say civilizations) were those religions. Just look at the Middle East for an example of this continuing phenomenon. Those who exercised freedom of thought were imprisoned or killed. Fortunately, we in the West have most religious thinking protected by a Constitution. This freedom provides us an overriding freedom of thought and expression.

But, even in this modern day, most of us were trained in early childhood and still believe in a "parental god" who sees all, knows all, and punishes/rewards little boys and girls accordingly. It is our God meme, and this internal meme is still alive and well in most people who subliminally play out this role either in the "child" or the "parent" psychological state in their daily lives throughout life. It is our most important meme for directing our external behavior.

What is a meme? If you skipped my Forward, then here is a mini-review.

Memes are the learned ground of consciousness. They can result in behavioral habits, but in the brain, it is a nexus of neural networks that provide conceptual sensory/emotional feedback to behavior. It is the basis of conceptual thought. It is the subtle, mental imagery that guides the thought process to its conclusions. Memes are a series of memories, connected to a larger, go-to memory/associated bank of familiar emotions, most of which were formed by the time you were five-years-old. That's why I say that religion is the basis for thought-formation for most people.

We retained religion to reinforce this psychological underpinning in our daily interactions with other human beings who are themselves (mostly) religious. It is mostly beneficial if one decides to play out this life in what is called the Astral. It is a hard habit to break when the memes are all in place. But escaping the pseudo-reality of them is finding new life.

Unfortunately, few can escape. But the easiest and most effective method to rid one of her/his auto psychotic thought processes and lifestyle is to commit one's self to becoming rigorously and, at times, brutally honest with oneself and others. I know it sounds trite, but in simple terms, this means *live truthfully*. To say that this is hard is an understatement. But it soon leads to an enlightened realization that we are (or were, such as the case with me) living in an ancient superstition, a mindset that is truly outdated, ineffective, and is a non-reality world that has nothing to do with god as you will (or have) come to know God!

Erik Bern, MD, wrote a book titled *The Games People Play* (Grove Press, New York, 1961) and in it, he described the psychodynamics of the adult/parent/child communications. Calling the method of communication "Transactional Analysis" he demonstrated in diagrammatic style, the structures of communications. In doing so, he adeptly laid out the dynamics of causes of disruptive behavior. He showed what he called the "crossed transactions" that result when one party speaks in say, the parental imperative mode of conversation he expects to receive a communication back in the "child" mode of conversation. These conversations are generally congruent. Though a lot of times they are not. But when an "adult" speaks to a "parent," generally the communication falls flat. As B.F. Skinner noted, operant conditioning is broken, and one party feels an emotional angst.

Here is a sample of parent/child disruptive conflict that is resolved by a shift to the adult mental mode.

"Be home by 10:00 o'clock! "(parent)
"Aw, that's too early, why do I have to be in that early?' (child)
"Just because I said so" (parent)
"Let's make it 10:30, ok? (child)
"Well, okay. But don't be late." (adult/congruency resolving conflict)

Okay, let's put this mechanism on the religious stage.
"You had better live the life that God is telling you to live." (parent/preacher)
"That's too strict, (demanding, dull, morose, joyless, etc.) why do I have to live the way you say?" (child)
"I'm God's spokesman. Do it or you will go to hell." (parent/preacher)
"I can't believe in a God that is unreasonable." (child…of God)
"Well, let's re-read the scripture." (reconciliation adult/parent)

Taking the states-of-being first used by Sigmund Freud in general terms, these three components and distinct aspects were the id, ego, and the suprego. I won't discuss Freud too much because he was not aware of contemporary psychology. But it was Freud's belief that a healthy balance of these three components of the mind is needed to be well-balanced and to produce reasonable mental health and stability in an individual. Some texts today speak of the id as the primitive brain, the ego as the learned brain, and the superego as the meme brain. So, with that, take a deep breath and try to bear with me as I try to describe the three states of consciousness.

According to Freud, the id functions in the emotional part of the mind. The id is the personality component made up of unconscious psychic energy that works to satisfy basic urges, needs, and desires. It is the "fight or flight" component of our animal nature. The id also operates on the pleasure principle, which demands immediate gratification of desires. It is the primitive and instinctive component of the personality. It is the impulsive and unconscious part of the psyche responding directly and immediately to our instincts. It was the id that ancient religions continually tried to appease, control, and/or suppress. This might be what Bern calls the "parent/child."

Freud said the ego was the rational thought process. It was, according to Freud, the part of the mind we are aware of. Think of mindfulness. This is what Freud said was the more active part of the mind. The ego is basically in control until overcome by the id (immediate pleasure, or fear/fight/flight) all responding to the five senses.

Freud's superego is the ethical meme component of the personality and provides the moral standards by which the ego operates. The superego provides criticisms, prohibitions, and inhibitions that form a parent state of conscience, and its positive aspirations and ideals represent one's idealized self-image or "ego ideal." This might be what Bern calls the "parent".

Thus, a typical parental statement is not necessarily rationally based on a factual description of events or needs leading up to the request in the here and now. In human behavior terms, it is simply "stimulus/response." In other words, the action at hand stimulates either the child or (conversely) adult meme in our emotional, stimulus/response reactionary mind. There is no adult rationale to it. Fight or flight is and will always be reactionary.

The early twentieth-century psychologist, B.F. Skinner wrote an entire psychology theory and many books on it on stimulus/response. His thesis was solidly built on habitual response to certain stimuli. His results in studying the theory were primarily demonstrated in animals. He called his primary book *The Behavior of Organisms, an Experimental Analysis*, B. F. Skinner, published by Appleton-Century-Crofts (1966).

Skinner was one of the most influential of American psychologists of the 20th century. As a behaviorist, he developed the theory of operant conditioning -- the idea that behavior is determined by its consequences. Think about this. This means that the expressed thought by one person when communicated already carries an expectation for an operant response. This makes it likely that the same behavior will occur again… and again…and again.

So, stimulus/response, cause/effect, operant conditional, and Newton's 3rd law of thermodynamics, the dual worlds of the astral plane, emotion wins again…and again… Habit prevails, (operant conditioning) nobody learns. Everybody just reacts to their emotions. The writer that most influenced my thinking on living in habitual behavior (call it autopilot) was Dr. Joe Dispenza who wrote a number of books on the subject. The book that that most influenced it was *Breaking the Habit of Being Yourself* (Hay House, Inc., Carlsbad Ca. 2012). In his book and tapes, he demonstrated unequivocally how the majority of people in the world simply live the same life that they lived the day before. Over and over and over… He showed how to break this no-growth habit though meditation.

Conflict invariably arises when the ego or logical adult of one person expects to communicate as the "adult" in the room with another "adult," but the other adult, who, unfortunately, perceives the communication in the id (emotional or "astral" state), then responds in a state of parent or child id, an operant conditioned state. Both are emotional, and both are controlled by unconscious memes.

It is immediately obvious to the ego "adult" that a conversation between the two parties is impossible unless the other party can shift from the id emotional state of a parent/child to a rational, ego state of an adult. Then, two adults can quickly rationalize and conclude with an outcome that both understand and accept. I know the above paragraph is difficult to understand, but not to worry, you got it subliminally.

Bern said the only response of an adult to a parent/child/id-based statement is something like this: "I'll try to cooperate." We all know that for an adult to argue logically with the parent/child verbal dynamic is futile. Neither understand intellectual logic. You have the intellect trying to rationalize with an emotional state. End of story, it is futile. Everything that you say will be met with a "yes, but…" Which again, brings us to religion.

Religion does not function in the adult. Religion functions in parent or child and in the past or future. (Be good and God will bless you.) Religion cannot function in the here and now. Who can logically differ with the emotionally based belief of religion?

Why insist on insulting modern intelligence with ancient cultural myths and legends which were surely expressions of allegorical folklore. Religion gets around this obstacle by demanding faith (belief) over rationality. If one differs from "faith" with a rational argument contrary. Then he/she is quickly disenfranchised from the group. Belief is based on faith and hope. One is based in future; the other in the past.

This doesn't mean that the truths conveyed in some of the ancient myths and legends don't communicate a truth from one age to the next. But religion has a wily way of inserting racial, ethnic, political, and other prejudicial biases just as the ancient Hebrews did to differentiate their monotheistic and aesthetic Jewish cultures from all others. The insistence that they were "chosen" from all the other peoples of the earth certainly builds on this idea.

There are no "adults in the room" in religion.

As I write, American television is full of made-up hatred for the country of North Korea. North Korea has done nothing wrong except to not obey (the disobedient child) an out-of-date agreement it made decades ago. The agreement was a quid pro quo. North Korea says America and the West have broken the quid pro quo. Ergo, North Korea says the quid is null and void. Who's right and who's wrong?

So, Mr. President, are we ready to go to war and kill millions of Koreans from both North and South Korea? In doing so. we will probably lose some tens of thousands of American boys and girls. Does anyone remember Vietnam? You can't bully or bomb a determined cultural meme out of existence. But that's okay, we have elected parent leaders (that's what Presidents do, right?) and we're being the parent to the world. We are in the "it's just because we said so!" state of being. Bully for us! The parent invariably wins over the child.

"Why?" (child-we-the-people)

"Because I (parent-the-church-the-politicians the President) say so!"

"Um, could we the (sane adults talk about this?")

"Of course not!" (Parental, authoritarian, patriarchal, Presidential)

Of course, the current anachronistic, conservative, religious, Christian approach is to simply double down, conjure up more hatred of the "bad guys" and admonish more diligent reading of the scriptures, to "put god back in the classrooms," more attendance of church and often, to "shun" worldly trappings. It's a simplistic, outmoded, and ineffective way of creating the spiritual change that the country sorely needs. They would do just as well to use self-flagellation on themselves.

Most of the "baby boomers" have left Christianity, except for the few "born again-ers," who are largely offspring of fundamentalist evangelicals. The "millennials" and the "digitals" are turning away from religion in huge numbers too, having assessed and rejected the shallow, "show-biz pantomime" religion shamelessly promoted by the "Christian business managers" (a huge professional group of religious hacks living off grant money endowments from politically rich 501-c non-nonprofits such as Koch Brothers. (https://www.huffingtonpost.com/topic/koch-brothers National Christian Foundation, (https://www.ncfgiving.com) Christian Aid Ministries, https://christianaidministries.org/ The J. Bulow Campbell (Foundation https://fconline.foundationcenter.org/grantmake profile/index? Key=CAMP007) (all public domain) and other religious, tax-avoiding, conservative religious/political organizations who are now in charge of selling "the Christian life" and who have high-jacked the Gospel of Jesus Christ to suit their own fringe ideals, which of course is money and power.

It's no wonder that religious ego-driven, "big business" personalities like the multimillionaire televangelist Kenneth Copeland, ww.deceptioninthechurch.com/kcopeland.html Benny Hinn, https://www.bennyhinn.org. Pat Robertson, www.patrobertson.com Bishops Eddie Long, (deceased) and T. D. Jakes, www.tdjakes.com and of course, Joel Osteen, (whom I personally like) https://www.joelosteen.com (all public domain) can continue to rake in hundreds of millions of dollars from these so-called paganized Christian productions or houses of idolatry, complete with mini-shopping malls, food courts, souvenirs, niche counseling, and of course remote TV for continuous viewing while munching on your cheeseburger and French fries. While the whole world looks on in amazement. "God is just blessing me, brothers and sisters!"

Hmm…say what?

owadays, any nut-case can start a "Christian Crusade" by simply taking a day off and writing a grant proposal (they will even write it for you) getting money, videos, tracts, and other material to speak the gospel of ignorant, superficial, special-interest "Christianity" to a world desperate for truth.

It is simply appalling the hypocritical way Evangelicals take Christianity and use it in any profitable manner. A good example is when the GOP right-wing (mainly evangelicals) cried out in Christian indignation when the proverbial shit finally hit the fan under the Obama administration with Lois Lerner, the former head of the Internal Revenue Agency (IRS) https://www.washingtontimes.com/.../lois-lerner-holly-paz-wanttestimony-sealed-per (public domain) who tried in vain to stop the phony exploitation of religious exemptions to the tax code. She was viciously attacked by Republicans for even investigating the tens of thousands "tax-free grants" for Christian 501-C charities that were both advertised and sold openly. The religious exemptions laws, of course, were put in place by the Republicans. She had to resign. Here is an ad I Googled up:

("We Form Your 501c3 for a low fee of $395 in Texas. Limited Time Only…Services: Obtaining Federal ID Number, Drafting Corporate Bylaws…")

Most, if not all, of these tax-evading gimmicks were set up by religious groups to simply avoid paying taxes like everyone else. The unfortunate woman who was head of the agency was figuratively run out of town on a rail.

Yes, sir, Christianity has a business to run folks!

Chapter 23

Dead and Alive -- Can They exist Cooperatively?

The Walking Dead Check List

Well yes, you can be dead
And alive
At the same time.
Where do you go when you dream?
Where are you when you awaken?

Do you visit heaven often?
Or not enough?
See your body lying below.
In that state.
Are you not dead until living?

Where are you?
In your soul?
In your brain?
First consciousness?
Left-brain religious rote?
Mindfulness or mindlessness?
Is something dead?
Something else is alive!

(*poem on pot-smoking and soul-travel ca. 2014*)

Let's digress briefly to my first visit to my sibling sister Mary Helen in the fall of 1974, which was my turning point that each of us has in karmic time ("And as it is appointed unto men once to die, but after this the judgment..."). Death of the *old* man (or woman) is death of the *illusionary* (*memes*) reality we brought with us from a karmic past. And yes, religion reinforces that illusion. When I said goodbye to my dear sibling on that fall day I truly thought that I would never see her again. I was clinging to the old illusion with my *memes* telling me that anyone who dared to *be Jesus* deserved to die. It too, was an old myth. Death was in that illusion too. I had operated within this meme *all my life.*

Leaving my visit left me totally exhausted physically, emotionally, mentally, and spiritually. I had said good-bye to every member of my family now, except Dorothy Louise. I had mixed emotions spiraling about me. She would be the last good-bye.

Heading home, I felt that the very air was going out of my life. *Being Jesus* was killing me. But what could I do? The little puddle-jumper Bombardier out of Kalispell stopped in Spokane so I could connect with a 737 Frontier to San Francisco. When I arrived in Spokane, I felt it was finally over; just like Jesus must have felt late in his second year of ministry, my time had come. Yes, and I wanted it over. I had *detached* from everything material. I was holding on to nothing in the astral world. It was though I had divorced myself from life itself. I could see death just over the horizon.

When I disembarked in Spokane, I knew that I could not connect with *anything* that would bring me out of my death spiral. I could feel life running out of me faster than I could put it back. But oddly, I was encompassed within a strange dream-like calm. The time to catch my airline connection with Frontier passed. I don't know how long I sat in the little terminal. I kept thinking, *where can I go to die?*

I'll take a taxi to a good hospital and die there, I thought, as energy continued to drain from my entire being. I was weak and unsteady. I could hardly put one foot in front of the other. *This is really death,* I was thinking…*finally* it's going to happen! But was it? Whatever it was, I was ready for it.

"Hello, what can I do for you?" the pleasant little nun at the reception desk of St Joseph Hospital asked.

"Sister, I need to check in and die," as I let out a long sigh.

She looked at me, smiled and said, "Oh dear… now tell me, what is the problem?" What a relief, I felt, for some reason, I didn't get the usual outright rejection and dismissal of my strange remarks. She's serious, I thought.

"Sister," I enunciated slowly, "I am *Jesus* and my time has come… I am dying. I became Christ, and now is the time to give this life back to

God… and may I sit down?"

"Of course, my dear. Now, first let me have your name."

C'mon, I thought. Do I fill out a form to get to die? Too weary to argue, I gave her my name and provided her with all the details, just like I would have had I come here for gall bladder surgery.

Finally completing her paperwork, she looked up and sighed, "I just love you evangelical charismatics."

"What?" I asked. "What do you mean?" I hardly considered myself a charismatic. And certainly not evangelical in a thousand years!

"Oh, you're not the first to come in here for this, she said. And you're all just alike…so loving!"

With that I was ushered to a room and told to don the hospital gown laid out for me. Soon a doctor entered the room. "Hi there," he piped, "I'm Dr. Hudson. *(fictitious)* I'm the staff psychiatrist here at St Joseph's."

"I'm *Jesus*," I said. "I just want a simple place to die. I've taken on his life of materiality and now it is finished, I can't live it any longer."

"Do you hurt anywhere?" he queried, ignoring my Jesus talk. He began taking my vital signs.

"No," I said, "I'm just so tired. I'm *really* tired and ready to die."

And I was. I had carried this burden of *at-one-ment* in the here and now, *WWJD* in real time, naked and afraid, as they say for the past five years. I knew that I had done something no one else had ever done, that is, challenged the mythology of a vengeful god head-on. I deserved to die and I knew it. And at last, I was ready. I surrendered all.

"Okay, let's get this IV started," he said, "and we'll make you as comfortable as possible."

I closed my eyes. The life and burden of being *Jesus* that I had carried so many years was leaving. I surrendered my life to death. I heard the doctor's voice like coming out of a cave.

"This is normal saline with sodium pentothal and it will put you into a drowsy sleep state."

Yeah right, I thought. That's what the warden tells those poor souls on death row when execution time finally arrives. They know the next moment the warden will nod his head to the executioner. And that's exactly what I expected…honestly.

Weird, the closer I came to my death, the more logical and calm I became.

"I want to ask you a few questions," I faintly remember him saying.

And then that was all.

I gave up the *ghost*, and I died…this is the end… I thought.

Sunlight was streaking in through the hospital window onto my face as I awoke. The nurse was setting breakfast up for me.

"Where am I?" I asked. She looked at me with a quizzical expression.

"Why, good morning" she said, "you're in St. Joseph's hospital… ready to eat breakfast?" she asked sweetly.

"Breakfast?" I asked. "Am I alive?" Before she could answer, in walked the same doctor I saw the night before.

He sat down and got right to it: "David, you can play God all you want, but you *cannot* replace God."

I looked at him. I had never heard that expression before. "Replace God?" I asked.

"Yes, that's what you have been trying to do." He said. "You can *play* God, but you cannot *replace* God." He repeated. "No one has. Even Jesus! It just doesn't work."

I was taken aback. I had never thought that I was *replacing* God. I was just *being Jesus* as completely as I could, wherever I happened to be. Sort of "what would Jesus do…*in person*, in the here and now moment…If he were me.

"It's the same thing," he said. "There's only God. Jesus is part of that one God.

"Yes, but *Jesus* is the son of God, and I'm *that*," I persisted.

"Well yes, but then you're trying to replace Jesus, aren't you?"

"I didn't know that I was trying to *replace* Jesus, I'm just representing him in person here on the earth plane."

"Well just relax now, eat your breakfast and I'll see you later. We want to do an EEG, if that's alright with you." I nodded and began eating my scrambled eggs and toast.

I stayed in the hospital three days. The staff ran a multitude of tests and I checked out normal on all of them.

Still in a state of amazement, I was subsequently discharged, and bag in hand, caught a cab to the airport to continue my (eternal) journey back home.

What happened to me? I wondered. I thought I had finally made the ultimate surrender – just like Jesus did. I felt different—lighter and relieved – almost euphoric. As I looked around me, the thought almost shouted in my ears, I beat the curse! Yeah, I'm alive. I beat death!

But that was not all. It was not the end of my search by any means.

Now I had to live with the *victory* over death. That meant that I had to live with the *truth* of my knowledge. I *had* to tell the story. Now I have.

Dr. David P. Summers

Chapter 24

Why Do We Die?

When Death is Defeated

Why not take a trip
To heaven
And check it out?

You might be surprised.

You might like having a mind that queries
That explores adventure,
Tries something new,
A mind that rises from the dead.

Me? I dance where the
Shadow Once danced,
Where flowers once blossomed.
I trembled
When melodies were sung,
I heard cymbals
When the raindrops fell
And I shed tears
Over and over
Like a repetitious sonnet.

I felt the very brush of Death's wings,
Waging war with other imperfect beings.

Finally, clothed in the scales of Death
I was a hero to the end,
Deep in the grave of perfection
Unaware of my own inner-death.

(poem on my LSD use in the 70s ca. ca. 1970)

Why *should* we die? That's the *better* question. Why is it that when have finally plateaued into the golden years of life, having married, (or remained single) raised a family, acquired a little wisdom and certainly the experiences to go with it, do we have to die and leave all this…where we found it, in the unfathomable and infinite pool of spirit? Why die?

Of course, there are many reasons, but one is because many get it into their heads that they are required to transition to something that is far better than the life that we have. As consequence, not only is there little desire to live, the life they once lived seems so much better, the experiences of the past outweigh the prospects of the present life. Then, there are those who live for the *future* instead of just living. When they finally give up on the future to redeem our lives, it leaves them.

Finally, there are those who live in the present. This is the *self-realized* person. Granted, the quantum field of *all potentiality* is a good place to leave all that wisdom and experience, but why not live *with* it – at least *re-experience* ourselves, but this time with the knowledge and wisdom we have acquired through hard lessons? Does religion deny us the right? Has religion put artificial limits to eternal life here, in the here and now?

I believe it *has* contributed to our abbreviated life.

The mythological excuse is to say, "well, God called her/him home."

But why would an omnipotent, inexhaustible, omniscient and omnipresent God *need* to *call* someone home? This is perhaps the biggest non-sequitur of our age, isn't it?

In plain words, it just doesn't make sense.

Why would God *not* enjoy having mankind *finally* learn how to get along, how to cure disease, and how to fairly use mother earth and *stay alive to enjoy it*? Why would God *not* enjoy living *with us* instead of living *up there*? (in heaven)

We, as humans enjoy seeing our kids grow up, find good jobs and professions, marry and produce grandkids, then why not God? It just doesn't seem to make sense to die, at least so quickly after achieving the primary goals in life. Then why die?

I'll try to answer this in as few words as possible.

I don't think we die because the telomeres on our chromosomes lose their enzyme coating. Or our DNA proteins wear out. I don't think we die because we reach the limit of reproduction of our cells, although those are accepted causes of aging and death. I think we die because we squander our vital energies on chasing *illusion*. Chasing *non-realities*. Chasing the *past* or the *future* both fall into the category of non-realities. Instead of living in the *real world* of the *present* state of *here and now*, we anguish over the things that we cannot change in the *past* or the things that have not yet manifested in the *future*. No one is alone in this; our whole culture does it. And religion is complicit in this squandering. It promotes it.

The question then arises, why not use this energy where we can make a difference? Why not use it in the only manner that is truly effective? If we did use it only in the present, use it only when events *manifest*, use it only when we can touch, feel, smell, taste, or hear the manifestation wouldn't we find far more joy and comfort than in the opposite lifestyle? It is amazing what the body does to promote longevity when it is in a state of homeostasis – a stress-free balance of congruency with itself. This is the condition that the medical world calls…well…healthy. And it is a condition of happiness and joy.

Truthfully, life only happens in the *present state, the here and now of manifested, created energy.* A corollary is that freedom is only found in the present state.

And it ends there.

Let me now pause and give you, dear reader, the opportunity to accept or reject the above suggestion: Living in the past and future is a waste of time and energy (a) yes (b) no. If yes, we shall proceed with some ideation that fills the page. If no, then you, dear reader, please provide a single example that bears out your position.

Here is the real question; why die if you don't *need* to die? That's the question.

Let me shout this out in following word/symbols:
Life is the expression of OMNIPOTENT energy.
We CO-CREATE WITH GOD OUR OWN life by manifesting that which we need or want.
NEEDS and WANTS are two distinctly different expressions OF ENERGY. NEEDS are naturally fulfilled by *coexistence* with the *immanent God*. In the sayings of Jesus, *"Look at the birds of the air; they do not sow or reap or store away in barns, and yet your heavenly Father feeds them. Are you not much more valuable than they?"*
WANTS ARE FULFILLED BY USING OUR OWN ENERGY TO *CHANGE* THE UNIVERSAL energy TO MANIFEST our WANTs. It's a zero-sum game. Each of these two expressions define the person.

As I said, wants are fulfilled by the sacrifice (or reapportionment) of standard values for achievement or fulfillment of desire. There is a choice for which is the most important to one's "being." As Jesus' disciple James said "Therefore, whoever wishes to be a friend of the world makes himself an enemy of God" (James 4 KJV). In other words, friendship with materialism is an anathema to your true potential. But when one lives in balance with God and nature, all needs are met.

Death exchanges nothing in return for our lives. Death is a thief. The same is for living the past or future. You get nothing out of it. So, you might say that a person who spends all her/his waking time dwelling upon the past or future is living in a *state of death*.

I'm not saying that you shouldn't think of the past or future. It's okay to *find out* where you came from and to where you are going; take your ideas and use them as the blueprint and foundation for your life. But then commit the ideas, blueprints and foundations to God. Leave them there! To take your vital energy and squander it by chasing one idea after another is nothing more than trying to become rich by borrowing more and more money to achieve it.

Might we become the first generation since Noah or Enoch that lived in a state of fulfilled needs?

My psychologist friend Vivian Collins (*with permission*) and Christian provocateur puts it like this: "Never chase affection or attention. If it isn't given freely by another person, (or God*) it isn't worth having."

It's living on borrowed hope and illusion for that hoped-for pot of gold. It simply almost always *fails* to happen, and in real life, and…get this, you always must pay for your wasted effort. Your life has only so much energy allotted to give and once you become obsessed with more cars, bigger houses, bigger bank accounts, etc., you misappropriate the vital spirit of living today in return for a dream of tomorrow that rarely ever materializes. Why not live in comfort, here today, and live and love now?

As historian and philosopher Joseph Campbell said, "follow your bliss!"

My friend and fellow writer, Ken Dahl wrote in his more recent book, *Honesty: The Final Frontier*, (iUniverse, Ken Dahl Books, 2017), "As expressions of the Divine, the love we feel toward one another and all of life is an evolution and a manifestation of Natures' capacity and potential to love. The highest degree of love that a person could feel for another human or for an animal or the earth IS the Cosmos, loving itself."

Dr. David P. Summers

Chapter 25

The Gift Must be Opened!

Open Upon Receiving

Listen to the crass
Preaching of
"Getting there,"
But nothing about "being here."
Which makes sense as much
As a map to nowhere.

I'll not give the ending away,
But it's hiding in plain sight.
I'm certain
What's the problem?
Religion has pulled the truth
Behind the curtain.

Look closer:
If you find pleasure
You may merge yourself
In their pleasure
Into the potential of laughter
And the at-one-ment at the end of day
Simply because
The cat that plays
May show you the way!

(poem on life's disappointment in religion)

In closing, let me talk just a little more about living in the present state of the "here and now" which I think is what St. Paul was talking about when he completed the sentence with... "and once to die, after that, the judgement" in the 9th chapter of Hebrews (KJV). It is a judgment mechanism, not of the mind, but of the universe. There is no "divine or holy" right way or wrong way. Religion created all that. But, every action is judged by the energy that is taken from the universe, and each action has an immediate reaction throughout the entire universe. (That's why astrophysicist scientists will tell me that just one little electron affects the entire universe.)

Jesus commanded us to simply love God and love one another. You can hardly do one without the other. So, why is this so hard for us to do? It's not.

Become Jesus for a while and see how easy it is. Forget what you were *taught* to believe and open your senses to Christ's immanent love. Step out! Sometimes Christ's love is subtle, other times it's easily discernable.

Sometimes it's so dramatic that you think it's due to something else. But remember, it's your world. And when your actions are from love, you are co-creating it with Christ.

I am a curious person. Nowhere in the bible does God say; "thou shalt not be curious..." Curiosity is the bane of religion. "Believe, don't ask!" It is religion that suppresses curiosity, not Spirit. Spirit leads one continually into new dimensions of experience by stimulating one's curiosity.

I had already said *yes* to life, so when the thought of becoming Jesus hit me, two things happened to my mind. First, I said *yes* to a closed mind which began to open. Saying *yes* opened it. Secondly, I took the opportunity to step into Jesus when the Jesus portal opened to me. Here is what I had to do. Remember, each of us is unique and will approach the *at-one-ment* moment with Christ differently.

Well, maybe three things.

I had to find some way to turn off the drilled-into-me, relentless, left-brain-logical-audible-memeically-imaging-biblical-life instructions. I had attended hundreds of meetings that offered a way to peace and contentment but always found that they required that I give up a freedom that I was currently experiencing for a vow to become a habitual believer in some future redemption that would set me free once again.

It was like asking a free man or woman to go to prison so that she could know what freedom was like! This is why I turned to marijuana. I had been to the "come to Jesus" confessional literally hundreds of times prior to trying it. And it cost me nothing. And it was temporary. But it was up until then, my only highway left out of the *hell* that I lived in.

And really, there was no magic to it. All it did was open my eyes. Why my destiny chose the little herb for my *yes* to Jesus is still a mystery to me. But *Being* Jesus liberated me. It was by far the most enlightening, illuminating, and mind-expanding experience that I ever, ever, had. Even afterwards, when old habits tried to take over, the will to find that instant reaction from the universe when I could contact Jesus in the present moment kept leading me back to the immanent Christ.

It wasn't through prayer that I found the immanent God. If prayer was the answer we would by now be living in a heavenly paradise here on earth. Unfortunately, prayer is a habit and not a de novo experience for most and I didn't have time left for old habits. Maybe it was the supplication part that I didn't have time for, I really don't know.

I know that statement is incomprehensible to the *true believer*.

But to momentarily opt out of the busy world of money, greed and power and retire to nature and sit down on a log and light up a marijuana blunt was where I found peace, joy, and satisfaction in the moment. Yes, that was back in the 70s – almost fifty years ago. Back then, when I turned my thoughts to Jesus and his love for the world as he knew it, I could internalize him and find a new world of freedom and spiritual power. He gave me the keys to the kingdom. And most of all, I found the immanent power of his love which was truth, the power of love, and wisdom.

And of course, it changed my life.

That's what God is. God is not bought and sold. You cannot continue to believe in and try to realize the ancient, mythological stories of God and ignore the reality of the present immanence. God is always in congruence with mankind and moves with it as man advances. This fact places God right in the present tense, right in the here and now – this is the "joy unspeakable and full of glory…" that St. Peter wrote of.

It is a transformation.

Some find the Christ in meditation, some need a preacher to hold their hand, others need to go to the woods and tune in and turn off. And some need all the above.

Communion.

Obviously, no religion provides the exclusive path to Christ. You might think an entrance ticket can only be bought out of the bible. Perhaps.

But unless you "hire" a translator who can bring into plain, common, vernacular, everyday language what was inarguably written by ancient tribesmen before paper and books, even before the internet, it will likely take you all your life. That's a lot to waste as the love of Jesus Christ is, as

I keep repeating, is immanent, free, and now! And get this: one can enter the *being* of Christ as much as one cares to. The door is open. Always.

Think of taking a casual morning walk with your soul-mate or lover, holding hands while walking along a well-tended garden, with hedge rows interspersed with climbing roses, beds of flowers of all genre, and an occasional bench for rest. Ahh…how cool!

Now, think of the subtle tug, the ever-so-tightened grip on your hand from that soulmate when he/she gently signals that the beauty at hand simply must be lovingly assimilated into your entire being. Your moment in ecstasy is this moment *at-one-ment*.

It can be indescribable.

This, almost imperceptible, energy is the feeling of unconditional love that permeates and expresses itself constantly in the present moment, presenting myriad opportunities of life *present* and *real*. In *being* Jesus, you entered the life-spirit of Christ and once there, there are no limits. As Jesus said, "once you put your hand to the plow, there is no turning back." I know that's an old and venerable saying, but this meaning is obvious.

This is the *Immanent God* manifesting, not some archaic story passed on from some prophetic ancient time, threatening to rain fire down from heaven in some Middle eastern place; it's not even momentous Jesus feeding the multitude or turning the water into wine, a story which I love; it is unconditional love at *every* moment in the experience of living *everywhere*.

And, I find that at times, when Jesus and I still become *at-one-ment*, I know that I'm not *replacing* the Jesus of the 1st century. I am *at-one-ment* with the *here and now Christ* as often as I desire. This is the true experience of Christ's unconditional love.

I now meditate, and I do find the same immanent presence that I could only once find by completely shutting down my left brain with pot. My left brain has now come to terms with my right brain.

When I put the physical world (usually that means the left-brain) in its place and meditate, even for a moment or two, allowing the immanent presence of here and now come through, I begin to *see* the future and what is going to happen next. Maybe my prediction is simply my next breath or next blink of an eye. But in my holistic right brain, I *am* predicting my future. I know that I need only ask.

Dr. Joe Dispenza said, in one of his books, "science tells us that we become totally unconscious in the micro-moment of the blink of our eye, regaining consciousness the moment the blink is over." If you tallied up the total time that you were unconscious during a lifetime it would come to about seven years.

Yes, seven years of total unconsciousness.

That's a lot of waking coma, right? The future is like that. One knows that the blink of the eye is but a *pause* in eternity. One knows that life *resumes* after a blink of an eye. That's predictable. Take it from there!

The eternal, immanent, and unconditional love of Christ, whether the man-made *myth* of a story retold in myriad written accounts for two thousand years, or of a *real* human being, retold, over and over, is real or symbolic, it *is* the divine *gift* of love and eternal joy.

With joy, one needs nothing else, for joy preempts everything! So, I at last come to the central truth of this book. *It is love*!

Being Jesus *is being in love* with creation, here and now. You *are a co-creator* with the *Imminent* God and that *is* JOY!

So, stop and think about it.

JOY!

I'll leave it there.

The end!

Dr. David P. Summers

Afterward

But, as I said about smoking pot in Texas where it is still illegal, if you want to really get down to it, it's simply illegal to be Jesus. Religion saw to make it so. The *Archie Bunkers* of my beloved state that make me a criminal when I want to have a little right-brain bliss in my life always *need* a bad guy to chase, don't they?

They do the same for a *Jesus* on the street corner. It was the same in Jesus' day. The world has not accepted alternative paths to God. You can get killed for choosing either. Both are acts of faith.

I think I have said enough for now. I'm glad we remained friends throughout this little trip and hope we will remain friends – forever!

And despite my life-long attempt, I was never quite able to convey my (spiritual) love to Lester. Nor he to me. So, that little preoccupation is gone forever. We both had lessons to learn before moving on. We'll just have to make do with the bits and pieces of joy we both found in each other!

It was good enough for me -- I hope, good enough for him.

But, what is forever? *(I just can't help myself, can I?)* Forever is just *today, thinking about tomorrow*, isn't it?

So, until we meet again, I love you all.

Forever!

"The history of mankind will probably show that no people has ever risen above its religion, and man's spiritual history will positively demonstrate that no religion has ever been greater than its idea of God. Worship is pure or base as the worshiper entertains high or low thoughts of God." A.Z. Tozer, "The Knowledge of the Holy," 1961, Harper, San Francisco

"*So, does free will exist? Yes, if not in ultimate reality, then at least in the operational sense necessary for sanity and thereby for the perpetuation of the human species.*" Edward O. Wilson, "The Meaning of Human existence," 2014,

Norton & Company, New York

Dr. David P. Summers

The end. (Really)

1. Remember, memes are raw sensory signals transformed into a brain representation of the world that surrounds us. Investigators have now uncovered the contributions to perception of a brain region called posterior parietal cortex. They show that posterior parietal cortex contributes to the merging of signals from different sensory modalities, as well the formation of memories about the history of recent stimuli.

www.ingramcontent.com/pod-product-compliance
Lightning Source LLC
LaVergne TN
LVHW050023080526
838202LV00069B/6890